Methodologies for Conducting Research on Giftedness

Methodologies for Conducting Research on Giftedness

EDITED BY

Bruce Thompson and Rena F. Subotnik

American Psychological Association

Washington, DC

Published by
American Psychological Association
750 First Street, NE
Washington, DC 20002
www.apa.org

To order
APA Order Department
P.O. Box 92984
Washington, DC 20090-2984
Tel: (800) 374-2721; Direct: (202) 336-5510
Fax: (202) 336-5502; TDD/TTY: (202) 336-6123
Online: www.apa.org/books/
E-mail: order@apa.org

In the U.K., Europe, Africa, and the Middle East, copies may be ordered from
American Psychological Association
3 Henrietta Street
Covent Garden, London
WC2E 8LU England

Typeset in Goudy by Circle Graphics, Columbia, MD

Printer: Maple-Vail Books, York, PA
Cover Designer: Minker Design, Sarasota, FL

The opinions and statements published are the responsibility of the authors, and such opinions and statements do not necessarily represent the policies of the American Psychological Association.

Library of Congress Cataloging-in-Publication Data

Methodologies for conducting research on giftedness / [edited by] Bruce Thompson and Rena F. Subotnik. — 1st ed.
    p. cm.
  ISBN-13: 978-1-4338-0714-5
  ISBN-10: 1-4338-0714-9
  1. Gifted children—Research. 2. Gifted children—Ability testing. I. Thompson, Bruce, 1951- II. Subotnik, Rena Faye.

  BF723.G5M48 2010
  155.45'5072—dc22

                                        2009032682

British Library Cataloguing-in-Publication Data

A CIP record is available from the British Library.

Printed in the United States of America
First Edition

CONTENTS

CONTRIBUTORS

Kathleen M. T. Collins, Associate Professor, Department of Curriculum and Instruction, University of Arkansas, Fayetteville

Jennifer R. Cross, Postdoctoral Research Fellow, Center for Gifted Education, College of William and Mary, Williamsburg, VA

Tracy L. Cross, Jody and Layton Smith Professor of Psychology and Gifted Education & Executive Director, Center for Gifted Education, College of William and Mary, Williamsburg, VA

Geoff Cumming, Emeritus Professor, School of Psychological Science, La Trobe University, Bundoora, Melbourne, Australia

Brian G. Dates, Director of Evaluation and Research, Southwest Counseling Solutions, Detroit, MI

Fiona Fidler, ARC Post Doctoral Fellow, School of Psychological Science, La Trobe University, Bundoora, Melbourne, Australia

Robin K. Henson, Professor, Department of Educational Psychology, University of North Texas, Denton

Qun G. Jiao, Professor and Librarian, Newman Library, Baruch College, City University of New York, New York, NY

Kevin M. Kieffer, Associate Professor and Chair of the Department of Psychology, Saint Leo University, Saint Leo, FL

Jason E. King, Associate Director, Evaluation and Research, Office of Continuing Medical Education, and Associate Professor, School of Allied Health Sciences, Baylor College of Medicine, Houston, TX

Rex B. Kline, Associate Professor, Department of Psychology, Concordia University, Montréal, Québec, Canada

Nancy L. Leech, Associate Professor, School of Education and Human Development, University of Colorado–Denver

Lindsey Martin, Doctoral Student, Department of Teaching and Learning, Southern Methodist University, Dallas, TX

D. Betsy McCoach, Associate Professor, Measurement, Evaluation and Assessment, University of Connecticut, Storrs

Kim Nimon, Assistant Professor, Department of Learning Technologies, University of North Texas, Denton

Paula Olszewski-Kubilius, Director, Center for Talented Development, Professor, School of Education and Social Policy, Northwestern University, Evanston, IL

Anthony J. Onwuegbuzie, Professor, Department of Educational Leadership and Counseling, Sam Houston State University, Huntsville, TX

Robert J. Reese, Assistant Professor in the Department of Educational, School, and Counseling Psychology, University of Kentucky, Lexington

J. Kyle Roberts, Associate Professor, Department of Teaching and Learning, Southern Methodist University, Dallas, TX

Robert J. Sternberg, Dean, School of Arts and Sciences, Tufts University, Medford, MA

Rena F. Subotnik, Director, Center for Psychology in Schools and Education, American Psychological Association, Washington, DC

Bruce Thompson, Distinguished Professor of Educational Psychology, and of Library Science, Texas A&M University, College Station, and Adjunct Professor of Allied Health Sciences, Baylor College of Medicine, Houston, TX

Tammi Vacha-Haase, Associate Professor, Department of Psychology, Colorado State University, Fort Collins

FOREWORD

ROBERT J. STERNBERG

Everyone likes to receive gifts. Yet the field of giftedness has not been accepted happily into the broader realm of education. Indeed, giftedness has become more like that gift of an ugly tie you receive from your in-laws that you quickly stuff in a drawer, pulling it out only when the in-laws visit and hoping it has not become too wrinkled. Any observer of this reaction might wonder why the study of gifts has not been welcomed in the ways gifts usually are. Next, that observer might wonder why the gifted themselves often are not welcomed into the U.S. educational system.

To take the second question first, the gifted often are not welcome because they seem too much like the rich uncle who wants you, in your relative poverty, to help him become richer at your expense. Many educators feel that the gifted are the last ones to need special services and thus feel put upon when they are asked or even required to provide such special services. And many gifted students want nothing less than to stand out from all their fellow students, marked as being not quite special, but rather as especially dorky. Yet these gifted students are often those who most need special services to alleviate the repetition and excruciating boredom they may experience in a typical classroom.

To take the first question second, the field of giftedness has been less blessed by strongly designed research than have some other fields in education, including the field of developmental disabilities; this field deals with children on the opposite end of the spectrum and typically receives more than 99% of the resources—both for research and for special education. If we want to strengthen the field of giftedness, one way to do it certainly is to have stronger research, but without adequate funding, it becomes a chicken-and-egg problem. Funding is lower, in part, for the lack of strong research. But the weak funding discourages the strongest investigators from entering the field. And the stigma attached to the field, and often to the gifted themselves, helps matters not at all.

There have been efforts to enhance and systematize the research on giftedness. For example, the *International Handbook of Giftedness and Talent* (Heller, Mönks, Sternberg, & Subotnik, 2000) has provided a key reference for studying the field, and the second edition of *Conceptions of Giftedness* (Sternberg & Davidson, 2005) has attempted to survey a wide variety of different views of what giftedness is and what it means. But these volumes, and others in the field, have tended to dwell on substantive issues—who the gifted are and how we can best identify, study, and educate them. Methodological issues have tended to be a sideshow, largely because the field did not even have enough sophisticated methodologists to render a compendium doable. That was then.

This is now: The field is ready. This book is a grand departure from past volumes in the field of giftedness. It tackles seriously and comprehensively, for the first time, the central issues of methodology in the field of gifted education—the methods without which the central questions in the field—such as Who is gifted? and How can we best educate the gifted?—cannot definitively or even plausibly be answered. The book covers the gamut of methods, including methods that focus on individual differences, such as factor analysis, and other methods that focus on the techniques commonly used in experimental research, such as analysis of variance. There is also ample discussion of mixed methods in research, in which investigators employ multiple methods in order to converge on a single set of conclusions that transcend the methodologies used to elicit them.

The book represents a major step forward for the field of giftedness, in part because it serves as an existence proof that a book focusing on methodology in the field of giftedness is possible. There are probably no issues in the book that apply only to the field of giftedness. Most of the arguments could be applied as well to the field of developmental disabilities or equally to studies of, say, experts and novices. But this book has an advantage over more general books on methodology in that it focuses specifically on studies concerned with a special population—in this case, the gifted.

Why does one even need such a book as this one? Consider the most basic question addressed in the field and in the book: How do we identify the gifted and distinguish them from anyone else? Part of what has held the field back is the difficulty of answering even this most basic question. To answer it, one must grapple with fundamental questions such as whether giftedness is unidimensional or multidimensional and whether giftedness is defined in terms of a discrete group or rather represents merely a region on a broader continuum. And these questions, in turn, can be answered only when we have methodological tools sufficiently sophisticated to address them in a meaningful way. The book's coverage is deep and broad, including topics such as mixed data collection, factor analysis, confidence intervals, hierarchical linear modeling, and structural equation modeling.

When I learned that this book was in preparation, I gladly agreed to write the foreword because I thought the topic to be such an important one. At that point, it was all a gamble because I had not yet read the chapters that would constitute the book. Having now read these chapters, I have learned that readers with levels of knowledge ranging from fairly rudimentary to highly sophisticated will acquire knowledge that will serve them well in the field. The gamble paid off for me, and your taking the time to read the book will be a gamble that pays off well for you, too!

REFERENCES

Heller, K. A., Mönks, F. J., Sternberg, R. J., & Subotnik, R. F. (Eds.). (2000). *International handbook of giftedness and talent*. Amsterdam: Elsevier.

Sternberg, R. J., & Davidson, J. E. (Eds.). (2005). *Conceptions of giftedness* (2nd ed.). New York: Cambridge University Press.

Methodologies for Conducting
Research on Giftedness

INTRODUCTION: A PROMISING FUTURE FOR RESEARCH IN GIFTED EDUCATION

RENA F. SUBOTNIK AND BRUCE THOMPSON

The editors envision this volume as a handbook for researchers in psychology and education who target exceptional populations in their work, and particularly individuals exhibiting gifts and talents. The research tools described here can help to move the scholarship on giftedness and talent development to a new level of rigor and encourage the testing of program models, as well as predictive validity of theoretical or conceptual frameworks (see for example Sternberg & Davidson, 2005). Of course, the methods described in these chapters can also be usefully applied in general populations or in studies dealing with specialized subpopulations other than gifted and talented.

The scholars who contributed to the first nine chapters of this volume are pioneers in the field of measurement and statistics, and they show us most elegantly how the methodologies they have mastered or developed can apply to samples that, by their nature, make statistical analysis more challenging. We tasked our contributors to address the following four barriers, and one facilitator, associated with gifted education research:

- Definitions of giftedness and talent are not standardized.
- Test ceilings can be too low to measure progress or growth.

- Comparison groups are difficult to find for extraordinary individuals.
- Participant attrition in longitudinal studies may compromise tests of hypothesized effects.
- Qualitative research conducted with gifted populations can be enhanced due to highly articulate study participants.

LACK OF STANDARDIZATION IN DEFINITIONS OF GIFTEDNESS

When high IQ was the most common criterion for identifying individuals as gifted, many assumptions and comparisons of outcomes could be reasonably made across studies. Yet even under conditions where most scholars equated giftedness with high IQ, scholars disagreed as to whether group tests were sufficiently rigorous when compared to individual tests. Another dispute arose with regard to cutoff scores for services. Some services or programs designed for gifted students selected children who scored in the top 1% on tests of intelligence, while others included the top 3%. Other approaches have emerged in response to the domain-specific nature of giftedness and talent, as well as the limited predictive validity of IQ scores beyond school achievement. As a result of challenges by scholars such as Sternberg (1981), Bloom (1985), Gardner (1983), Renzulli (1978), and others, more attention has been directed to identifying children and youths with domain-specific abilities, creativity, or practical intelligence rather than profiles of general ability reflected in high IQ.

What does this all mean for research on gifted populations? It means that the field is progressing to a more sophisticated and evidence-based level. Concurrently, however, it is nearly impossible to conduct meta-analyses of effect sizes when the study samples come from populations identified in such different ways. If professionals in the field of giftedness studies are to focus on more rigorous methods of research, they must make proactive efforts to resolve definitional issues (see chaps. 1 and 11, this volume). Meta-analyses will then be more useful in helping us achieve generalizations relevant to policy and practice.

CEILING EFFECTS

A conundrum experienced by researchers working with gifted and high-achieving students is measuring outcomes of an intervention for individuals clustered around the top of the scoring range. How valid are these scores? How do such outcomes affect what can be learned about participants' potentials and how participants differ from one another? Olszewski-Kubilius (see chap. 10, this volume) discusses an important tactic used by many in the field of gifted studies—off-level testing. Without access to a highest point of potential performance, it is hard not only to judge effectiveness of an intervention but also to determine what might be appropriate services for such individuals. However, off-level tests are normed on individuals of a different age, which leads to potential problems with score validity. This volume offers suggestions on addressing the ceiling effect conundrum (see chaps. 5 and 6, this volume).

COMPARISON GROUPS

To test the effects of an intervention, researchers need a comparison group. The ideal candidates for a comparison group are those who qualify for participation in a program but are randomly assigned to a control group. Because of the high status associated with participation in a gifted program, very few qualified candidates will turn down an opportunity to participate. As mentioned by McCoach (see chap. 12, this volume), as a field, gifted education has not been accountable to its clients by testing program effects. Sometimes this stems from poor funding of programs, which leaves no extra funds for quality control. But more often, this is due to the assumption that any program is beneficial for students and that therefore withholding treatment is inherently unethical. Without the statistical techniques addressed in this volume, we are blinded to program or other intervention outcomes. We may, in fact, be supporting programs that are not particularly effective at the expense of those that might be more appropriate.

PARTICIPANT ATTRITION

All researchers fear the loss of participants during the course of a study, so this problem is not unique to research with gifted individuals. However, when the numbers of potential participants are already small, and when comparison groups are hard to find, participant attrition is especially painful (Subotnik & Arnold, 1994). The suggestions offered by King and Dates (see chap. 9, this volume) on missing data help to alleviate this problem methodologically. Yet accounting for missing data is not the same as explaining why a person leaves a program or a career trajectory. Such explanations might be incredibly useful to those who are concerned about continuous improvement of programs. As recommended by Onwuegbuzie, Collins, Leech, and Jiao (see chap. 6, this volume), interviews with "leavers" enrich quantitative analyses. In a study of Westinghouse Science Talent Search winners (Subotnik, Duschl, & Selmon, 1993), 40% of the women who reported wanting to pursue science, technology, engineering, and mathematics (STEM) careers when they graduated from high school had already switched out of STEM majors by the end of their sophomore year in college. Several of these women did not respond to surveys for years. Later, a few got back in contact to say that the reason they did not respond to earlier surveys was because they were embarrassed to be part of the leaver statistic.

Chapters in *Methodologies for Conducting Research on Giftedness* also address the question of sample size. Innovative approaches such as Q-technique factor analysis capitalize on this situation by turning a potential problem into a strength (see chap. 2, this volume). Using confidence intervals can accommodate an otherwise problematic sample size (see chap. 3, this volume).

VERBAL ABILITY

One advantage, at least from the first author's experience, of working with gifted populations is that most tend to be articulate. This can be helpful in qualitative research when participants are asked to respond to interview protocols or open-ended survey instruments. This attribute can also be useful in responding to more complex items on instruments or following more intricate sets of directions.

RESEARCH AGENDA FOR THE FIELD OF GIFTED EDUCATION

In an earlier publication, Subotnik (2006) set out a research agenda for the field of gifted education that argued for the following investigative goals:

- ensuring that sufficient numbers of high-quality scientists, technology professionals, engineers, and mathematicians are prepared to meet our society's future needs
- evaluating whether our public schools are serving all members of the community well, including gifted and talented students
- determining the value added of gifted education for all children
- determining the value added of educating a gifted student to full capacity by way of special programming. (p. 354)

Ensuring that sufficient numbers of high quality scientists, technology professionals, engineers, and mathematicians are prepared to meet our society's future needs. With regard to engaging the talents of future participants in the STEM enterprise, researchers would want to know the following (among other possible questions):

- What variables are the best predictors of ability in specific domains of mathematics and science?
- What are the most common environmental obstacles to talent development?
- What are the most common psychosocial obstacles to talent development?
- What are the most powerful environmental and psychosocial enhancers of talent development?

Evaluating whether our public schools are serving all members of the community well, including gifted and talented students. Federal, state, and local governments constantly evaluate our public schools for accountability purposes, particularly with regard to meeting levels of proficiency. However, many students are beyond proficiency. Some topics need to be investigated in order to find out what school reforms might be most effective in meeting the needs of all children in our schools, including gifted and talented students. A sample of such topics might be the following:

- What influence does a cohort of high-achieving, academically motivated students have on the rest of the school? If the effect is positive, how big must the critical mass of high achievers be?
- If only a small percentage of high-achieving students in a school are children of color, how well do the high achievers serve as role models and leaders for the rest of a diverse school population?

Determining the value added of gifted education for all children. Some colleagues in gifted education have argued that the field should stop labeling children as gifted and provide services to all children as if they were gifted (cf. Borland, 2003). Given the controversy that often surrounds gifted education as a form of stratification, elitism, or even racism (see chap. 11, this volume), it would be important to explore this topic in a scholarly manner. For example, we could ask,

- What would be the effect of randomly assigning students to gifted programs by way of a lottery?
- What if schools invited students who were academically motivated, but not necessarily labeled, to join gifted programs?

Determining the value added of educating gifted students to their full capacities by way of special programming. Olszewski-Kubilius (see chap. 10, this volume) and McCoach (see chap. 12, this volume) support testing the most basic of assumptions. How much value added do services for gifted students provide for identified gifted children? As these authors point out, researchers and practitioners operate under the assumption that such programs are valuable—so much so that we are reluctant to test this assumption by randomly assigning qualified students to a control group. To affect policy, we need to know how much human capital enhancement we get from investing in high-quality education for gifted students. Do gifted students who participate in gifted programs contribute significantly more as adults by way of ideas, products, or performances?

CONCLUSION

Gifted education is ready for intervention studies and other investigations with more complex designs (see chap. 8, this volume), but most scholars in the field (as well as many other fields) have not been trained to conduct or to design such studies (see chap. 4, this volume). We need to explore the effectiveness of our programs and identification schemas. We need to test the efficacy of our theoretical models. With this volume, we can come much closer to meeting these goals.

REFERENCES

Bloom, B. S. (1985). *Developing talent in young people*. New York: Ballantine.

Borland, J. H. (Ed.). (2003). *Rethinking gifted education*. New York: Teachers College Press.

Gardner, H. (1983). *Frames of mind: The theory of multiple intelligences*. New York: Basic Books.

Renzulli, J. S. (1978). What makes giftedness? Reexamining a definition. *Phi Delta Kappan, 60*, 180–184, 261.

Sternberg, R. J. (1981). A componential theory of intellectual giftedness. *Gifted Child Quarterly, 25*, 86–93.

Sternberg, R. J., & Davidson, J. E. (Eds.). (2005). *Conceptions of giftedness* (2nd ed.). New York: Cambridge University Press.

Subotnik, R. F. (2006). A report card on the state of research in the field of gifted education. *Gifted Child Quarterly, 50*, 354–355.

Subotnik, R. F., & Arnold, K. D. (Eds.). (1994). *Beyond Terman: Contemporary longitudinal studies of giftedness and talent*. Norwood, NJ: Ablex.

Subotnik, R. F., Duschl, R., & Selmon, E. (1993). Retention and attrition of science talent: A longitudinal study of Westinghouse Science Talent Search winners. *International Journal of Science Education, 15*, 61–72.

I

ADVANCED TECHNIQUES

1

USE OF FACTOR ANALYSIS TECHNIQUES IN THE STUDY OF GIFTEDNESS

ROBIN K. HENSON

Factor analysis is often used to summarize relationships among many variables into a manageable, smaller set of factors. The methodology is frequently employed in instrument development and assessment of score validity, but it has other applications as well. This chapter reviews some common applications of factor analysis, provides an accessible treatment of how to conduct and interpret the analysis with a heuristic example, and discusses some potential benefits and problems that may be faced when conducting factor analysis in the study of giftedness.

Factor analysis has enjoyed a long history of use across the social sciences. With most approaches, factor analysis is employed when researchers seek to reduce many variables to a smaller set of factors. The factors can then be thought of as a synthesis, or representation, of the many variables from which the factors were created. There are other uses of the methodology, such as Q-technique factor analysis, which can be used to identify types of people (see chap. 2, this volume), but most often variables are the subject of the analysis and therefore are the focus of this chapter.

Put yet another way, factor analysis allows us to summarize the correlations present among a set of variables. One major use of factor analysis, for example, is in the development of assessment instruments consisting of many items, some of which are correlated with each other but not with other items. Each subset of correlated items would then be clustered together as a factor, yielding a simpler, summarized way to reflect the correlations among the original items.

EXPLORATORY VERSUS CONFIRMATORY APPROACHES

A less than perfect distinction can be made between factor analytic methods that are exploratory or confirmatory. Exploratory factor analysis is used to search for possible factors that may be present among the variables, with no or limited theory about what those factors should be. Confirmatory factor analysis is used when there is an established expectation for what factors should exist in a data set based on given theory or scientific evidence. As Gorsuch (1983) explained, "Whereas the former [exploratory factor analysis] simply finds those factors that best reproduce the variables . . . , the latter [confirmatory factor analysis] tests specific hypotheses regarding the nature of the factors" (p. 129). Typically, structural equation modeling techniques (see chap. 7, this volume) are used to conduct confirmatory factor analysis.

Differences between these two approaches are sometimes not clear. For example, the factors underlying many items on an instrument may very well be informed by prior theory, and therefore test items are developed to reflect certain domains (e.g., we may expect self-concept domains in academic and social settings). However, the expectation that the items reflect anticipated factors may not have been adequately tested, and therefore we do not have sufficient empirical evidence that the items cluster together in expected ways. In this case, we have both exploratory and confirmatory purposes; we hope to evaluate what factors are present in the data, and we also hope to determine whether these factors align with our theoretical expectations that guided item development. Nevertheless, generally an exploratory approach would be preferred in this example because the instrument lacks prior support. Readers are referred to Kieffer (1999), Stevens (2002), and Thompson (2004) for other treatments of both exploratory and confirmatory factor analysis. This chapter focuses on exploratory factor analysis.

FACTOR ANALYSIS IN THE STUDY OF GIFTEDNESS

Since its roots in IQ measurement, factor analysis has been applied to a wide variety of fields, including assessment within the study of giftedness. For example, using participants with some form of gifted background, researchers have examined the factor structure of scores from instruments measuring IQ (Watkins, Greenawalt, & Marcell, 2002), time perspective (Worrell &

Mello, 2007), social coping (Rudasill, Foust, & Callahan, 2007), academic self-concept (McCoach & Siegle, 2003), and multiple intelligences (Chan, 2006). These are just a few recent examples employing the method with gifted samples.

Factor Analysis, Construct Measurement, and Score Validity

In such studies, factor analysis is often used to explore or confirm how individual variables, such as items on an assessment, cluster together to form constructs. Factor analysis is thus closely linked to issues of construct measurement. Thompson and Daniel (1996) noted that the factors, or constructs, "can be seen as actually causing the observed scores on the measured variables" (p. 202). Henson and Roberts (2006) stated that "factor analysis at once both tests measurement integrity and guides further theory refinement" (p. 395).

Construct measurement is important in a wide variety of fields, including the study of giftedness, where researchers are often interested in unobservable (or latent) constructs such as social competence or mathematics achievement. Of course, some constructs may appear to be more observable than others. However, this difference is often a reflection of our familiarity with the construct. Mathematics achievement and its assessment, for example, are pervasive in educational environments, and therefore it may seem that we can clearly observe this construct. In fact, what we observe are students' responses to items that purport to assess underlying mathematics capacity, rather than the construct directly. The observable scores we obtain from mathematics assessments are reflections of the underlying construct. The scores can then be factor analyzed to (a) develop and refine the instrument and (b) assess the applicability of the theory guiding the process.

Factor analytic methods can also be used for data reduction purposes other than instrument development. It may be useful in some cases to reduce a large number of predictor variables into a smaller set of factors for multiple regression analysis. Nevertheless, most uses involve some form of instrument development or construct measurement. Worrell and Mello (2007), for example, examined the factor structure (using both exploratory and confirmatory means) of Zimbardo Time Perspective Inventory (Zimbardo & Boyd, 1999) scores in a sample of academically talented adolescents. This 56-item instrument purportedly yields five subscales, or factors, including Past Negative, Past Positive, Present Hedonistic, Present Fatalistic, and Future perspectives. However, Worrell and Mello were not able to replicate this structure in their sample—a result that raises questions about the nature of the five constructs in similar samples.

This is an issue of score validity. If the five factors noted above are not replicable among academically talented adolescents, then use of scores on these five subscales is questionable. Thus, the factor structure of an instrument's scores can also be informative from a psychometric standpoint. As

Watkins et al. (2002) observed, "Factor analysis constitutes one major source of statistical evidence regarding the construct validity of a test. Construct validity comprises the evidence supporting the appropriateness of inferences and actions taken on the basis of test scores (Messick, 1995)" (p. 165).

It is important to note, however, that construct validity support requires evidence from multiple substantive, structural, and external sources (Benson, 1998). Factor analysis informs only the second of these. Nevertheless, the factorial structure of the data can provide one type of critical evidence for construct validity.

Purpose

In spite of potential benefits, a statistical analysis is helpful only when it is employed and interpreted correctly. A number of other researchers have commented on appropriate practice when it comes to carrying out a factor analysis (cf. Fabrigar, Wegener, MacCallum, & Strahan, 1999; Henson, Capraro, & Capraro, 2004; Henson & Roberts, 2006; Hetzel, 1996). Unfortunately, these empirical reviews of factor analysis use in published research indicate that the methods are very often poorly handled and reported. Like most statistical methods, refinement of the methodology comes with time, and factor analysis is no exception. Recent advances in theory and technological capacity due to computing resources have allowed for the improvement of factor analytic methods.

Given this difficulty in published research and the continuing value of factor analysis, the current chapter is focused primarily on providing an accessible, introductory treatment on how to conduct an exploratory factor analysis. To meet that goal, I discuss the primary (and critical) decisions that researchers must make in the process. To help make the presentation concrete, a hypothetical data set of gifted students will be analyzed using SPSS (Version 15.0). Interested readers can use the data set to replicate and practice the methods discussed herein. Additionally, I review several possibilities and problems associated with using factor analysis that may have implications for the study of giftedness.

CONDUCTING AN EXPLORATORY FACTOR ANALYSIS

A Hypothetical Scenario

To demonstrate the use of factor analysis, let us consider the following hypothetical scenario. We will assume the role of a researcher interested in gifted adolescents admitted into a residential early college entrance program at a public university. More specifically, we wish to focus on the social competence of these gifted students as part of a larger agenda regarding the social development of gifted adolescents. On the basis of the extant (and still hypothetical) literature, it is believed that social competence can vary depending on whether the interactions are in academic settings (e.g., with faculty and fellow students) or in nonacademic settings (e.g., with friends and social acquaintances). However, there are no adequate instruments available to assess these constructs, and therefore we develop seven items—four for academic and three for nonacademic social competence. A 7-point Likert-type scale is used, and respondents indicate their level of agreement to behavioral statements presumably assessing social competence.

In this case, we are most interested in the constructs of social competence and less interested in the specific items that make up the structure. Factor analysis will allow us to determine if the structure of the data fits the theoretical expectation that there should be two subscales present in the seven items. Those items that assess the same construct should be reasonably correlated with each other and therefore be part of the same factor.

Assume that we have administered the seven-item instrument to 30 gifted adolescents who were admitted to an early college entrance program, and we now are interested in determining if the data indeed yield two factors as expected. Note that this is another example where there are both exploratory and confirmatory processes working together. The instrument's items are new and untested, thus calling for an exploratory beginning to the investigation. Yet the items were not created in a vacuum; they were generated from the theoretical expectation (presumably grounded in the extant literature) of two types of social competence. Table 1.1 presents the hypothetical data for this situation.

Decision Making and Reporting

Any exploratory factor analysis necessarily involves a series of decisions that must be made by the researcher. Henson and Roberts (2006) emphasized the need for these decisions to be made in a "thoughtful" (p. 396) manner and reported in such a way as to allow researchers "to independently evaluate the results obtained in an [exploratory factor analysis] study" (p. 400). The following sections walk through the major decisions to be considered in a factor analysis. Other sources treat these issues in a more comprehensive manner (see, e.g., Gorsuch, 1983; Thompson, 2004), and still others review them more succinctly (see, e.g., Henson & Roberts, 2006; Kieffer, 1999).

Matrix of Associations

All factor analyses begin by analyzing some matrix that characterizes the relationships between the variables. As noted previously, factor analysis

TABLE 1.1
Hypothetical Data for an Exploratory Factor Analysis

Participant	Nonacademic items			Academic items			
	1	2	3	4	5	6	7
1	2	4	3	1	1	2	1
2	3	3	2	2	2	2	4
3	4	2	4	3	3	3	3
4	3	3	1	2	2	4	2
5	5	2	4	1	3	3	2
6	4	1	5	2	4	3	7
7	3	2	6	5	5	4	3
8	4	3	7	6	6	3	2
9	3	2	6	7	7	4	1
10	5	1	3	5	6	5	4
11	4	2	5	6	7	6	7
12	5	1	2	7	6	7	6
13	4	2	3	7	5	6	2
14	3	3	4	4	4	5	3
15	4	5	7	5	5	6	1
16	5	6	5	6	4	7	3
17	4	5	6	6	5	6	6
18	5	4	7	7	4	7	5
19	6	3	5	6	3	6	7
20	5	2	6	5	2	5	4
21	7	3	7	6	2	6	7
22	6	4	6	7	3	5	1
23	5	4	7	6	2	4	2
24	6	5	5	5	1	3	1
25	7	6	4	4	2	2	2
26	5	5	5	3	3	3	4
27	6	4	6	2	2	2	2
28	7	5	7	3	3	3	6
29	5	4	6	2	2	1	3
30	6	5	7	1	1	2	7

focuses on summarizing these relationships. Different matrices can be analyzed. Phi or tetrachoric correlations may be employed with dichotomous data. When the data are continuous, either a variance–covariance or a Pearson correlation matrix may be analyzed. Because the Pearson correlation matrix is most often used in the literature and has certain advantages (cf. Henson et al., 2004; Henson & Roberts, 2006), this matrix is the type that is analyzed here. Table 1.2 presents the correlation matrix among the items for our heuristic data. SPSS was used for all analyses presented, and Appendix 1.1 provides the commands for interested readers.

Examination of these correlations is quite informative because we can see that the items within an expected subscale tend to be more highly corre-

TABLE 1.2
Correlation Matrix for Items on the Social Competence Instrument

Item	1	2	3	4	5	6
2	<u>378</u>					
3	<u>.402</u>	<u>.364</u>				
4	.109	−.107	.240			
5	−.322	−.455	.006	(.584)		
6	.007	−.170	.032	(.778)	(.534)	
7	.288	−.183	.136	(.030)	(.110)	(.276)

Note. Items 1 through 3 are intended to measure nonacademic social competence, and Items 4 through 7 are intended to measure academic social competence. The correlations within the nonacademic subset are underlined, and those within the academic subset are in parentheses. All other correlations are between items from different subsets.

lated with each other than with items for the other subscale. This would suggest the possible presence of two factors in the data. However, there are two noteworthy exceptions. First, Item 5 has a moderate correlation with an item outside its expected subscale (Item 2), although Item 5's within-subscale correlations are still higher. Second, Item 7 tends to be weakly related to any of the other items. These issues will be revisited when interpreting our analysis.

Factor Extraction

There are many ways to extract factors from the matrix of associations, and each uses different methods to summarize the relationships. The two most common approaches are principal components analysis (PCA) and principal axis factoring (PAF, or common factor analysis). There has been considerable debate about the differences between these methods, but space precludes a full explication of the issues here. Let it suffice to say that PAF is generally thought to be the appropriate method for examining constructs, and PCA is better used for data reduction rather than assessment of latent constructs (for a more complete discussion, see Fabrigar et al., 1999). However, the differences between the methods shrink when factoring large numbers of variables, as is often the case, and when the variables have high reliability (Henson & Roberts, 2006; Thompson, 2004). As such, and for ease of communication, both approaches are referred to as *factor analyses* in this chapter. PCA is used in the current demonstration because its results are often comparable with those of PAF under the above circumstances and it is most commonly used in the literature.

Determining the Number of Factors

Factor extraction is simply the method for summarizing the variable relationships; it does not determine how many factors are present in the data, which is a decision that the researcher must make. It is absolutely critical to extract the right number of factors because this directly impacts the interpretation of the final results.

Eigenvalue-Greater-Than-One (EV > 1) Rule and Scree Plot

There are many guidelines to inform this decision, including the EV > 1 rule (Kaiser, 1960) and the scree plot (Cattell, 1966). Historically, both of these rules have seen frequent use, and they remain the most commonly employed guidelines in spite of repeated arguments regarding their inaccuracies (cf. Henson & Roberts, 2006; O'Connor, 2000; Zwick & Velicer, 1986).

Each factor comes with a statistic called an *eigenvalue*, which is a representation of how much variance the factor can reproduce out of all the variance present within and between the items in the matrix of associations. If there were no correlations ($r = 0$) among any of the items, then there would be no shared variance, and subsequently there would be no way to summarize the correlations into more succinct factors. Each item would represent its own entity, with an eigenvalue equal to 1. In this case, there are no factors because there is no summarization of the items together. Therefore, when an eigenvalue greater than 1 is obtained, it represents more summative power than a single item and thus may represent a factor. (The full logic behind the EV > 1 rule is actually more complex than this, but I will not address that here.) The scree plot is a graphic display of the eigenvalues, and the researcher must interpret which eigenvalues represent substantive factors and which represent error or noise in the data.

Figure 1.1 presents a portion of the SPSS output from the initial PCA for our data (SPSS menu sequence is Analyze—Data Reduction—Factor). Under the initial eigenvalues portion, we can see the eigenvalues for the seven components (or factors) extracted from the correlation matrix. In PCA, the sum of eigenvalues for all possible factors will equal the number of variables

Total Variance Explained

Component	Initial Eigenvalues			Extraction Sums of Squared Loadings			Rotation
	Total	% of Variance	Cumulative %	Total	% of Variance	Cumulative %	Total
1	2.471	35.294	35.294	2.471	35.294	35.294	2.412
2	1.886	26.948	62.241	1.886	26.948	62.241	1.927
3	1.102	15.749	77.991	1.102	15.749	77.991	1.302
4	.675	9.645	87.635				
5	.463	6.610	94.245				
6	.283	4.045	98.290				
7	.120	1.710	100.000				

Extraction Method: Principal Component Analysis.

a. When components are correlated, sums of squared loadings cannot be added to obtain a total variance.

Figure 1.1. Partial SPSS output for initial principal component analysis.

factored. Therefore, if we took the time to compute it, the sum of the eigenvalues equals seven, or the total number of items.

Hypothetically, if the correlations among the seven items in Table 1.2 were all 0, then each of these eigenvalues would be 1. Instead, we see that the eigenvalues move from larger to smaller, with some above and below values of 1. This is a function of the extraction process, whereby the first factor is created to explain as much of the correlation matrix as possible. The second factor is extracted to explain as much as possible out of what is left over (called the *residual correlation matrix*, analogous to error scores in a regression), and so on. The output also shows us the percentage of variance from the correlation matrix that is reproduced by each factor (e.g., Factor 1 reproduced 35.29%).

Keeping and interpreting all seven of these factors would eradicate the purpose of a factor analysis. In fact, some of these factors simply represent noise or error variance and are not reliable or meaningful at all. Thus, we must determine which factors likely represent reliable variance and keep only those.

The right-hand portion of Figure 1.1 shows that only those factors with an EV > 1 were retained upon extraction. This is the default option in SPSS and most other statistics packages and, as Thompson and Daniel (1996) noted, "may be the most widely used decision rule, also by default" (p. 200). Empirical studies have verified that the EV > 1 rule remains the most commonly employed guide (Henson et al., 2004; Henson & Roberts, 2006). This is highly unfortunate because the EV > 1 rule is often inaccurate (see, e.g., Byrd & Henson, 2007; Zwick & Velicer, 1986) and can lead to retaining too many factors, particularly when there are large numbers of items (Zwick & Velicer, 1982). As a matter of course, other guidelines for determining the number of factors should also be considered and reported.

The scree plot shown in Figure 1.2 is commonly used but requires a level of subjective interpretation to determine the location of the break in the line of plotted eigenvalues separating reliable from noise factors. Ideally, there would be a clear flattened line to the right of the plot representing noise factors, with a clear upward turn toward the left indicating reliable factors. Figure 1.2 is ambiguous in this regard, although there is a slight bend after the first three factors.

Parallel Analysis and Minimum Average Partial

Fortunately, there are other more accurate guides for determining the number of factors, including parallel analysis using a minimum average partial criterion. Only parallel analysis is exampled here, but both are discussed elsewhere (e.g., O'Connor, 2000; Zwick & Velicer, 1986).

The logic behind parallel analysis is straightforward. Factors are supposed to summarize reliably shared variance among variables and should at

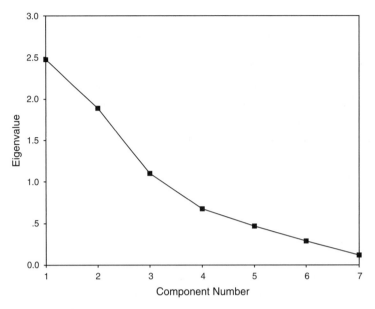

Figure 1.2. Scree plot for initial eigenvalues.

least explain more variance than factors generated from random variables, regardless of the magnitude of the eigenvalues. In parallel analysis, one or more random data sets are created with the same number of cases and variables as the real data set. The random data are then factored, and the random data eigenvalues are compared with the eigenvalues for the real data. Only factors from the real data whose eigenvalues are larger than the eigenvalues from the respective factors in the random data are retained.

Table 1.3 presents results from several approaches to conducting a parallel eigenvalue analysis. Thompson and Daniel (1996) provided SPSS commands to generate a random data matrix from which to generate factored eigenvalues. However, the creation of random data is, well, random, and therefore one random matrix may vary slightly from the next, thus affecting the eigenvalues. O'Connor (2000) provided a very useful SPSS (and SAS and MATLAB) routine to generate many random data matrices and then compute the average and 95th percentiles of the eigenvalues. The O'Connor results in Table 1.3 were computed with 1,000 random data sets. In this case, and in contrast to the EV > 1 rule, all three approaches (O'Connor's program for mean and 95th percentile EVs, and Thompson and Daniel's program for random EVs) agree that there are two factors more reliable than the random data. More specifically, the third factor's eigenvalue (1.102) is lower than its random counterparts. Research has clearly demonstrated the improved accuracy of parallel analysis and minimum average partial approaches over

TABLE 1.3

Eigenvalues for Real and Random Data from Parallel Analyses

Factor	Obtained EVs	Mean EVs[a]	95%ile EVs[a]	Random EVs[b]
1	2.471	1.759	2.074	1.843
2	1.886	1.404	1.599	1.529
3	1.102	1.159	1.304	1.305
4	.675	.949	1.088	.770
5	.463	.760	.899	.758
6	.283	.577	.715	.413
7	.120	.392	.521	.382

Note. EV = eigenvalue. [a]Using SPSS commands recommended by O'Connor (2000). [b]Using SPSS commands recommended by Thompson & Daniel (1996)

traditional retention rules (Zwick & Velicer, 1986). Given their benefits, use of these methods should be a matter of course when determining the number of factors.

Theoretical Considerations

Beyond the options thus far discussed, researchers must also consider the theoretical implications of the factors. In other words, factors should make sense in terms of the items that they entail. This is taken up further in the next section, and given the retention rules above, we will consider that two factors are likely present in our current data.

Factor Rotation and Interpreting the Pattern and Structure Coefficients

Eventually, we must determine what items are related to what factors, and this requires interpretation of factor pattern and structure coefficients. This is not unlike interpretation of standardized weights and structure coefficients in regression or other analyses (Courville & Thompson, 2001; Henson, 2002), where higher coefficients indicate (generally) greater relevance. Each item will have a coefficient for each factor retained.

Before interpretation, though, it is typically necessary to rotate the factors to make the meaning of the factors more apparent. *Rotation* refers to redistributing the variance explained by the factors so it becomes clearer which items apply to which factors. There are many rotation strategies, but they generally fall into two categories. *Orthogonal* rotations (e.g., varimax, quartimax) ensure that the factors are left uncorrelated during the process, which allows for distinct interpretation of each factor as the variance it represents is not shared with any other factor. *Oblique* rotations (e.g., promax, direct oblimin) allow the factors to correlate in the end, and therefore factors can explain some of the same variance in the original matrix of associations.

Readers are referred to Kieffer (1999) and Thompson (2004) for explanations of how rotation occurs and more detail about various strategies. The decision between orthogonal and oblique strategies basically hinges on whether the researcher thinks the constructs being measured should be correlated or not, which is often a theoretical consideration and which may not be clear in an exploratory situation. In our example, though, one might expect some positive correlation between academic and nonacademic social competence because one might think that overall social competence is reflected in both areas.

Unless the expectation is quite certain about the factor correlations, researchers "should first obliquely rotate results, examine the factor intercorrelations (and report them), and then make judgments about whether an orthogonal or oblique rotation is most warranted" (Henson & Roberts, 2006, p. 410). Too often, researchers simply assume uncorrelated factors and use an orthogonal rotation. If the correlations are not noteworthy (say, about .40 or better), then an orthogonal rotation may be considered. Orthogonal rotations do have the advantage of being more parsimonious and therefore potentially more generalizable if the factors are relatively unrelated. Of course, oblique rotations better honor reality if the factors are indeed correlated.

However, some methodologists do take the opposite view (cf. Thompson, 2004) and suggest that orthogonal rotation be performed first and, if the goal of simple, interpretable structure is achieved, that the oblique rotation not be used unless theory demands otherwise, especially when scores on the factors are not in turn being used in subsequent analyses. The thinking behind these views emphasizes first that interpretation clarity is the major objective of rotation and second that replicability is important. Theoretically, because orthogonal rotation estimates fewer parameters and therefore is more parsimonious, if both rotations for given data are approximately equally interpretable, the orthogonal rotation might be preferred because simpler solutions under these circumstances are theoretically more replicable.

Returning to our example, Table 1.4 presents the rotated pattern and structure coefficients after an oblique rotation for the default option of retaining three factors under the EV > 1 rule. The pattern coefficients provide information about "the importance of a given variable to the factor with the influence of the other variables partialled out" (Weigle & Snow, 1995, p. 5). The structure coefficients are the simple correlations between the item and the factor. In this case, an oblique rotation called *promax* (with kappa = 4) was used so we can evaluate factor correlations. With oblique rotations, researchers should interpret both the pattern and structure matrices. With orthogonal rotations, the pattern and structure matrices are the same, and therefore only one set of coefficients needs to be interpreted. For more, see Henson and Roberts (2006) or Thompson (2004). In either case, the term *loading*, which is often seen in the literature, should not

TABLE 1.4

Factor Pattern and (Structure) Coefficients for Initial Three-Factor Solution
Rotated to the Promax Criterion (kappa = 4)

Item	Factor I	Factor II	Factor III
4	.964 (.908)	.255 (.124)	−.127 (.063)
6	.855 (.871)	.062 (−.043)	.132 (.293)
5	.780 (.815)	−.311 (−.414)	−.024 (.105)
2	−.159 (−.320)	.770 (.775)	−.330 (−.323)
3	.256 (.160)	.766 (.733)	−.017 (.100)
1	−.076 (−.099)	.744 (.772)	.394 (.415)
7	−.011 (.164)	.019 (.065)	.957 (.956)

		Factor correlations	
II	−.130		
III	.185	.047	

Note. Items with factor pattern coefficients above .40 are underlined. Coefficients are ordered based on magnitude within a factor.

be used because it is ambiguous and does not specify which type of coefficient is being referenced.

Examination of the coefficients in Table 1.4 indicates that Items 4 through 6 are salient on Factor I, with much lower coefficients on the other two factors. Factor I, then, is primarily a function of the correlations between these three items, and therefore we can consider naming this factor based on their content. Although we do not have the exact items in this example, we do know that these were three of the four items representing *academic social competence*, and thus it would be reasonable to name the factor as such. Likewise, Items 1 through 3 were salient on Factor II, and we could name this factor *nonacademic social competence*. Note as well that Item 5, which had a moderate correlation with Item 2 in the nonacademic domain (see Table 1.2), has the largest out-of-factor coefficients when examining the first two factors. However, its coefficients for Factor I are still substantially larger.

Factor III presents a difficulty. Only one item is relevant for this factor, and it makes little sense to have a factor with just one item. In spite of the fact that this factor was initially retained because of the EV > 1 rule, factors are supposed to summarize correlations among several items. In fact, at least three items would normally be expected. Instead, the parallel analysis was on target, indicating two factors; the third factor is too weak and should not be retained.

Item Deletions, Factor Correlations, and Reextraction

Because Item 7 does not relate to either of the first two factors, it is reasonable to delete this item from the analysis. Furthermore, it may be reasonable to delete items that had high coefficients on more than one factor in order to simplify interpretation of the factors, assuming the factors were not strongly correlated. Yet if the factors were allowed to correlate (perhaps because the constructs should be related in theory and we wished to examine that expectation), then one would probably have greater tolerance for items on more than one factor, because this is what would make factors correlate in the first place. This is one reason why the interpretation of oblique solutions is potentially more complex.

Once we make item deletions, the correlation matrix changes, and therefore we must rerun the factor analysis to get results with just Items 1 through 6. It is very important in this process to recheck the number of factors present after item deletions. Because the pattern and structure coefficients will change as the matrix of associations changes, it would be insufficient to simply assume that the same number of factors would be present.

Table 1.4 informs us that the correlations among the factors are very small, with the largest being .185 (just 3.4% shared variance). Because the factors are not correlated, an orthogonal rotation was used when rerunning the factor analysis. Table 1.5 presents the final results after deleting Item 7, but this time with an orthogonal rotation (varimax). Because of the orthogonal rotation, the pattern and structure coefficients are the same. The two factors explained 71.1% of the variance in the original matrix of associations, which is more than the average of 52.03% observed in Henson and Roberts's (2006) review of factor analytic practice.

Table 1.5 also reports the communality coefficients, which represent the proportion of variance in the original item that is reproduced across the retained factors. For example, the factors were able to reproduce 87.8% of the variance of Item 4, which is a substantial amount. It follows, then, that when communality coefficients are high, more variance in the matrix of associa-

TABLE 1.5
Factor Pattern/Structure Coefficients for Two-Factor Solution
Rotated to the Varimax Criterion

Item	Academic social competence	Nonacademic social competence	h^2
4	.920	.178	.878
6	.877	.016	.769
5	.788	−.369	.757
1	−.022	.796	.635
3	.206	.744	.597
2	−.292	.737	.628
Trace	2.364	1.899	
% of variance	39.403	31.654	

Note. Items with factor pattern coefficients above .40 are underlined. Percentage of variance is postrotation. The prerotation eigenvalue of the third, unretained factor was .682. h^2 = communality coefficient.

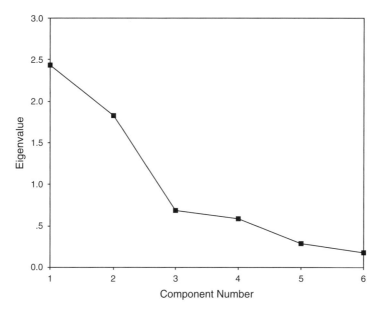

Figure 1.3. Scree plot for final solution.

tions will be explained, and therefore the total variance explained will be higher. The note in the table also reports the eigenvalue for the first factor that was not retained. This helps the reader to evaluate the decision to retain two factors. Figure 1.3 presents the scree plot for the final solution, which clearly indicates the presence of two factors.

In the end, we have found pretty strong support for our expected subscales, with all items except one behaving as anticipated. Although we did expect a positive correlation between the factors, this was not observed, suggesting that adolescents are not necessarily high or low on both subscales simultaneously. This provides important structural validity support for our scores, but again, it does not mean that we have truly assessed social competence. To this point, we have only the content validity of the items to support this possibility. Additional work would be needed to examine score validity fully.

SOME CONSIDERATIONS FOR USING FACTOR ANALYSIS IN THE STUDY OF GIFTEDNESS

Sample Size

In the heuristic example, the sample size is likely too low to yield a trustworthy solution. Although representativeness of a sample is more important than sample size, the sample size still must be large enough to warrant the analysis. Factor analysis usually employs many variables, so many cases are required. This poses a challenge in the study of giftedness because of the inherently restricted size of the population. Nevertheless, sufficient effort and time must be extended to gather enough participants to justify the analysis.

Many authors have proffered rules of thumb for how big a sample needs to be for factor analysis, but MacCallum, Widaman, Zhang, and Hong (1999) demonstrated that these rules can sometimes be misleading and that one key determinant of whether the sample size is large enough is the magnitude of the communality coefficients. While an eigenvalue speaks to how much variance a factor reproduces across all the items, a communality coefficient informs how much of an item's variance is reproduced across all the extracted factors. For example, a communality of .50 would indicate that the factors were able to explain 50% of that item's variance. Generally, when communalities for the items are high, fewer participants can be used, and when communalities are low, more are needed. Of course, communalities are not known before the analysis, making a priori sample size determinations difficult. At the unavoidable risk of oversimplifying the matter, I will simply state that researchers probably want at least a 5:1 participant to variable ratio as a bare minimum, and ratios more in the range of 10:1 are preferred.

Test Ceilings and Limited Variance

The nature of gifted students often creates assessment difficulties in the form of ceiling effects, where students perform at the high end of the scale. One ramification may be restricted variance on the variables being assessed, as compared with the variability in the scores that may be observed within a more general population. The ceiling may prevent some students from scoring as high as their abilities would otherwise indicate.

Restricted variance may lead to reduced correlations between variables in some cases (Shavelson, 1996; Thompson, 2006). It is important to emphasize, though, that restriction of range does not always reduce correlations as a matter of course, and in some cases the relationships can actually become stronger (cf. Huck, 1992; Huck, Wright, & Park, 1992). However, if range restriction is indeed an issue, this may reduce the magnitude of the correlations in the matrix of associations, thereby weakening the factor analysis. It is difficult to know the full extent of this potential problem, but if norms or prior studies are available for the variables of interest, we could at least examine whether the gifted sample has comparable variance as is reflected in the prior data. If there is a reasonable explanation for why item variances might be artificially restricted (as with a ceiling effect), we could consider correcting correlation coefficients among items for attenuation (Greener & Osburn, 1979) and then analyze these corrected correlations. The corrected correlations would generally be larger and reflect stronger relationships among the variables, thereby increasing the feasibility of a factor analysis.

Multigroup Factor Analysis and Factor Invariance

Because factor structure is a function of the correlations among scores, and because scores are a function of particular samples, obtained structures can vary from sample to sample or between subsamples within a more broadly defined population. There are multiple implications of this fact for studying gifted students.

First, it would typically be presumptuous to assume that scores from an instrument developed with nongifted students would have the same factor structure when used with gifted students. Of course, it would also be presumptuous to assume the structure would be different. The point here is simply that the factor structure should be empirically examined with gifted students before too much faith is placed in scores.

It may be that the nature of some constructs differs even within subgroups of gifted populations. Does the structure of social competence differ between gifted boys and girls or based on ethnicity or perhaps varied socioeconomic status variables? These considerations are not unique to the study of giftedness, and they apply any time a factor structure is assumed to extend to different types of samples. If our interest is in generalizing factor structure across varied groups, then we are seeking evidence for factor invariance.

Multigroup factor analysis is one method by which to test for factor invariance across groups (e.g., male versus female, gifted versus nongifted). This approach is normally undertaken within a confirmatory factor analysis framework using structural equation modeling and therefore is beyond the scope of this chapter. Interested readers are referred to Byrne (1989) for more detail on this valuable methodology.

Domain Specificity in Gifted Constructs

Social science research is often challenged by issues of domain specificity when operationalizing constructs. We often wish to identify and study constructs that are generalizable across many persons, which may require relatively broad-spectrum definitions of constructs. However, this can come with the risk of losing applicability in some specific circumstances.

For example, the study of self-efficacy involves examining people's beliefs regarding whether they can execute the courses of action necessary to be successful at certain tasks (Bandura, 1997). Both theory and research indicate that these beliefs can be rather specific regarding the task at hand, and people's beliefs can vary considerably regarding other tasks. A gifted adolescent, for instance, may be quite efficacious in one subject area but not in others. Therefore, measuring self-efficacy should occur for relatively specific tasks rather than as some global measure of general self-efficacy, which may not be useful when studying the construct in a particular area (Pajares, 1996).

Domain specificity is ultimately a theoretical concern and therefore dependent on the nature of the construct being studied. However, factor analysis may come to bear on the theory because we often use the analysis to explore whether the domains hypothesized are actually present in the data, as in the social competence example offered earlier. As such, factor analytic results can inform the theory regarding the specificity of our constructs. As Nunnally (1978) stated, "factor analysis is intimately involved with questions of validity . . . [and] is at the heart of the measurement of psychological constructs" (pp. 112–113).

CONCLUSION

For readers new to factor analysis, it is hopefully apparent from this chapter that this methodology requires the researcher to make a number of decisions that may influence later results and that there is an inherent level of subjectivity in this process. Nevertheless, these decisions can be made thoughtfully and on the basis of current research. And the decisions should be adequately reported so others can externally evaluate them.

Factor analysis is remarkably useful for summarizing data and informing instrument development. It is also helpful for evaluating whether constructs supported by theory in one group of study subjects are present in other groups as well.

The specific approach to factor analysis taken in the example above should not be taken as the only method. There are many nuances and other ways to conduct the analysis, depending on the data collected and the purposes of the research. Indeed, entire courses are taught on the method. The primary purpose of this chapter was to present an accessible treatment of one common approach to factor analysis, with an emphasis on making informed decisions along the way. Researchers are strongly encouraged, for example, to consider modern rules for determining the number of factors in a data set. Given its utility, factor analysis will continue to be used often across the literature in general and in the study of giftedness in particular.

APPENDIX 1.1
SPSS COMMANDS FOR FACTOR ANALYSIS EXAMPLE

```
* Examine correlations among the items.
CORRELATIONS
   VARIABLES=q1 q2 q3 q4 q5 q6 q7 /
   PRINT=TWOTAIL NOSIG /MISSING=PAIRWISE .


* Run initial PCA with oblique (promax) rotation.
FACTOR
   VARIABLES q1 q2 q3 q4 q5 q6 q7 /MISSING LISTWISE /
   ANALYSIS q1 q2 q3 q4 q5 q6 q7 /
   PRINT UNIVARIATE INITIAL EXTRACTION ROTATION /
   FORMAT SORT /PLOT EIGEN ROTATION /
   CRITERIA MINEIGEN(1) ITERATE(25) /EXTRACTION PC /
   CRITERIA ITERATE(25)/ROTATION PROMAX(4) /
   METHOD=CORRELATION .


* Run final PCA after dropping item 7 with orthogonal
  (varimax) rotation.
FACTOR
   VARIABLES q1 q2 q3 q4 q5 q6 /MISSING LISTWISE /
   ANALYSIS q1 q2 q3 q4 q5 q6 /
   PRINT INITIAL EXTRACTION ROTATION /FORMAT SORT /
   PLOT EIGEN ROTATION /
   CRITERIA MINEIGEN(1) ITERATE(25) /
   EXTRACTION PC /CRITERIA ITERATE(25) /
   ROTATION VARIMAX /METHOD=CORRELATION .
```

REFERENCES

Bandura, A. (1997). *Self-efficacy: The exercise of control*. New York: Freeman.

Benson, J. (1998). Developing a strong program of construct validation: A test anxiety example. *Educational Measurement: Issues and Practice, 17*(1), 10–17, 22.

Byrd, J., & Henson, R. K. (2007, April). *A comparison of four factor retention methods in nonnormal data*. Paper presented at the annual meeting of the American Educational Research Association, Chicago.

Byrne, B. M. (1989). Multigroup comparisons and the assumption of equivalent construct validity across groups: Methodological and substantive issues. *Multivariate Behavioral Research, 24*, 503–523.

Cattell, R. B. (1966). The scree test for the number of factors. *Multivariate Behavioral Research, 1*, 245–276.

Chan, D. W. (2006). Perceived multiple intelligences among male and female Chinese gifted students in Hong Kong: The structure of the Student Multiple Intelligences Profile. *Gifted Child Quarterly, 50,* 325–338.

Courville, T., & Thompson, B. (2001). Use of structure coefficients in published multiple regression articles: β is not enough. *Educational and Psychological Measurement, 61,* 229–248.

Fabrigar, L. R., Wegener, D. T., MacCallum, R. C., & Strahan, E. J. (1999). Evaluating the use of exploratory factor analysis in psychological research. *Psychological Methods, 4,* 272–299.

Gorsuch, R. L. (1983). *Factor analysis* (2nd ed.). Hillsdale, NJ: Erlbaum.

Greener, J. M., & Osburn, H. G. (1979). An empirical study of the accuracy of corrections for restriction in range due to explicit selection. *Applied Psychological Measurement, 3,* 31–41.

Henson, R. K. (2002, April). *The logic and interpretation of structure coefficients in multivariate general linear model analyses.* Paper presented at the annual meeting of the American Educational Research Association, New Orleans. (ERIC Document Reproduction Service No. ED 467 381)

Henson, R. K., Capraro, R. M., & Capraro, M. M. (2004). Reporting practices and use of exploratory factor analyses in educational research journals: Errors and explanation. *Research in the Schools, 11*(2), 61–72.

Henson, R. K., & Roberts, J. K. (2006). Use of exploratory factor analysis in published research: Common errors and some comment on improved practice. *Educational and Psychological Measurement, 66,* 393–416.

Hetzel, R. D. (1996). A primer on factor analysis with comments on patterns of practice and reporting. In B. Thompson (Ed.), *Advances in social science methodology* (Vol. 4, pp. 175–206). Greenwich, CT: JAI Press.

Huck, S. W. (1992). Group heterogeneity and Pearson's r. *Educational and Psychological Measurement, 52,* 253–260.

Huck, S. W., Wright, S. P., & Park, S. (1992). Pearson's r and spread: A classroom demonstration. *Teaching of Psychology, 19*(1), 45–47.

Kaiser, H. F. (1960). The application of electronic computers to factor analysis. *Educational and Psychological Measurement, 20,* 141–151.

Kieffer, K. M. (1999). An introductory primer on the appropriate use of exploratory and confirmatory factor analysis. *Research in the Schools, 6,* 75–92.

MacCallum, R. C., Widaman, K. F., Zhang, S., & Hong, S. (1999). Sample size in factor analysis. *Psychological Methods, 4,* 84–99.

McCoach, D. B., & Siegle, D. (2003). The structure and function of academic self-concept in gifted and general education students. *Roeper Review, 25,* 61–65.

Messick, S. (1995). Validity of psychological assessment. *American Psychologist, 50,* 741–749.

Nunnally, J. C. (1978). *Psychometric theory* (2nd ed.). New York: McGraw-Hill.

O'Connor, B. P. (2000). SPSS and SAS programs for determining the number of components using parallel analysis and Velicer's MAP test. *Behavior Research Methods, Instruments, & Computers, 32*, 396–402. Retrieved July 12, 2009, from http://flash.lakeheadu.ca/~boconno2/nfactors.html

Pajares, F. (1996). Self-efficacy beliefs in academic settings. *Review of Educational Research, 66*, 543–578.

Rudasill, K. M., Foust, R. C., & Callahan, C. M. (2007). The Social Coping Questionnaire: An examination of its structure with an American sample of gifted adolescents. *Journal for the Education of the Gifted, 30*, 353–371.

Shavelson, R. J. (1996). *Statistical reasoning for the behavioral sciences* (3rd ed.). Boston: Allyn and Bacon.

Stevens, J. (2002). *Applied multivariate statistics of the social sciences* (4th ed.). Mahwah, NJ: Erlbaum.

Thompson, B., & Daniel, L. G. (1996). Factor analytic evidence for the construct validity of scores: A historical overview and some guidelines. *Educational and Psychological Measurement, 56*, 197–208.

Thompson, B. (2004). *Exploratory and confirmatory factor analysis.* Washington, DC: American Psychological Association.

Thompson, B. (2006). *Foundations of behavioral statistics: An insight-based approach.* New York: Guilford Press.

Watkins, M. W., Greenawalt, C. G., & Marcell, C. M. (2002). Factor structure of the Wechsler Intelligence Scale for Children—Third Edition among gifted students. *Educational and Psychological Measurement, 62*, 164–172.

Weigle, D. C., & Snow, A. (1995, April). *Interpreting where detected effects originate: Structure coefficients versus pattern and other coefficients.* Paper presented at the annual meeting of the American Educational Research Association, San Francisco. (ERIC Document Reproduction Service No. ED 383 766)

Worrell, F. C., & Mello, Z. R. (2007). The reliability and validity of Zimbardo Time Perspective Inventory scores in academically talented adolescents. *Educational and Psychological Measurement, 67*, 487–504.

Zimbardo, P. G., & Boyd, J. N. (1999). Putting time in perspective: A valid, reliable individual-difference metric. *Journal of Personality and Social Psychology, 77*, 1271–1288.

Zwick, W. R., & Velicer, W. F. (1982). Factors influencing four rules for determining the number of components to retain. *Multivariate Behavioral Research, 17*, 253–269.

Zwick, W. R., & Velicer, W. F. (1986). Factors influencing five rules for determining the number of components to retain. *Psychological Bulletin, 99*, 432–442.

2

Q-TECHNIQUE FACTOR ANALYSIS AS A VEHICLE TO INTENSIVELY STUDY ESPECIALLY INTERESTING PEOPLE

BRUCE THOMPSON

Especially gifted and creative people are in relatively short supply, but are also very interesting. Because Q-technique factor analysis is especially suited for the intensive study of a small number of especially interesting people, Q-technique factor analysis is especially suitable for inquiry about giftedness and creativity. The purpose of the present chapter is to provide a primer on using Q-technique factor analysis in the intensive study of gifted or creative people, or other especially interesting people. Additional resources for the interested reader are Kerlinger (1986, chap. 32), Brown (1980), Carr (1992), and Thompson (2000, 2004).

Origins of Q- and Other Factor Analytic Techniques

Factor analysis was conceptualized by Spearman (1904), coincident with Alfred Binet's creation of the first intelligence test in France, at which point questions about measurement validity arose. Although factor analysis can be used for various purposes (Thompson, 2004), there has always been an intimate linkage between factor analysis and measurement validity questions. Indeed, "construct validity has [even] been spoken of as . . . 'factorial validity' "

(Nunnally, 1978, p. 111). Joy Guilford's (1946) discussion some 60 years ago illustrates this application:

> Validity, in my opinion is of two kinds . . . The *factorial validity* [italics added] of a test is given by its . . . [factor pattern coefficients on] meaningful, common, reference factors. This is the kind of validity that is really meant when the question is asked "Does this test measure what it is supposed to measure?" A more pertinent question should be "What does this test measure?" The answer then should be in terms of factors . . . I predict a time when any test author will be expected to present information regarding the factor composition of his [sic] tests. (pp. 428, 437–438)

In this application of factor analysis, and in the way that most applied researchers unconsciously think about factor analysis, the data matrix is constituted by different participants defining the data matrix rows, and different variables (e.g., IQ test items, IQ subscale scores) defining the columns of the data matrix. A matrix of association coefficients (e.g., Pearson r, Spearman rho, covariance, sum of the squared cross products, polychoric correlation) among the columns is computed, and then factor are extracted from the v-by-v association coefficient matrix in the manner explained by Thompson (2004, pp. 22–24), using one of the many factor analytic methods (e.g., principal components analysis, principal axis analysis, image factor analysis, canonical factor analysis).

The purposes of such factor analyses are to determine (a) how many factors underlay the response patterns of the participants, (b) how associated the variables are with the factors, and in some cases, (c) what scores might be created on the factors, and used in place of the original data in subsequent analyses, such as multiple regression (Thompson, 2006), descriptive discriminant analysis, or predictive discriminant analysis (Huberty, 1994). The association matrix is the actual basis for factor analysis, and we are analyzing the relationships among the columns in the data matrix. The accuracy or replicability of our association coefficients is dependent on the ratio of the number of rows in the data matrix to the number of columns in the data matrix. Typically, we expect the ratio of data matrix rows to columns to be at least 2:1, and perhaps much greater, so that our association coefficients, and in turn our factors, will be reasonably trustworthy.

However, during the 1940s, some psychologists began wondering what would happen if the data matrix was transposed, such that variables delineated data matrix rows, and people delineated the data matrix columns. These psychologists (e.g., Stephenson, 1935, 1953) reasoned that the mathematics of factor analyzing association matrices do not know whether they are analyzing variables, people, or even time.

Researchers interested in factor analyzing people rather than variables quite rightly point out that psychologists are frequently more interested in talking about types of persons (e.g., Type A personalities, compulsive persons) than about types of variables (e.g., introversion, spatial ability). Thus, on its face the factor analysis of people is appealing.

However, when the possibilities of factoring people were first conceptualized, heated arguments regarding the utility and the meaning of person factors erupted, especially between William Stephenson and Sir Cyril Burt (Burt & Stephenson, 1939). Burt was the first psychologist knighted for his contributions to testing, and later was the subject of controversy as to whether he had fabricated some or all of his data in studies of identical twins raised separately. Stephenson outlived his rival by some 18 years, and remained academically active until the very end of his life in his late 80s, even editing a journal dealing exclusively with factor analyzing people.

Out of this controversy grew a recognition that analyzing variables, or people, or time, could all be useful for different purposes. Raymond Cattell (1966) summarized eventually six primary factor analysis choices in conceptualizing his "data box," with the three axes of the box involving (a) either one or more than one *variable*, (b) either one or more than one *person*, and (c) either one or more than one *occasion of measurement*. Cattell termed these three features of the data, *modes*, and suggested that six "*techniques*" could be delineated on three surfaces of the "box" by using the three axes in various pairwise combinations.

Specifically, Cattell (1966) suggested that researchers could factor:

1. *variables* as the columns of the data matrix, with *people* constituting the matrix rows, which Cattell labeled *R-technique* factor analysis (e.g., Thompson, Cook & Heath, 2003);
2. *people* as the columns of the data matrix, with *variables* constituting the matrix rows, which Cattell labeled *Q-technique* factor analysis (e.g., Thompson, 1980b);
3. *variables* as the columns of the data matrix, with *occasions* constituting the matrix rows, which Cattell labeled *P-technique* factor analysis (e.g., Cattell, 1953)—here the analysis might involve a single participant, or location statistics (e.g., means, medians, Huber estimators) summarizing for each variable and each occasion all the scores as a single number;
4. *occasions* as the columns of the data matrix, with *variables* constituting the matrix rows, which Cattell labeled *O-technique* factor analysis (e.g., Jones, Thompson & Miller, 1980)—here again the analysis might involve a single participant, or location statistics summarizing for each variable and each occasion all the scores as a single number;

5. *occasions* as the columns of the data matrix, with *people* constituting the matrix rows, which Cattell labeled *T-technique* factor analysis (e.g., Frankiewicz & Thompson, 1979); or

6. *people* as the columns of the data matrix, with *occasions* constituting the matrix rows, which Cattell labeled *S-technique* factor analysis.

R-technique is the most frequently published of the analyses, followed by Q-technique reports, but articles have been published using five of the six two-mode factor analysis techniques.

Purpose of the Present Chapter

Q-technique factor analysis requires that the number of people be less than approximately half the number of variables. Of course, there are limits to how many variables can be measured in a given study before participants become fatigued, or unwilling to provide additional responses. The limitation on the number of variables that can reasonably be measured implies, in turn, a limitation as to how many people can be factored, especially because we may only study a number of people that is a fraction of the number of variables. Thus, as Kerlinger (1986) noted,

> One can rarely generalize to populations from Q person samples. Indeed, *one usually does not wish to do so* [italics added]. Rather, one tests theories on small sets of individuals carefully chosen for their "known" or presumed possession of some significant characteristic or characteristic. (p. 521)

In short, a "strength of Q is its suitability for intensive study of the individual" (Kerlinger, 1986, p. 517), achieved by asking one extraordinarily interesting person to repeatedly provide data, or *the intensive study of a small number of especially interesting people*.

THREE DATA COLLECTION STRATEGIES

Any of three data collection strategies (Thompson, 1980a) may be employed in studies invoking Q-technique factor analysis: (a) Q sorts, (b) normative ratings, and (c) mediated rankings. Each of these strategies will be illustrated here using hypothetical data, so as to make the discussion of these methods more concrete. The interested reader is encouraged to replicate the reported analyses using the SPSS syntaxes that are also provided.

In each example, we will presume that participants were asked to provide data with respect to 27 paintings recently sold at auction. The paintings

TABLE 2.1
Twenty-Seven Famous Paintings Recently Sold at Auction

Painting	Painter
01. *Rideau, Cruchon et Compotier [7]*	Paul Cézanne
02. *Irises*	Vincent van Gogh
03. *Peasant Woman Against a Background of Wheat*	Vincent van Gogh
04. *Portrait de l'artiste sans barbe*	Vincent van Gogh
05. *Portrait of Dr. Gachet*	Vincent van Gogh
06. *Vase with Fifteen Sunflowers*	Vincent van Gogh
07. *A Wheatfield with Cypresses*	Vincent van Gogh
08. *Portrait of Duke Cosimo I de'Medici*	Jacapo Pontormo
09. *Bal au moulin de la Galette, Montmartre*	Pierre-Auguste Renoir
10. *Massacre of the Innocents*	Peter Paul Rubens
11. *Portrait of Adele Bloch-Bauer I*	Gustav Klimt
12. *Portrait of Adele Bloch-Bauer II*	Gustav Klimt
13. *Police Gazette*	Willem de Kooning
14. *Woman III*	Willem de Kooning
15. *Acrobate et jeune Arlequin [8]*	Pablo Picasso
16. *Au Lapin Agile*	Pablo Picasso
17. *Dora Maar au Chat*	Pablo Picasso
18. *Femme assise dans un jardin*	Pablo Picasso
19. *Femme aux Bras Croisés*	Pablo Picasso
20. *Garçon à la pipe*	Pablo Picasso
21. *Le Rêve [9]*	Pablo Picasso
22. *Les Noces de Pierrette*	Pablo Picasso
23. *Yo, Picasso*	Pablo Picasso
24. *False Start [5]*	Jasper Johns
25. *No. 5, 1948*	Jackson Pollock
26. *White Center (Yellow, Pink and Lavender . . .)*	Mark Rothko
27. *Green Car Crash (Green Burning Car I)*	Andy Warhol

Note. The square brackets represent painting versions.

are listed in Table 2.1. The example is used to emphasize that the data being collected can involve degrees of agreement about attitude items, but can involve anything, including objects such as paintings, photographs, or sculptures. In each example, we presume here that the researcher has elected to study intensively the very interesting students at L'École Magnifique, a hypothetical boarding school for gifted and/or creative women located in the first arrondissement in Paris, hospitably near Le Louvre.

Q Sorts

The Q sort is the most commonly-used strategy for collecting Q-technique factor analysis data. However, Q-technique factor analysis can be conducted with data collected in other ways, and not all Q sort studies use Q-technique factor analysis.

In a Q sort, participants are required to sort a fixed number of objects (e.g., statements on index cards, photographs of famous paintings) into a fixed number of categories, based on some criterion (e.g., extent of disagreement/ agreement, degree to which paintings are deemed aesthetically appealing). In our example, participants are asked to sort the photographs of the 27 paintings to indicate how artistically appealing they find the paintings. The paintings are rated from 1 = *most appealing* to 7 = *least appealing*, subject to the restriction that *exactly* the following number of paintings must be placed into each of the seven categories:

	Most Appealing				Least Appealing		
Categories	1	2	3	4	5	6	7
Numbers	2	3	5	7	5	3	2

Given a decision to investigate 10 women, but to investigate them intensively, as against less intensively investigating a large number of participants, we presume that the researcher has carefully selected 10 women of special interest. Geri, Camie, Jan, and Murray have all been admitted to L'École Magnifique based on their extraordinary artistic abilities. Carol J, Shawn, and Peggy have been admitted based on their exceptional accomplishments in literature. And Anne, Mary, and Catherine have been admitted based on their exceptional science abilities. The 10 participants rate the 27 paintings in the manner reported in Table 2.2.

Let's presume that the Table 2.2 data are entered in Word or WordPerfect into a file named Q_RENA2.TXT, which is saved as an ASCII text file, and that the ID variable is entered in the first two columns, and then the data for the 10 participants are entered with one space separating each participant's data from the other data. We can then use the computer package SPSS, and type the following syntax to implement our analysis.

```
DATA LIST
  FILE='c:\spsswin\q_rena2.txt' FIXED RECORDS=1 TABLE/1
  id 1-2
  Geri Camie Jan Murray CarolJ Shawn Peggy Anne
  Mary Catherin 3-22 .
list variables=id to Catherin/cases=99 .
FACTOR VARIABLES=Geri TO Catherin/
  PRINT=ALL/PLOT=EIGEN/
  CRITERIA=FACTORS(3)/EXTRACTION=PC/ROTATION=VARIMAX/
  SAVE=REG(ALL FSCORE) .
sort cases by fscore1 (A) .
list variables=id fscore1/cases=99/format=numbered .
```

TABLE 2.2
Q-sort Data for Ipsative Ratings of the Table 2.1 Paintings

Painting/statistic	Geri	Camie	Jan	Murray	Carol J	Shawn	Peggy	Anne	Mary	Catherine
					Gifted people					
1	1	1	2	2	4	7	5	4	5	5
2	1	2	3	2	5	4	6	3	3	3
3	2	3	1	2	7	5	6	5	4	4
4	2	1	2	1	4	6	5	6	6	6
5	2	3	1	3	6	4	7	3	3	3
6	3	2	2	1	4	6	4	7	5	5
7	3	3	3	3	6	5	4	4	4	4
8	3	3	3	4	5	7	7	5	7	6
9	3	4	3	3	6	5	7	6	6	7
10	3	4	3	3	5	5	4	4	4	4
11	4	3	4	4	1	1	1	3	3	3
12	4	4	4	4	1	2	1	5	5	5
13	4	4	4	5	2	1	3	4	4	4
14	4	4	4	4	2	2	2	4	4	3
15	4	5	5	4	2	3	2	3	3	4
16	4	5	4	5	3	2	3	5	5	4
17	4	4	4	4	3	3	2	4	4	5
18	5	4	5	4	3	3	3	3	3	3
19	5	5	5	4	3	3	3	6	6	5
20	5	4	4	5	3	4	3	4	5	6
21	5	5	5	5	4	3	4	5	4	4
22	5	6	5	6	4	4	4	7	7	7
23	6	5	6	5	4	4	4	2	2	2
24	6	6	7	7	5	4	5	1	1	1
25	6	7	6	6	7	5	5	1	1	1
26	7	6	7	6	5	4	6	2	2	2
27	7	7	6	7	4	6	5	2	2	2
Sum	108	108	108	108	108	108	108	108	108	108
M	4.000	4.000	4.000	4.000	4.000	4.000	4.000	4.000	4.000	4.000
SD	1.610	1.610	1.610	1.610	1.610	1.610	1.610	1.610	1.610	1.610
Skewness	0.000	0.000	0.000	0.000	0.000	0.000	0.000	0.000	0.000	0.000
Kurtosis	−0.505	−0.505	−0.505	−0.505	−0.505	−0.505	−0.505	−0.505	−0.505	−0.505

```
sort cases by fscore2 (A) .
list variables=id fscore2/cases=99/format=numbered .
sort cases by fscore3 (A) .
list variables=id fscore3/cases=99/format=numbered .
```

In this example, we are factor analyzing an association matrix consisting of the Pearson r correlation coefficients among the 10 participants. SPSS will output this matrix as a single triangle, because the two off-diagonal triangles of this symmetric matrix are redundant. Table 2.3 presents the Pearson product–moment correlation matrix for our data. For our hypothetical data, the correlation coefficients are sufficient to suggest that the 10 participants will group into three person factors reflecting the kinds of the giftednesses of the women (i.e., art, literature, or science).

For the Table 2.3 correlation matrix, the first three eigenvalues, which quantify how much variability is captured by each person factor upon initial factor extraction, are 4.90, 2.57, and 1.48. Because these values are greater than 1.0, and the fourth eigenvalue (i.e., 0.43) is less than 1.0, these results suggest that three person factors underlie the ratings of the 27 paintings (Guttman, 1954). A scree plot of the eigenvalues (see Gorsuch, 1983, 2003; Thompson, 2004) also suggests that the eigenvalues level off after the third initial factor, which also supports the extraction of three person factors (i.e., factors here consisting of people, rather than of variables).

Factors upon initial extraction are almost never interpretable. Thus, factor rotation is almost always necessary to clarify the factor structure, and an algorithm called *varimax* quite often works suitably for this purpose (see Gorsuch, 1983, 2003; Thompson, 2004). Table 2.4 presents the varimax-rotated matrix reported on the computer output produced by our previously-presented SPSS syntax.

We typically ask three questions when interpreting Q-technique factor analyses. First, how many person factors underlay the patterns in the ratings? In this example, the answer was three.

Second, which people define the person factors? Here, as suggested by the factor pattern/structure coefficients reported in Table 2.4, Camie, Murray, Geri, and Jan were highly correlated (r_S = 0.94, 0.93, 0.92, and 0.88, respectively) with Factor I; Mary, Catherine, and Anne were highly correlated (r_S = 0.95, 0.94, and 0.91, respectively) with Factor II; and Carol J, Peggy, and Shawn were highly correlated (r_S = 0.94, 0.92, and 0.82, respectively) with Factor III. The person factors in the present example reflect the forms in which the talents of the 10 hypothetical women are manifested. The results suggest that those talented in visual art, literature, or science systematically vary in what they find appealing in paintings based on their domains of talent. (Such are the pleasantries of hypothetical data in which results can be fashioned to be clear cut.)

TABLE 2.3
SPSS Output Pearson Correlation Matrix for the Table 2.2 Data

	GERI	CAMIE	JAN	MURRAY	CAROLJ	SHAWN	PEGGY	ANNE	MARY	CATHERIN
GERI	1.00000									
CAMIE	.87143	1.00000								
JAN	.90000	.81429	1.00000							
MURRAY	.87143	.91429	.85714	1.00000						
CAROLJ	-.15714	.05714	-.14286	-.07143	1.00000					
SHAWN	-.25714	-.21429	-.24286	-.25714	.65714	1.00000				
PEGGY	-.20000	-.01429	-.17143	-.10000	.85714	.61429	1.00000			
ANNE	-.42857	-.42857	-.51429	-.48571	-.12857	.10000	-.10000	1.00000		
MARY	-.44286	-.42857	-.48571	-.40000	-.15714	.17143	-.12857	.91429	1.00000	
CATHERIN	-.44286	-.40000	-.48571	-.41429	-.14286	.18571	-.10000	.87143	.94286	1.00000

TABLE 2.4
Varimax-rotated Pattern/Structure Coefficients, Squared Pattern/Structure Coefficients, and Communality Coefficients Extracted from the Table 2.3 Correlation Matrix

Participant	Pattern/structure coefficients			Squared coefficients			
	I	II	III	I	II	III	h^2
Camie	**0.94**	−0.20	0.02	88.4%	4.0%	0.0%	92.4%
Murray	**0.93**	−0.21	−0.08	86.5%	4.4%	0.6%	91.5%
Geri	**0.92**	−0.22	−0.16	84.6%	4.8%	2.6%	92.0%
Jan	**0.88**	−0.29	−0.14	77.4%	8.4%	2.0%	87.8%
Mary	−0.24	**0.95**	−0.04	5.8%	90.3%	0.2%	96.2%
Catherine	−0.24	**0.94**	−0.01	5.8%	88.4%	0.0%	94.1%
Anne	−0.28	**0.91**	−0.04	7.8%	82.8%	0.2%	90.8%
Carol J	−0.03	−0.14	**0.94**	0.1%	2.0%	88.4%	90.4%
Peggy	−0.07	−0.12	**0.92**	0.5%	1.4%	84.6%	86.6%
Shawn	−0.14	0.18	**0.82**	2.0%	3.2%	67.2%	72.4%

Note. Pattern/structure coefficients greater than |0.50| are presented in bold.

Third, which of the sorted objects (i.e., here, paintings) were the primary basis for defining the person factors? We examine the factor scores to address this last question. In Q-technique factor analysis there is one factor score for each rated object (here, 27) on each factor (here, 3).

The factor scores are in z score form, which means these scores have a mean of 0.0, and standard deviations and variances of 1.0. We define cut values to determine which rated objects were most salient to the creation of the person factors, and which rated objects were not especially salient to creating the person factors. Often, cut points one standard deviation above and below the factor score means of zero (i.e., $|1.0|$) are used to decide which objects were salient to the person factor results. Table 2.5 presents the salient factor scores on the three person factors.

In the present context, (a) the large pattern/structure coefficients were all positive, and (b) the rating system used lower numbers for most appealing. This means that *lower* factor scores for paintings on a given person factor indicate that the persons associated with the person factor found these paintings *most appealing,* while *higher* factor scores for paintings on a given person factor indicate that the persons associated with the person factor found these paintings *least appealing.* For example, the Table 2.5 factor score for the van Gogh painting *Irises* had a factor score of −1.57, which was the lowest factor score on Factor I, indicating that the women defining the first person factor most liked this painting.

The Table 2.5 factor scores indicate that the four women (i.e., Camie, Murray, Geri, and Jan) who defined Factor I found most appealing paintings

TABLE 2.5
Salient ($z > |1.0|$) Factor Scores on the Three Person Factors

	Painting artist	Factor			
		I	II	III	I – II
2	van Gogh	−1.57	−1.13		−0.44
1	Cézanne	−1.56			
4	van Gogh	−1.38			
5	van Gogh	−1.29	−1.02	1.06	−0.27
3	van Gogh	−1.21		1.31	
6	van Gogh	−1.11			
25	Pollock	1.23	−1.56	1.23	2.79
24	Johns	1.30	−1.59		2.89
26	Rothko	1.48			
22	Picasso	1.62	2.37		−0.75
27	Warhol	1.73			
23	Picasso		−1.10		
19	Picasso		1.16		
8	Pontormo		1.43		
9	Renoir		1.49	1.46	
11	Klimt			−2.15	
12	Klimt			−1.84	
14	de Kooning			−1.38	
13	de Kooning			−1.32	
15	Picasso			−1.17	

Note. The differences between Factor scores on Factors I and II are reported in the rightmost column for paintings that were salient on the first two Factors.

by the impressionist painters, and especially the Cézanne painting and four of the van Gogh paintings. These women found least appealing paintings in the abstract school.

The Table 2.5 factor scores indicate that the three women (i.e., Mary, Catherine, and Anne) who are talented scientists were defined especially by their distaste for portraits that are dark in coloring, and especially their dislike ($z = +2.37$) for Picasso's *Les Noces de Pierrette*. And the artist women and the science women differed most strongly in their ratings of the Pollock and the Johns paintings (I and II = 2.79 and 2.89, respectively).

The Table 2.5 factor scores indicate that the three women (i.e., Carol J, Peggy, and Shawn) whose talents arise in literature were distinguished by their affection for the works of de Kooning. These women found especially appealing paintings by Klimt, whose work is symbolic and often erotic.

Normative Ratings

Ipsative (Cattell, 1944) ratings invoke a forced-choice response format in which responses to one item inherently constrain the possible choices for subsequent items. The data in the previous example were ipsative (e.g., the decision to place a painting in the 1 = *most appealing* category meant that only one other painting could be placed in that category).

Normative (Cattell, 1944) ratings employ a response format in which one response does not mechanically constrain any other responses. Thus, if I decide to rate one teacher as 1 on warmth using a 1-to-5 Likert scale, I can mechanically rate the same teacher anything I want on friendliness. Logically, I may be constrained to rate the teacher similarly on both criteria, because the criteria seem very similar, but there are no mechanical constraints, given my first response, with respect to my second response.

The Q sort data collection method forces the data columns to have *exactly* the same shape (i.e., skewness and kurtosis). The shapes of the entities being correlated are relevant to the computation of the Pearson *r* coefficients among the people. As Thompson (2006) explained,

> . . . the Pearson *r* asks the following two questions:
> 1. How well do the two variables order the cases in exactly the same (or the opposite) order?, and
> 2. To what extent do the two variables have the same shape?
> This second consideration comes into play, because *a straight line can catch all the asterisks in a scattergram if and only if (iff) the two variables have the same shape.* (p. 119)

The Pearson *r* can reach its mathematical limits of +1 and −1 iff the two variables (or, in the present context, the two people being correlated) have the same shapes (i.e., the same skewness and the same kurtosis). Note that this does *not* mean that the two variables or the two people must have scores that are normally distributed.

The ironies of conventional analytic traditions are evident in the obsession that many Q-technique investigators have about analyzing only data that have identical shapes, while R-technique and other investigators pay considerably less attention to these issues, even though the factor analytic mathematics are identical in both cases. Given that people using the Pearson *r*, or R-technique factor analysis, or canonical correlation analysis, worry in only limited ways about shape, a logical conclusion would be that Q-technique factor analysis might reasonably be employed even when participant data are collected using normative measurement, and the data are not identically shaped.

Now we will presume that 10 other L'École Magnifique students (i.e., Deborah, Eileen, Susan, Barbara, Donna, Wendy, Kathy, Jill, Allegra, and Carol) are also intensely interesting, and so are included in a different Q-technique study. These 10 participants are asked to rate the 27 paintings on a scale from 1 = *no artistic appeal* to 7 = *extraordinary artistic appeal*, which yields the normative data presented in Table 2.6.

TABLE 2.6

Q-sort Data for Normative Ratings of the Table 2.1 Paintings

Painting/statistic	Gifted people									
	Deborah	Eileen	Susan	Barbara	Donna	Wendy	Kathy	Jill	Allegra	Carol
1	7	6	7	7	6	5	7	6	7	7
2	7	7	7	7	7	3	5	5	5	4
3	6	7	6	6	7	1	3	3	3	2
4	7	6	5	7	7	4	6	6	6	5
5	6	6	7	7	6	1	3	3	2	3
6	6	6	7	7	6	2	4	4	4	4
7	7	7	6	6	7	4	6	5	6	6
8	7	6	7	5	7	1	3	2	2	2
9	6	5	7	6	6	5	7	6	6	6
10	7	7	6	7	7	1	2	2	3	3
11	4	6	5	5	6	7	6	6	7	5
12	5	7	7	7	7	7	7	7	6	6
13	2	4	3	3	3	7	6	6	6	7
14	3	4	4	5	5	6	7	7	6	7
15	3	4	5	4	5	7	6	6	7	7
16	6	7	7	7	7	7	6	5	7	7
17	3	4	4	4	5	6	6	6	7	6
18	3	5	4	5	5	6	6	6	7	6
19	3	5	5	5	4	7	7	7	6	7
20	1	3	3	3	3	6	6	6	5	6
21	3	5	5	5	5	7	7	6	6	7
22	4	6	5	6	5	6	7	7	6	6
23	1	3	2	3	3	6	5	7	6	6
24	1	3	2	2	3	6	7	6	7	7
25	1	3	2	2	2	7	7	6	6	7
26	2	4	4	3	4	7	6	6	7	7
27	5	7	7	6	7	6	6	7	7	7
Sum	116	143	139	140	145	283	293	150	153	153
M	4.296	5.296	5.148	5.185	5.370	5.241	5.426	5.556	5.667	5.667
SD	2.140	1.409	1.693	1.634	1.543	1.865	1.852	1.474	1.515	1.587
Skewness	-0.147	-0.314	-0.489	-0.533	-0.607	-1.029	-1.274	-1.292	-1.354	-1.178
Kurtosis	-1.434	-1.261	-0.911	-0.920	-0.721	-0.379	0.628	0.827	0.876	0.257

We can analyze the data using the following SPSS syntax:

```
DATA LIST
  FILE='c:\spsswin\q_rena3.txt' FIXED RECORDS=1 TABLE/1
  id 1-2
  Deborah Eileen Susan Barbara Donna Wendy
  Kathy Jill Allegra Carol 3-22 .
list variables=id to Carol/cases=99 .
descriptives variables=all/statistics=all .
FACTOR VARIABLES=Deborah TO Carol/
  PRINT=ALL/PLOT=EIGEN/format=sort/
  CRITERIA=FACTORS(2)/EXTRACTION=PC/ROTATION=promax/
  SAVE=REG(ALL FSCORE) .
sort cases by fscore1(A) .
list variables=id fscore1/cases=99/format=numbered .
sort cases by fscore2(A) .
list variables=id fscore2/cases=99/format=numbered .
```

This syntax conducts an alternative rotation of the person factors, which allows the factors to be correlated or oblique to each other. The oblique rotation method used, *promax*, is the second most widely used rotation strategy, although promax is necessary in only about 15% of factor analyses (Thompson, 2004).

Table 2.7 presents the pattern coefficients, mathematically analogous to the beta weights in regression, which are *not* necessarily correlation coef-

TABLE 2.7
Promax-rotated Person Factors for the Table 2.6 Normative Data

Person	Factor I		Factor II		
	P	S	P	S	h^2
Barbara	*0.992*	0.955	0.077	−0.400	91.6%
Eileen	*0.969*	0.954	0.031	−0.435	91.1%
Susan	*0.961*	0.946	0.031	−0.431	89.6%
Donna	*0.958*	0.965	−0.015	−0.476	93.2%
Deborah	*0.889*	0.959	−0.146	−0.573	93.6%
Allegra	0.107	−0.365	*0.982*	0.930	87.4%
Kathy	0.061	−0.409	*0.977*	0.948	90.1%
Jill	0.005	−0.451	*0.950*	0.947	89.7%
Carol	−0.069	−0.513	*0.926*	0.959	92.3%
Wendy	−0.140	−0.567	*0.889*	0.956	92.9%

Note. P = factor pattern coefficient; S = factor structure coefficient. $h^2 = (P_I \times S_I) + (P_{II} \times S_{II})$. For example, $h_{BARBARA}^2 = (0.992 \times 0.955) + (0.077 \times -0.400) = 0.947 + -0.030 = 91.6\%$. Salient pattern coefficients (i.e., $> |0.5|$) are presented in italics.

ficients (and in oblique rotation are not), and thus do *not* range only within the limits of −1.0 to +1.0. Table 2.7 also presents the factor structure coefficients, which are correlations of measured variables with latent variables, just as they are in regression (Thompson, 2006), canonical correlation analysis (Thompson, 1984, 1991), or any other analysis, and so do range within the limits of −1.0 to +1.0.

The SPSS output reports that these two promax-rotated person factors have a Pearson r of −0.481, and thus the two factors share 23.1% of their variance ($−0.481^2 = 23.1\%$). Whenever factors are correlated, as they are whenever oblique rotation methods are used, both the pattern and structure coefficients must be reported, just as both beta weights and structure coefficients are reported in regression whenever the predictor variables are correlated (Courville & Thompson, 2001; Thompson, 2006).

Normally, we would also inspect the factor scores to further understand which ratings patterns differentiated the person factors. However, here, in the interest of space, this exercise is left to the province of the gentle reader.

Instead, the Q-technique factor analysis of a matrix of Spearman rho correlation coefficients among the participants will be illustrated. This can be accomplished by tricking SPSS into believing that the Spearman rho matrix is a Pearson r matrix, which can be done using the following syntax:

```
nonpar corr variables=Deborah TO Carol/
  matrix=out(*) .
if (ROWTYPE_ eq 'RHO      ')ROWTYPE_ = 'CORR      '.
FACTOR matrix=in(COR=*)/
  PRINT=ALL/PLOT=EIGEN/format=sort/
  CRITERIA=FACTORS(2)/EXTRACTION=PC/ROTATION=VARIMAX .
```

We might elect to analyze the Spearman rho matrix either because we believe (as some people do) that Likert scale ratings are not intervally scaled, or because we want the factors to be unaffected by shape differences. Furthermore, analyzing the same data in alternative ways (e.g., using both Pearson r and Spearman rho coefficients) is a method for investigating whether our results are artifacts of analytic choice. We prefer factors that are invariant (i.e., stable, replicable) across a variety of alternative analyses (Thompson, 2004). Table 2.8 presents the varimax-rotated factor pattern/structure coefficients computed in this manner.

Mediated Rankings

What drives reliability of scores is having greater variance in our data (Thompson, 2003). Historically, there was considerable debate about whether

TABLE 2.8
Varimax-rotated Pattern/Structure Coefficients
Extracted From the Spearman rho Matrix

Person	Factor I	Factor II	h^2
Eileen	*0.93*	−0.19	90.1%
Barbara	*0.92*	−0.20	88.6%
Donna	*0.91*	−0.29	91.2%
Susan	*0.91*	−0.18	86.1%
Deborah	*0.88*	−0.38	91.9%
Carol	−0.29	*0.87*	84.1%
Kathy	−0.17	0.83	71.8%
Wendy	−0.34	*0.81*	77.2%
Jill	−0.23	*0.80*	69.3%
Allegra	−0.10	*0.75*	57.3%

Note. Salient pattern/structure coefficients (i.e., > |0.5|) are presented in italics.

it might be desirable in attitude measurement to employ a 1-to-7 Likert scale, as against a 1-to-5 scale; whether a 1-to-9 scale might be more preferable still; and so forth. Certainly, more response alternatives allow participants to provide more variable responses, if they wish to do so. As Nunnally (1967) explained, "It is true that, as the number of scale points increases, the error variance increases, but at the same time, the true-score variance increases at an even more rapid rate" (p. 521). Thus, Guilford (1954) suggested that "it may pay in some favorable situations to use up to 25 scale divisions" (p. 291). As Thompson (1981) noted, "use of a large number of scale steps only becomes undesirable when subjects become confused or irritated at being confronted with a cognitively overwhelming number of response alternatives" (p. 5).

Theoretically, data should be more reliable, and factors more replicable, if the data have greater score variance. Thus, asking participants to rank order objects may be superior to asking participants only to sort objects as part of a Q sort. However, rank ordering numerous objects (e.g., 27, as in the present example, or a much larger number) could easily overwhelm and frustrate participants.

Mediated ranking (cf. Thompson, 1981; Thompson & Dennings, 1993) has been suggested as a vehicle for achieving this objective without unduly frustrating participants. In *mediated ranking*, the ranking task is accomplished in two discrete steps. First, participants are asked to perform a conventional Q sort. Second, participants are then asked to rank order with no ties the objects previously placed within each Q sort category.

As a final analytic example, Table 2.9 presents the mediated rankings data for the 27 paintings after evaluation by five additional students from L'École

TABLE 2.9
Mediated Ranking Data for Ipsative Rankings of the Table 2.1 Paintings

Painting/ statistic	Molly		Nancy		Lynn		Ida		Kelly	
1	1	2	2	3	1	2	5	19	5	19
2	1	1	3	8	2	3	3	9	3	8
3	2	5	1	1	3	9	4	17	4	16
4	2	3	2	5	1	1	6	23	6	23
5	2	4	1	2	3	10	3	8	3	6
6	3	6	2	4	2	5	5	21	5	20
7	3	8	3	10	2	4	4	16	4	15
8	3	7	3	6	3	7	7	27	6	25
9	3	10	3	9	4	15	6	24	7	26
10	3	9	4	15	4	12	4	15	4	14
11	4	13	3	7	3	6	3	10	3	9
12	4	11	4	12	3	8	5	20	5	21
13	4	12	4	16	4	14	4	11	4	11
14	4	14	4	11	4	11	4	13	3	10
15	4	17	5	20	4	13	3	6	4	12
16	4	15	4	13	5	18	5	18	4	17
17	4	16	4	17	5	21	4	12	5	18
18	5	19	5	19	4	17	3	7	3	7
19	5	22	5	21	4	16	6	25	5	22
20	5	20	4	14	5	22	5	22	6	24
21	5	21	5	18	5	19	4	14	4	13
22	5	18	5	22	6	25	7	26	7	27
23	6	23	6	24	5	20	2	5	2	4
24	6	25	7	26	6	23	1	1	1	1
25	6	24	6	25	7	27	1	2	1	2
26	7	26	7	27	6	24	2	3	2	3
27	7	27	6	23	7	26	2	4	2	5
M		14.0		14.0		14.0		14.0		14.0
SD		7.9		7.9		7.9		7.9		7.9
Skewness		0.0		0.0		0.0		0.0		0.0
Kurtosis		−1.2		−1.2		−1.2		−1.2		−1.2

Note. The initial Q-sort data are presented in the leftmost column under each participant's name. The final rankings are presented in the rightmost column under each participant's name. Descriptive statistics are reported only for the final rankings data.

Magnifique. Each participant has ranked the paintings from 1 to 27 with no ties. The data are ipsative and have exactly the same mean (i.e., 14.0), *SD* (i.e., 7.9), and coefficients of skewness and kurtosis (0.0 and −1.2, respectively).

Table 2.10 presents the varimax-rotated factor pattern/structure and communality coefficients for the two person factors. Again, if we wanted to discern the basis for the creation of these person factors (i.e., which paintings were ranked most extreme by persons associated with each factor), we would consult the factor scores from the analysis.

TABLE 2.10
Varimax-rotated Pattern/Structure Coefficients
and Communality Coefficients for the Ipsative
Rankings Data

Person	Factor		h^2
	I	II	
Molly	*0.94*	−0.24	94.1%
Lynn	*0.94*	−0.14	90.3%
Nancy	*0.92*	−0.28	92.5%
Kelly	−0.18	*0.98*	99.3%
Ida	−0.26	*0.96*	98.9%

Note. Salient pattern/structure coefficients (i.e., > |0.5|) are presented in italics.

SUMMARY

Q-technique factor analysis (Campbell, 1996) was first conceptualized more than half a century ago. Q-technique factor analysis can be conducted with the same software (e.g., SPSS) used to conduct any factor analysis. Q-technique factor analysis theoretically should be of great interest to psychologists, because psychologists are often most concerned about types of people, and R-technique addresses questions about types of variables, and *not* questions about types of people.

Q-technique factor analysis is especially useful when scholars want to intensively investigate a small number of especially interesting people, as against broadly studying a large number of people. Because people who are especially gifted or creative are relatively few in number, but very interesting, Q-technique factor analytic methods may be especially useful within this specialized arena of study.

REFERENCES

Brown, S. (1980). *Political subjectivity: Applications of Q methodology in political science.* New Haven, CT: Yale University Press.

Burt, C., & Stephenson, W. (1939). Alternative views on correlations between persons. *Psychometrika, 4,* 269–281.

Campbell, T. (1996). Investigating structures underlying relationships when variables are not the focus: Q-technique and other techniques. In B. Thompson (Ed.), *Advances in social science methodology* (Vol. 4, pp. 207–218). Greenwich, CT: JAI Press.

Carr, S. (1992). A primer on the use of Q-technique factor analysis. *Measurement and Evaluation in Counseling and Development, 25,* 133–138.

Cattell, R. B. (1944). Psychological measurement: Normative, ipsative, interactive. *Psychological Review, 51*, 292–303.

Cattell, R. B. (1953). A quantitative analysis of the changes in the culture pattern of Great Britain, 1837–1937, by P-technique. *Acta Psychologica, 9*, 99–121.

Cattell, R. B. (1966). The data box: Its ordering of total resources in terms of possible relational systems. In R. B. Cattell (Ed.), *Handbook of multivariate experimental psychology* (pp. 67–128). Chicago: Rand McNally.

Courville, T. & Thompson, B. (2001). Use of structure coefficients in published multiple regression articles: β is not enough. *Educational and Psychological Measurement, 61*, 229–248.

Frankiewicz, R. G., & Thompson, B. (1979, April). *A comparison of strategies for measuring teacher brinkmanship behavior*. Paper presented at the annual meeting of the American Educational Research Association, San Francisco. (ERIC Document Reproduction Service No. ED 171 753)

Gorsuch, R. L. (1983). *Factor analysis* (2nd ed.). Hillsdale, NJ: Erlbaum.

Gorsuch, R. L. (2003). Factor analysis. In J. A. Schinka & W. F. Velicer (Vol. Eds.), *Handbook of psychology. Volume 2: Research methods in psychology* (pp. 143–164). Hoboken, NJ: Wiley.

Guilford, J. P. (1946). New standards for test evaluation. *Educational and Psychological Measurement, 6*, 427–439.

Guilford, J. P. (1954). *Psychometric methods*. New York: McGraw-Hill.

Guttman, L. (1954). Some necessary conditions for common-factor analysis. *Psychometrika, 19*, 149–161.

Huberty, C. (1994). *Applied discriminant analysis*. New York: Wiley.

Jones, H. L., Thompson, B., & Miller, A. H. (1980). How teachers perceive similarities and differences among various teaching models. *Journal of Research in Science Teaching, 17*, 321–326.

Kerlinger, F. N. (1986). *Foundations of behavioral research* (3rd ed.). New York: Holt, Rinehart and Winston.

Nunnally, J. C. (1967). *Psychometric theory*. New York: McGraw-Hill.

Nunnally, J. C. (1978). *Psychometric theory* (2nd ed.). New York: McGraw-Hill.

Spearman, C. (1904). "General intelligence," objectively determined and measured. *American Journal of Psychology, 15*, 201–293.

Stephenson, W. (1935). Correlating persons instead of tests. *Character and Personality, 4*, 17–24.

Stephenson, W. (1953). *The study of behavior: Q-technique and its methodology*. Chicago: University of Chicago Press.

Thompson, B. (1980a). Comparison of two strategies for collecting Q-sort data. *Psychological Reports, 47*, 547–551.

Thompson, B. (1980b). Validity of an evaluator typology. *Educational Evaluation and Policy Analysis, 2*, 59–65.

Thompson, B. (1981, January). *Factor stability as a function of item variance*. Paper presented at the annual meeting of the Southwest Educational Research Association, Dallas. (ERIC Document Reproduction Service No. ED 205 553)

Thompson, B. (1984). *Canonical correlation analysis: Uses and interpretation*. Newbury Park, CA: Sage.

Thompson, B. (1991). A primer on the logic and use of canonical correlation analysis. *Measurement and Evaluation in Counseling and Development, 24*, 80–95.

Thompson, B. (2000). Q-technique factor analysis: One variation on the two-mode factor analysis of variables. In L. Grimm & P. Yarnold (Eds.), *Reading and understanding more multivariate statistics* (pp. 207–226). Washington, DC: American Psychological Association.

Thompson, B. (Ed.). (2003). *Score reliability: Contemporary thinking on reliability issues*. Newbury Park, CA: Sage.

Thompson, B. (2004). *Exploratory and confirmatory factor analysis: Understanding concepts and applications*. Washington, DC: American Psychological Association.

Thompson, B. (2006). *Foundations of behavioral statistics: An insight-based approach*. New York: Guilford Press.

Thompson, B., Cook, C., & Heath, F. (2003). Structure of perceptions of service quality in libraries: A LibQUAL+™ study. *Structural Equation Modeling, 10*, 456–464.

Thompson, B., & Dennings, B. (1993, November). *The unnumbered graphic scale as a data-collection method: An investigation comparing three measurement strategies in the context of Q-technique factor analysis*. Paper presented at the annual meeting of the Mid-South Educational Research Association, New Orleans. (ERIC Document Reproduction Service No. ED 364 589)

3

p VALUES VERSUS CONFIDENCE INTERVALS AS WARRANTS FOR CONCLUSIONS THAT RESULTS WILL REPLICATE

GEOFF CUMMING

What is the difference in the numerical understanding of gifted Grade 1 children and their age peers? What is the relationship between social coping and academic performance in gifted adolescents? These are simple examples of questions asked by researchers on giftedness, but consider for a moment chemistry rather than giftedness. A chemist's question like the first might be, What is the difference in melting point of this new plastic compared with the conventional plastic? Chemistry researchers would expect an answer like 35.4 ± 0.2°C, where 35.4 is our best estimate of the increased melting point of the new plastic and 0.2 is the precision of this estimate. Correspondingly, the best answer to my first giftedness question would be an estimated difference in numerical understanding scores between gifted and age-peer first graders and information about how precise that estimate is. This is best expressed as, for example, 8.6 [4.5, 12.7] months, using an age-equivalent scale of numerical understanding: The 8.6 months is the mean difference in scores we observed between our gifted first graders and a control group of age peers, and [4.5, 12.7] is the 95% confidence interval (CI). The CI tells us we can be 95% confident

This research was supported by the Australian Research Council.

the true population difference in numerical understanding between gifted children and age peers lies between 4.5 and 12.7 months. The 8.6 is our best estimate of the population difference, and the CI gives information about precision of that estimate. Similarly, an answer to my second question might be that, based on the data, there is a correlation of .34 [.08, .56]. This tells us we observed a sample correlation of .34 and can be 95% confident the population correlation for gifted adolescents lies between .08 and .56.

The paragraph above might seem a statement of the obvious: Of course we want quantitative answers, plus some idea of precision. If so, why do giftedness researchers, and indeed researchers across the social and behavioral sciences, persist in using null hypothesis significance testing (NHST), which does not address such questions and cannot provide such answers? NHST cannot answer questions like "How large is . . . ?" or "What is the relationship . . . ?" Instead, it tests a null hypothesis—almost always a statement of zero effect or relationship—and gives a p value that, if sufficiently small, permits rejection of that hypothesis. For example, the researcher calculates $p = .012$, rejects the null hypothesis of zero correlation, and concludes there is a positive population correlation between social coping and academic performance. There are many problems with this NHST approach. One is that it hardly tells us anything: It is totally implausible that the correlation between social coping and academic performance is exactly zero, so concluding there is a nonzero correlation is not informative. In other words, however tiny the true correlation—provided it is not exactly zero—if you can afford a sufficiently large sample, your p will very likely be small enough to justify conclusion of a statistically significant correlation. As Thompson (1992) stated,

> Statistical significance testing can involve a tautological logic in which tired researchers, having collected data on hundreds of subjects, then conduct a statistical test to evaluate whether there were a lot of subjects, which the researchers already know, because they collected the data and know they are tired. (p. 436)

Whether you obtain statistical significance or not may simply reflect whether you can afford a large sample or how tired you are willing to become!

In this chapter, I argue that researchers of giftedness should shift emphasis from NHST to CIs and other preferred techniques. I start with a brief summary of arguments put forward by statistical reformers and describe basic features of CIs. I then report a small survey of current statistical practices in giftedness research and a comparison with practices in psychology generally. The main part of the chapter is a discussion of p values and CIs in relation to replication; I focus on the Pearson's r correlation, because r is so widely used in giftedness research. A simulation demonstrates the large variability in r, and even greater variability in p values, over replications of a simple experiment. Calculations confirm that a p value gives only very vague information about replication, and therefore any p value could easily have been very different, simply because of sampling variability (Cumming, 2008). The severe deficiencies of p values in relation to replication give an additional strong reason for giftedness researchers to turn from NHST and pursue statistical reform with vigor.

STATISTICAL REFORM: FROM NHST TO ESCIMAT

There is a large literature critical of NHST, well summarized in chapter 3 of the excellent book by Kline (2004). First, NHST as typically practiced in social and behavioral sciences is an incoherent mixture of proposals by Fisher and by Neyman and Pearson. Textbooks usually recommend the Neyman–Pearson practice of setting an α value—almost always .05—in advance, whereas researchers usually follow Fisher by reporting an exact p value and regarding this as an inverse measure of the strength of evidence against the null. Second, there is evidence that researchers, and even many statistics teachers, hold serious misconceptions about NHST. Many, for example, hold the inverse probability fallacy by wrongly believing p is the probability the null is true given the data, rather than the probability of the data (or more extreme) if the null hypothesis is true: If $p = .01$, this does *not* mean a 1% chance there is no effect; rather, it means that if the true effect is zero, there is a 1% chance of obtaining the observed result, or more extreme. Third, NHST often leads to decision making unjustified by the data and damaging to research progress. For example, a result that is not statistically significant often leads to a conclusion of a zero effect, but this is unjustified because small sample sizes, which keep statistical power low, mean that in practice a nonsignificant result is common even when the true effect is of considerable size.

Given cogent critiques published by leading scholars for more than half a century, it is disappointing that reliance on NHST remains so widespread. Kline (2004) gives a set of practical recommendations for making the transition from NHST to better techniques. Wilkinson and the Task Force on Statistical Inference (1999) and Thompson (2006) are other sources of excellent practical advice. I discuss three techniques that are better than NHST: effect sizes (ESs), CIs, and meta-analytic thinking (MAT), which together make the statistical reformer's slogan *ESCIMAT* ("ess-key-mat"). An ES is simply an amount of anything we are interested in. It can be as simple as a percentage, a correlation, or a difference between means; it may be expressed in original measurement units (e.g., months of reading age), or in standardized form (e.g., Cohen's d), or as a units-free measure (e.g., r), or it may be a percentage of variance (e.g., R^2 or η^2). We calculate from our data a sample ES and use this as an estimate of a population ES, which is usually our main focus—the advantage in numerical understanding or the correlation between social coping and academic performance. Discussion and interpretation of research should typically be centered on ESs.

Almost as fundamental as our best estimate of a population ES is an indication of how accurate that estimate is likely to be. The best way to report precision is usually a 95% CI, which is an interval surrounding the point estimate. A practical problem is that 95% CIs are often depressingly wide, indicating that typical experiments give imprecise estimates of target population ESs. We should not, however, shoot the messenger and disparage CIs for being so large: They simply indicate truly the extent of uncertainty. This useful information that CIs give can be contrasted with the dichotomous outcome of a statistical significance test (an effect is or is not statistically significant), which may give an unjustified air of certainty, or even truth, and delude us into thinking that little uncertainty remains.

Given that any single experiment is unlikely to give a definitive result, our best strategy is to combine evidence over studies. Meta-analysis is the quantitative way to do this. We should think of our experiment in the context of past similar studies and as foreshadowing future studies—all to be combined by meta-analysis. That is meta-analytic thinking (Cumming & Finch, 2001) and is highly recommended. I will argue that CIs and MAT may be especially beneficial in giftedness research because in this field it may be especially difficult to obtain large samples to ensure high statistical power.

CONFIDENCE INTERVALS

Suppose our result was a difference in numerical understanding of 8.6 [4.5, 12.7] months. There are a number of ways to think about the CI: The interval [4.5, 12.7] is the set of plausible values for the population difference, given our data. Values outside that interval are relatively implausible but not impossible. Further, note that values close to the center of the interval are relatively good bets for the true value, those near the lower and upper limits are less good, and values outside the CI are even worse bets. There is also a link with NHST: If a null hypothesized value lies outside the CI, it can be rejected at the two-tailed .05 level; if inside the interval, it cannot be rejected at this level. Cumming and Finch (2005) explained the advantages of using figures with CIs displayed as error bars. They suggested *rules of eye* that are practical guidelines for the interpretation of such figures. Cumming (2007) gave an elementary introduction to CIs and discussed ways to show a CI graphically.

STATISTICAL TECHNIQUES USED IN GIFTEDNESS RESEARCH

I report a brief analysis of statistical techniques used in recent articles in *The Australasian Journal of Gifted Education*, *The Gifted Child Quarterly*, *High Ability Studies*, and *Journal for the Education of the Gifted*. I located in each journal the 10 most recently published articles that reported quantitative data and then examined those 40 articles for the occurrence of selected statistical techniques. This is a small sample, intended to give only a broad outline of current statistical practices of giftedness researchers.

Just 33 of the 40 (82%) reported statistical inference, the others giving only descriptive statistics—usually frequencies, percentages, and means. All 33 reporting inference used NHST, and only 1 (2%) also reported CIs, which were shown as error bars in figures. Fully 37 articles (92%) used tables to report data, but only 11 (28%) included any data figures. Only 2 (5%) included figures with error bars: the one case mentioned above with 95% CI error bars, and one that included figures with standard error (*SE*) error bars and also figures with error bars that were not identified. Unfortunately, error bars can represent various quantities, including CI, *SE*, and standard deviation (*SD*), and so it is a serious omission not to state clearly in each figure caption what error bars represent.

Cumming et al. (2007) reported a survey of statistical practices in 10 leading psychology journals. They found that almost all empirical articles (97%) used NHST but that use of CIs had increased from 4% in 1998 to 11% in 2005–2006. There was a substantial increase in figures with error bars, from 11% in 1998 to 38% in 2005–2006. In psychology generally, therefore, NHST continues to dominate, but the large recent increase in reporting of figures with error bars is encouraging and suggests the time may be ripe for further statistical reform. In giftedness research, by contrast, CIs are rare, figures are used relatively infrequently, and error bars are rarely displayed in figures. The field seems to lag behind other areas of psychology in the reform of statistical practices, at least in relation to the central techniques I have discussed so far.

It has proved difficult in our past journal surveys to code reliably the use of ESs, and so I did not attempt to do that in my 40 giftedness articles. It was clear, however, that ESs were routinely reported and discussed. Means, percentages, and correlations were often the focus, and Cohen's d and η^2 were other frequently reported ES measures. This is excellent practice, to be encouraged.

One common and problematic practice was use of the term *significant*, which has both a statistical meaning—we can reject the null—and the everyday meaning of important. It was very common in my 40 giftedness articles for the term to be used ambiguously. Referring to "the significant proportion of underachievement" or saying "the children may show significant advancement" is ambiguous. Such ambiguity can easily lead to a belief that merely rejecting a null hypothesis establishes an effect as important. Kline (2004) recommended dropping the word entirely and referring to "a statistical difference" rather than "a statistically significant difference." Alternatively, researchers should avoid ambiguous uses and say either "statistically significant" or "important."

Pearson's r was reported in 18 (45%) of the articles and used implicitly in many more in the form of estimates of reliability or validity. NHST was often used to assess r values as statistically significant or not, against a null of zero, but a CI was never reported for r. Because r is used so often in giftedness research, and because a CI on r can be so informative, I choose r as the context for my discussion of replication, p values, and CIs.

REPLICATION AS A BASIS FOR KNOWING

Science generally requires replication before a finding achieves acceptance. If an effect is observed in a different laboratory, robustness is demonstrated. Even replication under identical conditions in the original laboratory reduces the risk the initial finding was merely a sampling fluctuation. Our statistical methods aim to quantify that risk: The p value is often taken as a measure of the strength of evidence against the null hypothesis: Very small p is taken as strong evidence that the null is false and that the observed effect was not just a chance fluctuation. Further, it is taken as an indication that replication will also give evidence against the null. Given the central place of replication in science, it is justified to ask what information a statistical method provides about replications of our original experiment.

Kline (2004, chap. 3) identified 13 pervasive erroneous beliefs about p values and their use. Fallacy 5 is the *replication fallacy*, or the belief that $1 - p$ is the probability a replication of the experiment will give the same result or a statistically significant result. Such beliefs are, however, seriously wrong. Obtaining $p = .04$, for example, does *not* indicate a 96% chance a replication will be statistically significant. Considering the importance of replication and the widespread belief in the replication fallacy, it is curious there has been almost no consideration of what information a p value *does* give about replication. In Cumming (2008), I explored the extent to which p varies over replications. My conclusion was that the variability of p with replication is astonishingly large: Repeat an experiment, and one is likely to get a very different p value. Correspondingly, any p value could easily have been very different, simply because of sampling variability, and therefore a p value gives only extremely vague information about what is true in the world.

INTUITIONS ABOUT THE CORRELATION COEFFICIENT

Before discussing replication, I invite you to consider your own intuitions about r, and to write down your estimates in response to the questions posed in this section. The answers appear later in this chapter. I ask this because I believe it is vital to build strong intuitive understanding of the measures we use, and my informal observation is that many people's intuitions about r are quite inaccurate. I use r values of .10, .30, and .50 because these were suggested by Cohen (1988) as small, medium, and large correlations. Note, however, that Cohen emphasized that his reference values are arbitrary and that interpretation of r values—and other ESs—requires knowledgeable judgment in the research context. In the following four questions, and throughout this chapter unless otherwise stated, I use two-tailed $\alpha = .05$ for statistical significance and statistical power. Here, I use a null hypothesis that the population correlation $\rho = 0$.

1. What is the smallest N for sample $r = .10$ to be statistically significantly different from zero? For $r = .30$? For $r = .50$?
2. What is the smallest N for sample $r = .10$ in one group of size N to be just statistically significantly different from sample $r = .30$ in another group, also of size N? For $r = .30$ and $r = .50$? For $r = .10$ and $r = .50$?
3. Consider sample r values of .10, .30, .50, and .80. Estimate the 95% CI for each of these r values for $N = 50$ and again for $N = 200$.
4. Suppose the population correlation is $\rho = .30$. What is the smallest N needed to achieve power = .80?

AN EXAMPLE OF REPLICATION

Suppose that, using well-standardized measures, the correlation of social coping and academic performance is $\rho = .30$ in a population of gifted adolescents. Suppose you obtain scores for a sample of $N = 43$ adolescents and calculate that $r = .34$, $p = .024$. (The two-tailed p value for testing, as usual, the null hypothesis $\rho = 0$.) This correlation is plotted as the large dot for Sample 1, at the bottom of Figure 3.1; p is shown to the left. Now suppose you took additional samples, each $N = 43$, from the same population, and for each you calculated r. What would be the variability in r? In p? Figure 3.1 shows a simulation of 25 such samples. The most striking thing about Figure 3.1 is the enormous variability in p: The column of p values ranges astonishingly, from < .001 to .91. Values are labeled using conventional *, **, and *** symbols, and .05 < p < .10

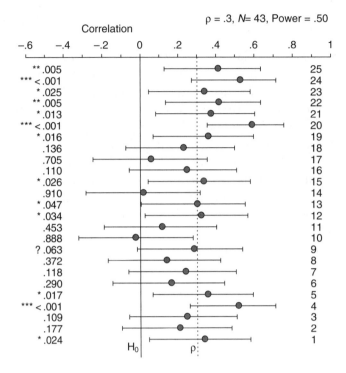

Figure 3.1. Simulation of 25 independent samples, each of $N = 43$ adolescents. The correlation r between scores of social coping and academic performance is plotted for each sample as a large dot. The 95% CI is shown for each r. The population correlation is assumed to be $\rho = .30$. At right is the index number of each sample, the first sample being at the bottom. At left is the p value for testing r against the null hypothesis of zero correlation in the population; p values are labeled *** for $p < .001$, ** for $.001 < p < .01$, * for $.01 < p < .05$, and '?' for $.05 < p < .10$. The power of this test is .50. Note the extremely large variation in p, from $< .001$ to .910.

is labeled as *?*. Any p value at all seems possible. How can p give useful information about what is true in the world if a mere sampling fluctuation—you happen to take a different sample—can give such a radically different value?

You may suspect some trick, some staged aspect of my example that gives unusually large variation in p. On the contrary, I have chosen an example typical of experiments in many fields in the social and behavioral sciences. The example assumes a medium ES in the population ($\rho = .30$) and sample size $N = 43$, which gives power = .50. A number of surveys (Maxwell, 2004, p. 148) have estimated that median power to find a medium ES, in published research in a number of fields in psychology, is around .50. I know of no evidence that statistical power is generally higher in giftedness research, and problems of limited participant pools may mean that the power of giftedness research is actually lower than for psychology generally. It is sobering to realize that conducting a typical experiment in psychology—or, very likely, in giftedness—amounts to merely obtaining a randomly chosen single p value from those exemplified in Figure 3.1.

Figure 3.2 shows the frequency histogram of p values expected in a large number of replications of my example experiment. The 25 p values shown in Figure 3.1 are consistent with that distribution. I used Fisher's r to z transformation to derive this histogram and for all calculations of p, CIs, and power. Howell (2002, chap. 9) and many introductory statistics textbooks explain that transformation and note it is an approximation. My simulations indicate it is an excellent approximation: The distributions of p I obtained in thousands of simulated samples closely matched the histograms, like that in Figure 3.2, that I calculated using the transformation.

Figure 3.1 also shows the 95% CI on each r. Besides the striking variability of p, there are several other aspects of Figure 3.1 worth noting. First, the CIs vary in length, with CIs on values of r closer to zero being longer. Also, the intervals are asymmetric, with the arm nearer to zero being longer; and the degree of asymmetry is greater for larger r values—see, for example, Sample 20. These variations reflect the operation of the r to z transformation. Second, the r values appear to generally cluster around .30 and to fall approximately evenly on either side of .30, as we expect, given that the samples were drawn from a population with $\rho = .30$. Third, we expect that in the long run, 95% of the CIs will include .30, and 5% will miss—usually by only a small amount. In the set of 25 samples, the CI for Sample 10 just misses to the left, and that for Sample 20 misses by a little to the right. Fourth, there is a functional relationship

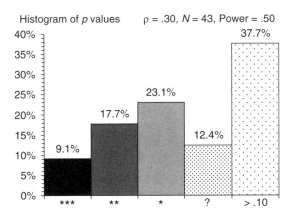

Figure 3.2. Histogram of p values expected in the long run on repeated sampling, assuming as in Figure 3.1 that $N = 43$ and $\rho = .30$, which gives power of .50. The *** column refers to $p < .001$, the ** column to $.001 < p < .01$, the * column to $.01 < p < .05$, and the '?' column to $.05 < p < .10$. Note that the sum of the percentages for the *, **, and *** columns equals the power, expressed as a percentage.

between p for a sample and the position of the CI in relation to the null hypothesized value of zero. Examine where the CIs fall and the corresponding p values: The closer r is to zero, the larger the p value, and the further the interval is to the right, the smaller the p. For Sample 13, the interval just misses zero, and p is just less than .05. With a little practice, it is easy to note where a 95% CI falls in relation to the null hypothesized value and to estimate p; Cumming (2007) discussed this relationship of CI position and p and suggested easily remembered benchmarks to help in the estimation of p.

Remember that Figure 3.1 describes results from a simulation. In real life, we do not know ρ and do not have the luxury of many repeats of our experiment—we have only a single value of r, with its CI. There is in principle an infinite sequence of r values and CIs, a small part of which is illustrated in Figure 3.1, but we have only our single r and CI. It is worth reflecting on the extreme variation in p shown in Figure 3.1 and the histogram of Figure 3.2. My example experiment is typical of much social research, because it has statistical power of .50 to find a medium-sized true effect—in this case a population correlation of $\rho = .30$. If there is actually a medium effect in the population, a researcher who runs such an experiment is sampling a single p value from the distribution in Figure 3.2. Obtaining a coveted ** or, even better, *** result is like winning a prize in a lottery, and the disappointment of ns results is frequent. This hardly seems an efficient or satisfying way to conduct and analyze research.

CIS OR p VALUES?

Given that we have only a single sample, what information about it would you prefer? Would you choose to know p, and perhaps r, as is commonly reported? Or would you prefer to be told r and its CI? Again, consider Figure 3.1: I suggest that a single p value gives hardly any information about the whole infinite sequence of potential samples; it gives little or no idea of the extent of variability in that sequence. In other words, the p value gives only extremely vague information about replication, about what is likely to happen next time. In Cumming (2008), I discussed in more detail the information a p value gives about replication and quantified just how vague that information is.

By contrast, the length of a CI gives some idea of the variability in the whole infinite sequence. A single CI gives some idea of the whole sequence and is a better exemplar of the sequence, whereas any single p value hardly seems to be an exemplar at all of the whole sequence. Further, the information a 95% CI gives about replication can be quantified: There is an 83% chance that r given by a replication will fall in the 95% CI of the initial experiment (Cumming & Maillardet, 2006). In other words, a 95% CI can be regarded as an 83% *prediction interval* for where *r* given by a replication will fall. Figure 3.1 illustrates this: Note whether each CI captures the *r* for the subsequent sample. The CIs for Samples 3, 9, and 14 fail to include *r* for the following sample; in all other cases, the CI captures the following *r*. So in 21/24 (87.5%) of cases, the 95% CI includes the replication *r*. In the long run, we expect 83% of CIs to capture *r* given by the following sample. We can therefore conclude that a 95% CI gives information about replication that is quantifiable and interpretable, whereas a *p* value gives only extremely vague information about replication. Advocates of statistical reform have explained several important advantages of CIs over NHST (Cumming & Finch, 2001, 2005; Kline, 2004). My comparison here of what information CIs and *p* values provide about replication gives a further strong reason for preferring CIs. The discussion here refers to *r*; Cumming and Fidler (2009) presented a similar discussion for means.

Distributions of *p* Values

Cumming (2008) explained that the distribution of *p* values, as in Figure 3.2, depends on statistical power. The distribution in Figure 3.2 applies whenever power is .50, and there are various combinations of ρ and *N* that give power of .50. Figure 3.3 shows the distribution of *p* for four values of power, ranging from .05, which is the power when $\rho = 0$ and the null is true, to .80, which is often chosen as the target level of power. Figure 3.3 also shows example pairs of ρ and *N* values for each level of power. The histograms show, as we would expect, a trend for large *p* when the null is true and successively smaller *p* as power increases. However, in every case, even at higher levels of power, there is great spread in the *p* values given by replications. Consider again our situation after running an experiment. We have a single *p* value, and we know *N* but not ρ. To what extent can our *p* diagnose which of the distributions in Figure 3.3 (or a distribution for some other level of power) applies, and thus what the true value of ρ is? If our *p* is very small (preferably < .001, or perhaps < .01), it suggests one of the lower distributions is a better bet, because these smallest *p* values are so infrequent in the upper, $\rho = 0$ distribution. However, any other value of *p* gives hardly any guidance as to which distribution applies and therefore hardly any information about the true value of ρ.

Considering NHST, can *p* indicate whether we can rule out the topmost distribution in Figure 3.3 and thus reject the null? Note again how impoverished this question is: We would like to know ρ, but NHST only attempts to rule out $\rho = 0$. As before, very small values of *p*, certainly *** and perhaps **, indicate that one of the lower distributions is a better bet. Very small *p* values do provide evidence against the null, but such values often arise from effects

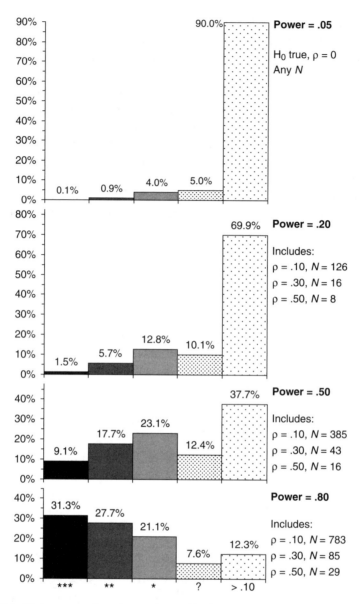

Figure 3.3. Histograms of *p* values expected in the long run on repeated sampling, for selected values of power. The histogram for power .50 is the same as that shown in Figure 3.2. Any particular value of power can be given by various pairs of values of ρ and *N*, and some example pairs are shown. The column labels are as in Figure 3.2.

that are obvious—that hit you between the eyes—and so it is hardly a triumph that p rules out a zero effect in such cases. Now consider * or ? results: The heights of the * and ? columns vary only modestly across all the distributions in Figure 3.3, so those p values cannot give much guidance as to which distribution is the best bet for describing truth for our experiment. The largest ratio of heights is 23.1/4 for * results, between power values of .50 and .05. This ratio of likelihoods of less than 6 can be contrasted with the mistaken idea that using a .05 criterion for p means the risk of error is only 1/20. A further implication of Figure 3.3 is that values of $p > .10$ also tell us little. They certainly do not provide evidence that $\rho = 0$, because there is only a ratio of 90/12.3, which is less than 8, between the likelihoods of $p > .10$ for the top and bottom distributions and much lower ratios for the intermediate distributions.

The conclusion must be that anything other than very small p values (say, .001 or perhaps .01) gives very little information indeed. A repeat of our experiment is likely to give a very different p value, and we do not have grounds for concluding anything much at all about ρ, the ES of interest.

Intuitions About r, Revisited

Figure 3.1 gives information about r, as well as p, in relation to replication. The 25 r values in Figure 3.1, and the CI widths, give some idea of the sampling distribution of r and of the variability of r with replication. These, together with the relation between CI placement and p, underlie the four questions I posed earlier. Here are the answers to those questions:

1. The smallest N for sample $r = .10$ to be statistically significantly different from zero is 385. For $r = .30$ it is 44, and for $r = .50$ it is 16.
2. The smallest N for sample $r = .10$ in one group of size N to be just statistically significantly different from $r = .30$ in another group of size N is 179. $r = .30$ and $r = .50$ needs $N = 137$, and $r = .10$ and $r = .50$ needs $N = 42$.
3. Figure 3.4 shows the 95% CIs for sample r values of .10, .30, .50, and .80, for $N = 50$, and for $N = 200$.
4. If $\rho = .30$, the smallest N needed to achieve power = .80 is 85. See Figure 3.3 for further examples of ρ and N value pairs that give particular values of power.

My conclusions are that 95% CIs on r tend to be surprisingly wide and that a large N is needed for short CIs. Quite large samples are required for statistical significance, but ES is an even stronger influence. In other words, even a small increase in r reduces markedly the N needed to achieve statistical significance. An especially large N is needed to demonstrate a statistically

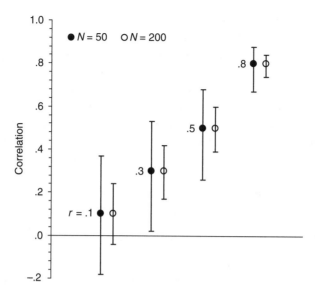

Figure 3.4. Selected values of *r* with their 95% CIs, for *N* = 50 and *N* = 200.

significant difference between two *r* values, although the *N* required drops markedly if the difference between the *r* values increases. All these obser-vations can be regarded as consequences of the "law of small numbers" (Tversky & Kahneman, 1971), which is the mistaken belief that small samples reflect their parent population quite closely. In other words, people have a strong tendency to severely underestimate the extent of sampling variability. As a result, the variability of the *r* values in Figure 3.1 may seem surprisingly large and the CIs in Figure 3.4 surprisingly wide.

SPECIAL FEATURES OF RESEARCH ON GIFTEDNESS

I chose *r* for my comparison of CIs and *p* values because *r* is used so often in giftedness research, but my discussion applies generally and does not rely on any particular features of giftedness. However, two features of giftedness research need to be considered. The first is the problem of score distributions. Measures used with gifted participants often hit a ceiling in which case scores are bunched near an upper limit and thus show negative skew. Conversely, if gifted participants are selected as scoring higher than, for example, 2.5 *SD* above the mean, scores on the selection variable—and perhaps on other vari-ables too—show positive skew. In either case, there may be severe departure from a normal distribution. NHST and CIs, as I discuss in this chapter, are both based on assumptions of sampling from normally distributed populations and, in the case of r, an assumption of bivariate normality. Departure from normality, which is a danger in giftedness research, should lead researchers to consider a transformation of the data and robust or nonparametric methods of analysis. Conventional NHST and CIs are based on similar theory, and both are to some extent sensitive to departures from normality, so the problem of nonnormality does not influence the choice between NHST and CIs.

A second feature of giftedness research is, however, relevant to that choice: There are often only limited pools of potential participants. Exceptional students are by definition in a small minority, and so it may be particularly difficult to achieve reasonable sample sizes and high statistical power. CIs will thus be discouragingly wide, and it may be especially tempting to turn to NHST and fervently hope that p will by chance be less than the magic .05. Using CIs may therefore be especially important in giftedness research.

DISCUSSION AND CONCLUSION

In Cumming (2008), I investigated replication for differences between means and concluded that the variability of p is astonishingly large and that anything other than very small p values gives hardly any useful information. Investigation of r in this chapter leads to the same conclusions. A possible response is to use a stricter criterion for statistical significance, perhaps .01. The trouble is that the bottom distribution in Figure 3.3 shows that even with power .80, there is a 41% chance of obtaining $p > .01$ and thus not rejecting the null. With power .90, which is often a forlorn hope, there is still a 25% chance of $p > .01$. Therefore, even with high power, we expect many experiments to give nonsignificant results and thus fail to reject null hypotheses that are false. Further, if only statistically significant results are published, much research effort will be wasted, and a skewed sample of research will appear in the journals because larger observed ESs—which give smaller p values—will be more often published. Meta-analysis of published results will thus overestimate population ESs. NHST cannot be salvaged by adopting a small α; other, better techniques need to be found.

I suggest that giftedness researchers should adopt a three-part response. First, be skeptical of conclusions based on p values. Bear in mind the enormous spread in the distributions in Figure 3.3 and the fact that any p value could easily have been very different simply because of sampling variability. Remember that p may mislead us into thinking little uncertainty remains merely because we luckily obtained a small p that permits rejection of the null.

Second, embrace statistical reform, especially by shifting emphasis from NHST; adopt Kline (2004, chap. 3) as a guide, and see Fidler and Cumming (2008) and Cumming and Fidler (in press). As a first step, report and interpret

CIs whenever possible, recognizing that they often give the best answers to the questions giftedness researchers typically ask. CIs give estimates of the effects we are interested in and don't merely suggest that an effect is nonzero. Show CIs as error bars in figures. CIs may seem wide, but they represent accurately the uncertainty in a study and provide a useful measure of the precision of estimates.

Third, try to achieve high power by investigating large ESs and by using large samples and other design strategies (Maxwell, 2004). Even so, recognize the limitation of most individual experiments, given that extremely high power is usually not practically achievable. Think of converging evidence, meta-analysis, and the combination of evidence over studies. Adopt meta-analytic thinking, and note that reporting CIs facilitates this and the carrying out of future meta-analyses. I argued above that achieving high power can be a particular challenge for giftedness researchers, who should therefore be especially conscious of the weaknesses of NHST. Correspondingly, using CIs and adopting meta-analytic thinking should be especially beneficial for giftedness research.

CIs give readily interpretable information about replication and encourage meta-analytic thinking. They help us think about point and interval estimates of an effect rather than only about whether or not an effect exists. Moving beyond the dichotomous thinking of p values to CIs can encourage psychology—and giftedness research—to develop a more quantitative and theoretically rich understanding of the world. The dramatic vagueness of p in relation to replication—and replication is at the heart of science—should motivate giftedness researchers to shift away from reliance on NHST and to adopt CIs and other, better techniques.

REFERENCES

Cohen, J. (1988). *Statistical power analysis for the behavioral sciences* (2nd ed.). Hillsdale, NJ: Erlbaum.

Cumming, G. (2007). Inference by eye: Pictures of confidence intervals and thinking about levels of confidence. *Teaching Statistics, 29,* 89–93.

Cumming, G. (2008). Replication and p intervals: p values predict the future only vaguely, but confidence intervals do much better. *Perspectives on Psychological Science, 3,* 286–300.

Cumming, G., & Fidler, F. (2009). Confidence intervals: Better answers to better questions. *Zeitschrift für Psychologie/Journal of Psychology, 217,* 15–26.

Cumming, G., & Fidler, F. (in press). The new stats: Effect sizes and confidence intervals. In G. R. Hancock & R. O. Mueller (Eds.), *Quantitative methods in the social and behavioral sciences: A guide for researchers and reviewers.* Mahwah, NJ: Erlbaum.

Cumming, G., Fidler, F., Leonard, M., Kalinowski, P., Christiansen, A., Kleinig, A., et al. (2007). Statistical reform in psychology: Is anything changing? *Psychological Science, 18*, 230–232.

Cumming, G., & Finch, S. (2001). A primer on the understanding, use, and calculation of confidence intervals that are based on central and noncentral distributions. *Educational and Psychological Measurement, 61*, 530–572.

Cumming, G., & Finch, S. (2005). Inference by eye: Confidence intervals, and how to read pictures of data. *American Psychologist, 60*, 170–180.

Cumming, G., & Maillardet, R. (2006). Confidence intervals and replication: Where will the next mean fall? *Psychological Methods, 11*, 217–227.

Fidler, F., & Cumming, G. (2008). The new stats: Attitudes for the twenty-first century. In J. W. Osborne (Ed.), *Best practices in quantitative methods* (pp. 1–12). Thousand Oaks, CA: Sage.

Howell, D. C. (2002). *Statistical methods for psychology* (5th ed.). Pacific Grove, CA: Duxbury.

Kline, R. B. (2004). *Beyond significance testing: Reforming data analysis methods in behavioral research.* Washington DC: American Psychological Association.

Maxwell, S. E. (2004). The persistence of underpowered studies in psychological research: Causes, consequences, and remedies. *Psychological Methods, 9*, 147–163.

Thompson, B. (1992). Two and one-half decades of leadership in measurement and evaluation. *Journal of Counseling and Development, 70*, 434–438.

Thompson, B. (2006). *Foundations of behavioral statistics: An insight-based approach.* New York: Guilford Press.

Tversky, A., & Kahneman, D. (1971). Belief in the law of small numbers. *Psychological Bulletin, 92*, 105–110.

Wilkinson, L., & the Task Force on Statistical Inference. (1999). Statistical methods in psychology journals: Guidelines and explanations. *American Psychologist, 54*, 594–604.

4

STATISTICAL SIGNIFICANCE, RESULT WORTHINESS, AND EVIDENCE: WHAT LESSONS ARE THERE FOR GIFTEDNESS EDUCATION IN OTHER DISCIPLINES?

FIONA FIDLER

Asher (1986) identified two factors that limit theory development and validation in gifted education research: imprecise measurement and small numbers of participants. He made this important point: "These two factors . . . combine to insure (sic) that results are obscure and that statistical significance is difficult to obtain" (p. 7). Asher was right about statistical significance being difficult to obtain: In fact, it may well be an unnecessarily difficult hurdle. The fact that $p < .05$ is difficult to obtain is only really a problem if statistical significance is considered the only acceptable evidence of result noteworthiness. In this chapter, I argue that it should not be and that falsely equating statistical significance with result noteworthiness has serious consequences. To demonstrate this, I draw lessons from other disciplines.

Schmidt (1996) identified the same factors as limitations in psychological research and added this dramatic claim: "Reliance on statistical significance testing . . . has systematically retarded the growth of cumulative knowledge in psychology" (p. 115). In this chapter I provide evidence in the

This research was supported by an Australian Research Council Postdoctoral Fellowship.

form of two case studies—one from psychology and one from medicine—for Schmidt's claim.

A brief survey of giftedness journals by Cumming (chap. 3, this volume) found that when authors made statistical inferences (rather than simply reporting descriptive statistics), they all relied on statistical significance testing (or null hypothesis significance testing [NHST]). Further qualitative investigation of these articles identified the following common reporting omissions and errors: failure to report the power of statistical tests; failure to report means and/or effect sizes for statistically nonsignificant results; reference to statistically nonsignificant differences, correlations, or changes as "no difference," "no correlation," or "no change" and/or interpreting statistically nonsignificant results as "due to chance"; use of the term *significant* ambiguously, therefore conflating statistical differences with theoretical or practically meaningful differences; and failure to report the precision of effect estimates with standard errors or confidence intervals (CIs).

The statistical reporting problems identified above are prerequisites for the stifling of cumulative knowledge Schmidt (1996) referred to. Because these reporting problems can be found with ease in the literature on giftedness research, it is important for researchers in this field to be vigilant of the damage that can be done to the progress of their discipline.

THREE REASONS WHY STATISTICAL SIGNIFICANCE IS NOT EQUIVALENT TO RESULT NOTEWORTHINESS

Francis Edgeworth coined the term *significant* to describe experimental results around 1885. But for Edgeworth, *significant* did not mean *important*; rather, it meant something like *not accidental* (Spiegelhalter, 2004). (There can be important nonaccidents, but there can also be trivial ones!) Ronald Fisher adopted the term too, and it is from him that our modern usage is inherited. He used it to "signify" results that may be worthy of further investigation (Salsburg, 2001). For Fisher, as for Edgeworth, the definition implied something weaker than *important*.

However, *significant* has, over the last 60 years or so, become synonymous with *result noteworthiness* in many scientific disciplines. It is now routinely misinterpreted as meaning *important* and/or *large effect*. In fact, statistical significance (e.g., $p < .05$) offers no direct evidence of theoretical or practical importance, and because it confounds effect size with sample size, it also falls short as a legitimate measure of magnitude.

Such misinterpretations are widespread, even in textbooks and expository articles. An article from *Gifted Child Quarterly* offers an example. The authors, perhaps in an effort to simplify their message directed at practitioners, mistakenly defined statistical significance as "the likelihood that the results did not occur by chance alone but rather are due to something other than chance" (Callahan & Moon, 2007, p. 309). This definition is in fact what Carver (1978) called the *odds against chance fantasy*. The misconception assumes that p = total probability of error. In other words, it fails to recognize that there are both Type I and Type II errors and that p values relate only to the former. More specifically, p is a conditional probability: the probability of obtaining results as extreme as or more extreme than those obtained, given the truth of the null.

To their credit, Callahan and Moon (2007) attempted to disentangle the concepts of statistical significance, effect size, and result meaningfulness. This is a worthwhile goal. However, the remaining ambiguity in their final definitions of these concepts has the potential to mislead:

> In intervention studies, current standards of research indicate that we should also look at an index of the meaningfulness of differences referred to as an effect size. Meaningfulness is a critical indicator of whether or not the size of the difference represents more than a trivial significant difference that may have occurred mathematically because of a large sample size (Callahan & Moon, 2007, p. 309).

Meaningfulness (or importance, sometimes denoted as "practical," "theoretical," or "clinical significance") is indeed a separate consideration from statistical significance. It is also a separate consideration from effect size. While it is true that larger effects are often more important than smaller ones, it is not the case that all large effects are important and all small effects are meaningless. In other words, effect size is not a formal index of meaningfulness—size doesn't guarantee importance. Sometimes small or subtle effects are crucially important; sometimes medium or even large effects are meaningless. Thompson (2006b) catalogued various situations in which small effects are noteworthy. For example, when the effects of an intervention cumulate over time, as might be the case in an educational intervention implemented in primary school grades, the small initial effect is amplified over time.

Callahan and Moon (2007) correctly established that sometimes statistically significant differences are trivial. However, it is important to note that the reverse is also true: Sometimes statistically nonsignificant differences are nontrivial and can be easily missed—even when of considerable size—if the sample size of a study is too small. They also equate statistically nonsignificant differences with "no effect"—for example, "there were no differences among groups in overall quality of writing" (p. 311). To stay with their example, the difference in writing quality between two groups is unlikely to ever be exactly zero; there usually is some difference. The question is whether the difference is meaningful. In other words, the issues at hand are whether the difference is trivial, meaningless, or unimportant or nontrivial, meaningful, or important and whether, despite these features, the statistical test has failed to detect it. In the following sections, I give three reasons—chosen from a potential list of many more—why statistical significance should not be equated with result noteworthiness.

1. p *values do not provide direct information about the probability of the* *hypothesis*.

The probability value (p value) that results from NHST does not offer direct information about the probability of null hypothesis or even the alternative hypothesis, for that matter. As any (good) statistical text will explain, the NHST p value provides the probability of getting a particular experimental result or a result more extreme (i.e., further into the tails of a null distribution), given that the null hypothesis is true: $P(D|H_0)$, where P = probability, D = data, and H = hypothesis. Unfortunately, the question of genuine interest is usually not "How likely are our data, given this hypothesis?" but rather "How likely is this hypothesis, given our data?" (Cohen, 1994). The latter is $P(H_0|D)$ and can only be solved using the mathematics of Bayes' theorem.

2. *Dichotomous decisions do not build good scientific theories*.

The dichotomous decision procedure—reject or accept (or, more correctly, fail to reject) the null—at the heart of NHST is largely irrelevant to the scientific process. It is may be useful in quality assurance of production (which was Neyman's and Pearson's concern), but it is almost certainly detrimental to the development of scientific theory. Good scientific theories develop through refining precise predictions of outcomes; simple accept–reject decisions offer virtually no scope for this. Kirk (1996) explained as follows:

> How far would physics have progressed if their researchers had focused on discovering ordinal relationships? What we want to know is the size of the difference between A and B and the error associated with our estimate; knowing A is greater than B is not enough. (p. 754)

What Kirk advocated in this quote, and what many others have also advocated, is a quantitative, estimation approach to science: p values are not enough.

3. NHST *violates the principles of falsificationism*.

Many scientists tend to think of themselves as Popperian (Mulkay & Gilbert, 1981). To them, the scientific method consists of proposing a hypothesis and then exposing it to tests that will disconfirm it, if indeed it is false. Such scientists are well aware of the dangers of looking only for confirmation and believe that NHST is doing the work of falsification for them. They believe that by following the rules of setting up null hypotheses and rejecting if $p > .05$, they are being the best Popperians they can be. These scientists are wrong.

They are not wrong because it is wrong to be Popperian (although many philosophers of science would argue it is, and many sociologists would say it is impossible to even try); they are wrong because using NHST is not Popperian. There is a sense—as we shall soon see, it is a superficial, trivial sense, but it is a sense nonetheless—in which NHST appears to uphold the principles of Popperian falsification. The language of NHST does conveniently map on to Popper's:

- Theories cannot be proved (we never accept the null hypothesis).
- Theories can, however, be shown to be false (we can reject the null hypothesis).
- Survival of a test merely means the theory is corroborated, not proved (again, we never accept the null hypothesis but rather continue to fail to reject; see Thompson, 2006a).

But the resemblance is trivial at best. In fact, NHST seriously violates Popper's falsifiability requirements.

Popper's (1959, 1963) most important demarcation criterion was that, to be considered scientific, there needs to exist a set of conditions that could expose a theory as false, if in fact it is, and that the theory must be subjected to risky tests, or tests that afford a high chance of exposing the theory as false. But typical statistical significance tests are not risky tests—the null hypotheses we use guarantee this. Virtually all null hypotheses in the social and life sciences are nil null hypotheses (e.g., of no correlation, of zero difference), and they are almost always a priori false. After all, it is usually the suspicion that some difference or correlation exists—that it is not zero—that motivates research to begin with!

Yet the null hypothesis (the one we never believed to begin with) is the only hypothesis exposed to the risk of rejection. Our real hypothesis remains protected from any risk because of the way we structure the statistical test. One might further argue that in statistically underpowered experiments, even these futile nil null hypotheses are not exposed to any real risk of rejection. Such tests have no chance of falsifying (of rejecting) anything—neither our real hypothesis nor our dummy hypothesis.

Why are nil null hypotheses almost always a priori false? Because in the behavioral and life sciences, almost everything is correlated with everything else to some extent, and the difference between two groups or conditions is rarely, if ever, exactly zero (Meehl, 1978). A more worthwhile null hypothesis would speculate about the actual magnitude of expected correlations or make predictions about the size of some difference based on relevant theory. Tests conducted on null hypotheses like this would be risky and much closer to the scientific standards Popper had in mind.

Despite these considerations, the superficial fit of NHST to falsification has been a remarkable force in perpetuating its use. In other words, Popperian rhetoric has thwarted many statistical reform efforts because researchers panic that in giving up NHST, they will have no means by which to test their hypotheses. This is simply untrue, and as we have seen, NHST, as typically practiced, is not a good test of a hypothesis anyway!

CHANGES IN STANDARDS OF EVIDENCE IN MEDICINE, ECOLOGY, AND PSYCHOLOGY

Standards of evidence not only are different in different disciplines, they also change over time. NHST was at the forefront of the inference revolution in the social and life sciences between 1940 and 1960. During this time, statistical significance became the new standard of scientific evidence in medicine, ecology, and psychology. But over 20 years ago, in the case of medicine, standards changed again: CIs usurped p values. In psychology and ecology, standards are changing, too. The question of how long such reforms will take to permeate education research remains open. The following accounts merely show how this change has occurred, or is currently proceeding, in other disciplines.

Medicine

In the 1950s, medicine faced a flood of new "wonder drugs" (Marks, 1997). Antibiotics and steroids were marketed for the first time, and important decisions about their effectiveness had to be made quickly. Prior to this, decisions about what drugs or procedures to employ were based largely on the expert recommendations of individual physicians. "Therapeutic reformers"—the champions of the randomized clinical trial—were concerned that decisions made in the traditional way (based on the expert opinion) were too time consuming, given the flood of new drugs, and too open both to individual biases and to pressure from pharmaceutical companies. The then newly arrived statistical significance testing techniques appeared to possess the qualities they were looking for: efficiency and objectivity.

Therapeutic reform was successful, and NHST was rapidly institutionalized as a routine step in clinical trial procedure. However, just over a decade after the institutionalization of NHST in medicine, its role in clinical trials was under scrutiny. Researchers began to worry that the technique was being misused and overrelied on and that statisticians, rather than physicians, had authority over the conclusions drawn from experiments (Cutler, Greenhouse, Cornfield, & Schneiderman, 1966). Statistical reform had begun, and by the end of the 1980s, strict editorial policies would profoundly change the way results were reported in medicine.

Kenneth Rothman was one journal editor leading the way in medicine's reform. In the early 1980s, he wrote the following in his revise-and-submit letters to would-be authors in *American Journal of Public Health (AJPH)*:

> All references to statistical hypothesis testing and statistical significance should be removed from the papers. I ask that you delete *p* values as well as comments about statistical significance. If you do not agree with my standards (concerning the inappropriateness of significance tests) you should feel free to argue the point, or simply ignore what you may consider to be my misguided view, by publishing elsewhere. (Rothman, cited in Fleiss, cited in Shrout, 1997)

In 1990, after leaving *AJPH*, Rothman became the founding editor of *Epidemiology*, where he instituted a similarly strict policy:

> When writing for *Epidemiology*, you can enhance your prospects if you omit tests of statistical significance. Despite a widespread belief that many journals require significance tests for publication, the Uniform Requirements for Manuscripts Submitted to Biomedical Journals discourages them, and every worthwhile journal will accept papers that omit them entirely. In *Epidemiology*, we do not publish them at all. Not only do we eschew publishing claims of the presence or absence of statistical significance, we discourage the use of this type of thinking in the data analysis, such as in the use of stepwise regression, (Rothman, 1998, p. 334)

During Rothman's term at *AJPH*, reports of *p* values dropped from 63% in 1982 to 6% in 1986 through 1989; in *Epidemiology*, there were none (Fidler, Thomason, Cumming, Finch, & Leeman, 2004).

By the mid-1980s, many major medical journals had followed suit, including the *New England Journal of Medicine*, *British Medical Journal*, *Lancet*, *British Heart Journal*, *Circulation Research*, and the *Journal of the American Medical Association*. What did their policies recommend instead of NHST? Without exception, they recommended that CIs replace *p* values. In 1988 the International Committee of Medical Journal Editors (ICMJE) backed up this recommendation. They revised their "Uniform Requirements for Manuscripts Submitted to Biomedical Journals" to include the following statement regarding statistical inference:

> When possible, quantify findings and present them with appropriate indicators of measurement error or uncertainty (such as confidence intervals). Avoid sole reliance on statistical hypothesis testing, such as the use of *p* values, which fail to convey important quantitative information. (ICMJE, 1988, p. 260)

By the time the manuscript guidelines went to press, more than 300 medical and biomedical journals had notified ICMJE of their willingness to comply with them. At that moment, CIs replaced NHST as the standard of evidence required by medical journals. Statistical reporting in medical journals continues to reflect change, with around 85% of medical articles reporting CIs (Coulson, Healey, Fidler, & Cumming, 2009).

Ecology

Before the 1950s, NHST was very rarely used in ecology. Fidler, Cumming, Burgman, and Thomason (2004) found that just over 5% of articles published in 1950 in two leading ecology journals reported NHST. However, by 1955, NHST appeared in one third (33%). By 1970, 60% of ecology articles relied solely on NHST, making it the dominant form of scientific evidence in this discipline.

Until very recently, there was little reason to think NHST had lost favor among ecological researchers in the decades that followed the 1970s. Despite growing criticisms of NHST in ecology over these decades, Anderson, Burnham, and Thompson (2000) reported that "the estimated number of p-values appearing within articles of *Ecology* exceeded 8,000 in 1991 and has exceeded 3,000 in each year since 1984" (p. 912). Similarly, in the *Journal of Wildlife Management*, there were more than 3,000 p values a year from 1994 to 2000 (Anderson et al., 2000).

However, very recently it has been possible to detect some change in statistical reporting. In 2001–2002, over 92% of empirical articles in two leading conservation biology journals used NHST; in 2005, this figure had dropped to 78% (Fidler, Burgman, Cumming, Buttrose, & Thomason, 2006). There were small but corresponding increases in the use of CIs and information theoretic and Bayesian methods. Recent instructional texts on these methods published for ecologists suggest increased adoption of these alternative methods in the future. In particular, the attention given to information theoretic methods (e.g., Burnham & Anderson, 2002) and Bayesian methods (e.g., McCarthy, 2007) suggests the uptake of these will grow rapidly in the next few years. Here, too, the standards of evidence are changing.

Psychology

In 1970, Morrison and Henkel wrote, "It is the social scientist's lack of theoretical development and of theoretical concern that make significance tests attractive" (p. 369). They were trying to explain why psychology was so rapidly seduced by NHST. It was perhaps not only the lack of theoretical development that made NHST attractive but also the false notion that NHST was itself a surrogate for theory.

Whatever the reason, psychology certainly took to the then-new technique: Sterling (1959) reported that in 1955, 81% of articles in four leading empirical journals reported NHST results. Similarly, Hubbard and Ryan (2000) surveyed articles published in 12 American Psychological Association (APA) journals between 1955 and 1959 and reported NHST use in 86%. Huberty (1993) examined 28 statistical texts written for behavioral scientists published between 1910 and 1949. He concluded, "It took about 15 years—from 1935 to 1950, roughly—for the Neyman–Pearson philosophy to be integrated (to some extent) into presentations of statistical testing in behavioral science statistical methods textbooks" (p. 323). By the mid-1950s, NHST was fully institutionalized in psychology journals, textbooks, and training programs. It has largely remained so, with roughly 96% of 2005–2006 articles in 10 leading psychology journals reporting p values (Cumming et al., 2007).

Although NHST remains entrenched in psychology, the discipline has produced more critics of the technique than any other. There are literally hundreds (perhaps now more than 1,000) articles in the psychology literature explicating the flaws and dangers of NHST. The most commonly recommended alternative is estimation: effect sizes and CIs. The APA (2001) *Publication Manual* included advice on effect sizes and stated that CIs are "in general, the best reporting strategy" (p. 22). Cumming et al. (2007) reported an increase in the use of figures with error bars (e.g., standard error bars, CIs) in articles published in 10 leading psychology journals from 11.0% in 1998 to 24.7% in 2003–2004 to 37.8% in 2005–2006. There are now at least 23 psychology and education journals whose editorial policies encourage alternatives to NHST or at least offer some warnings of its pitfalls (Hill & Thompson, 2004). The change from NHST to an estimation approach in psychology is still at an early stage but is slowly becoming substantial.

CASE STUDIES OF DAMAGE

One reason change was rapid in medicine is that drawing the wrong conclusion from research can, literally, be a life-and-death matter. In ecology, the increasing importance of properly analyzing and interpreting experimental results related to climate change, species extinction, and other environmental questions cannot be underestimated. Stakes such as these make statistical reform not merely a technical or philosophical issue, as it has largely been perceived, but a crucial ethical issue, one that is relevant to every researcher.

Avenues by which NHST could potentially damage the progress of science fall into four categories:

1. Time is wasted on searches for nonexistent moderating variables to explain illusory inconsistencies in the literature (i.e., "inconsistencies" due only to differences in statistical power, not in

existence or size of effect). We will see evidence of this in the situation-specific validity case described later in this section.

2. Time is wasted on incorrect, weak, or trivial theories because statistically significant results are interpreted as providing strong evidence in favor of the theory. Kline (2004) called this the "meaningfulness fallacy" (p. 66).

3. Research programs and sound theories are abandoned or there are unnecessary delays in the application of these programs because of the inability to produce consistent research results. We will see this in the streptokinase case below.

4. Research programs that never get started are lost because of their inability to jump the statistical significance hurdle. Cases of this kind are, of course, extremely difficult to document and make a systematic study of damage virtually impossible.

Categories 1, 3, and 4 are most likely to occur in literatures where the average statistical power is low and unreported. Category 2 is limited to cases where effect sizes are trivial and statistical power is unreasonably high or a few fortuitous early results became influential. Cases illustrating Category 2 are not provided here but can be found in Fidler (2005).

Low Statistical Power Is Common

In 1962, Jacob Cohen published the first survey of statistical power in the psychological literature. (Recall that statistical power = 1 − Type II error rate. In other words, statistical power is the probability of detecting an effect [of some specified size] that is really there. If a Type I error is equivalent to a false positive, a Type II error is equivalent to a false negative—for example, a pregnancy test result that tells you you're not pregnant when you are. Pregnancy tests always give their false positive and false negative rates; published psychology studies don't!) Because virtually none of the studies published reported power, Cohen calculated it himself. He calculated the average power for (arbitrarily designated) small, medium, and large effect sizes of 70 articles published in 1960 issues of the *Journal of Abnormal and Social Psychology*. For medium effect sizes, thought to be typical of psychological and educational effect sizes, the average power was .48.

The situation changed little in subsequent decades. Rossi (1990) conducted a similar survey roughly 20 years after Cohen. In those two decades, the average power to detect small, medium, and large effects had "risen" to .17, .57, and .83. For effect sizes most typical of the field, that's an increase in statistical power from .48 (Cohen, 1962) to .57 (Rossi, 1990)—hardly the desired improvement! Still worse news is to be found in Sedlmeier and Gigerenzer's

(1989) results. They also surveyed the *Journal of Abnormal Psychology*. In their sample, the average power for medium effect sizes was .50, virtually identical to the average power Cohen reported for 1960! Maxwell (2004) cited several other surveys—some more recent—of statistical power that give similar results (p. 148). Little wonder, then, that Hunter (1997) compared the average psychology experiment to flipping a coin! Yet despite low and unknown statistical power, many researchers continue to interpret statistical nonsignificance as evidence of no effect. This misconception has the potential to cause damage of various kinds in all disciplines.

The Case of the Theory of Situation-Specific Validity

Schmidt's (1996) claim quoted at the start of this chapter that reliance on statistical significance testing has slowed the growth of knowledge in psychology was motivated by a series of meta-analyses he, Jack Hunter, and their colleagues conducted throughout the 1970s and early 1980s (for an overview of meta-analysis, see Hunter & Schmidt, 2004). The orthodox doctrine of personnel psychology at that time was that the correlation between scores on cognitive ability or aptitude tests and on-the-job performance did not have general validity—that is, "A test valid for a job in one organization or setting may be invalid for the same job in another organization or setting" (Schmidt & Hunter, 1981, p. 1132). The doctrine seemingly applied even when jobs appeared to be superficially very similar.

This might seem strange at first, but it is not implausible: Imagine subtle differences in the clientele, training structure, or supervisory style. All could plausibly impact on job performance. A difficult supervisor at one branch might require staff at that branch to have better developed conflict resolution skills. Hence, the theory of situational specificity held that the validity of the tests depended on more than just the listed tasks in a given position description—it depended on the cognitive information processing and problem-solving demands of the particular workplace. The theory was empirically driven; its purpose was to explain the variability, or inconsistency, of empirical results.

However, the effect sizes in most studies were in fact reasonably similar. The apparent inconsistency was only in the statistical significance of studies— a simple product of the low and unreported statistical power of the literature. (With an average power of around 50%, it should not be surprising that half the studies are statistically nonsignificant.) This explanation went unrealized, however, and the theory of situational specificity grew structurally complex, with addition of many potential moderating variables. In fact, the search for such moderating variables became the main business of industrial or organizational psychology for decades, despite the fact that the variability they had been developed to explain was illusory. Schmidt and Hunter (1981) explained,

> If the true validity for a given test is constant at .45 in a series of jobs . . . and if sample size is 68 (the median over 406 published validity studies . . .) then the test will be reported to be valid 54% of the time and invalid 46% of the time (two tailed test, $p = .05$). This is the kind of variability that was the basis for the theory of situation-specific validity. (p. 1132)

How long did organizational psychology pursue this misdirected theory and its associated research program? In 1981, toward the end of their meta-analysis series, Hunter and Schmidt wrote, "The real meaning of 70 years of cumulative research on employment testing was not apparent. . . . The use of significance tests within individual studies only clouded discussion" (p. 1134).

The Case of Intravenous Streptokinase for Acute Myocardial Infarction

Between 1959 and 1988, a total of 33 randomized clinical trials tested the effectiveness of intravenous streptokinase for treating acute myocardial infarction. (Streptokinase is an enzyme that dissolves vascular thrombi, blood clots caused by atherosclerosis. Theory predicted it would benefit acute myocardial patients, because most cardiac arrests are caused by atherosclerosis—a gradual buildup of a fat-containing substance in plaques that then rupture, forming blood clots on artery walls.) The case below was reported in Hunt (1997) and included a useful illustration of a cumulative meta-analysis by Lau et al. (1992).

The vast majority of these trials (26 of 33) showed no statistically significant improvement at $p < .05$; the remaining seven trials did achieve $p < .05$. When described in this way—that is, as merely statistically significant or not—the results appear inconsistent. Yet upon inspection of the CIs for these trials, it is immediately obvious that many trials had extremely low precision (i.e., the CIs were very wide). A few trials, on the other hand, had intervals that were very narrow. This discrepancy alone should alert us to the fact that the inconsistency in results, in terms of statistical significance, is likely due to varying statistical power.

A cumulative meta-analysis (where consecutive trials are combined) showed that the odds ratios and CIs lined up on the favorable side of the null line as early as the fourth trial. By the seventh trial, the cumulative odds ratio was distinctly less than one (about .75), indicating that streptokinase had a positive effect on the treatment of myocardial infarction.

If results had been properly collated and interpreted, tests of this treatment could have ended in 1973 or even earlier. As it was, with dichotomous decisions based on NHST clouding the issue, testing continued until 1988 and included some 30,039 further participants. Assuming half of those were control group patients, approximately 15,000 patients were denied treatment that would have been effective for their condition. Of course, this figure does not even begin to account for the incalculable number of other patients who would have presented with this condition during the 15 years prior to 1988, when the Food and Drug Administration finally accepted the effectiveness of the drug.

HOW CAN GIFTEDNESS RESEARCH AVOID THESE PROBLEMS?

The types of questions driving research need to change. We need to move from asking dichotomous questions about whether an effect is statistically significant or not to asking how large the effect is and how uncertain the estimate is. The latter can be characterized in various ways, but standard errors and confidence intervals are the most familiar and are a good a place to start. Below, I outline three crucial components of an estimation approach to research: (a) meta-analytic thinking, (b) calculating and interpreting effect sizes, and (c) calculating and interpreting confidence intervals.

Think Meta-analytically

Meta-analytic thinking (Cumming & Finch, 2001) is thinking across the results of independent studies, acknowledging prior information with an emphasis on effect size rather than making dichotomous decisions based on the outcome of single experiments. It is the key to avoiding the types of damage the case studies in this chapter illustrate; it is how we stop systematically retarding the growth of cumulative knowledge (Schmidt, 1996).

Meta-analysis and meta-analytic thinking are especially important in fields like giftedness, where definitions (e.g., *giftedness, talent*) are not commonly agreed upon and measurement units therefore vary, making it difficult to compare across studies intuitively. Despite their importance, meta-analyses are relatively rare in giftedness research. A simple database search for meta-analyses in select giftedness journals returned few hits: For example, *Exceptional Children* has published only six meta-analyses since 1989 and *Gifted Child Quarterly* only one since 1991 (see Table 4.1). Focusing on estimation—effect sizes and CIs—is the first step toward improving this situation. Reporting these statistics ensures that adequate information is available for future meta-analysis, and thinking in estimation terms should itself naturally lead to increased rates of meta-analysis.

Calculate and Interpret Effect Sizes

Vacha-Haase and Thompson (2004) and Thompson (2006a) provided guides to effect sizes, both the calculation of relevant effect sizes and their

TABLE 4.1
Examples of Effect Sizes Used in Meta-analyses
in Two Giftedness Research Journals

Authors	Year	Journal	Types of ESs used
Bellini & Akullian	2007	*Exceptional Children*	Percentage of nonoverlapping data points (PND)
Sabornie, Cullinan, Osborne, & Brock	2005	*Exceptional Children*	Standardized effect size (ES): Cohen's *d*
Reid, Trout, & Schartz	2005	*Exceptional Children*	Standardized ES: Glass's *g* (when reported in original studies); mean diff/SD$_{pooled}$ (from Rosenthal, 1994) Corrected ES: Initial ES $* \sqrt{2}$ $(1 - R)$, where R = observed correlation between baseline and treatment data points (from Rosenthal, 1994)
Xin, Grasso, DiPipi-Hoy, & Jitendra	2005	*Exceptional Children*	PND
Hammill	2004	*Exceptional Children*	Standardized ES: Cohen's *d* Correlation: *r*
Vaughn & Feldhusen	1991	*Gifted Child Quarterly*	Standardized ES: Glass's *g*

interpretation. They offered the following taxonomy of effect sizes: "(a) standardized differences effect sizes [e.g., Glass's *g*, Cohen's *d*], (b) variance-accounted-for effect sizes [e.g., R^2], and (c) 'corrected' effect sizes [e.g., adjusted R^2]" (Vacha-Haase & Thompson, 2004, p. 474). The effect sizes used in the seven meta-analyses identified in two giftedness journals are classified in Table 4.1, using where possible the taxonomy provided by Vacha-Haase and Thompson.

Despite the fact that effect sizes provide the primary evidence necessary for drawing conclusions from research, effect size reporting is still not widespread, and effect size interpretation is even less common. Most researchers attempting effect size interpretation do not go beyond Cohen's (1988) benchmarks. However, rigid adherence to these benchmarks precludes more substantive and insightful interpretation. They were not designed to be uniformly applied in all fields of research; for example, what is a large effect in clinical psychology may be considered small in studies of visual perception. Cohen (1988) himself emphasized that

> these proposed conventions were set forth throughout with much diffidence, qualifications, and invitations *not* to employ them if possible [italics added]. . . . They were offered as conventions because they were needed in a research climate characterized by a neglect of attention to issues of [effect size] magnitude. (p. 532)

As noted elsewhere, "if people interpreted effect sizes [using fixed benchmarks] with the same rigidity that $\alpha = .05$ has been used in statistical testing, we would merely be being stupid in another metric" (Thompson, 2001, pp. 82–83). At least in relatively established areas of research, "there is no wisdom whatsoever in attempting to associate regions of the effect-size metric with descriptive adjectives such as 'small,' 'moderate,' 'large,' and the like" (Glass, McGaw, & Smith, 1981, p. 104).

Calculate and Interpret CIs

Cumming's survey in chapter 3 of this volume showed CI reporting was exceptionally rare in empirical studies of giftedness: 2%, 1 article in the sample of 40. There is much room for improvement. A detailed account of CIs, especially what they tell us about replication, is provided in chapter 3. As mentioned there, Cumming and Finch (2001) provided a guide to calculating CIs for various effect size measures, and Cumming and Finch (2005) provided a guide to interpreting CIs. The latter also includes warnings about common misinterpretations of CIs.

CONCLUSION

This chapter has demonstrated why the adoption of an estimation approach based on effect sizes, CIs, and meta-analytic thinking is important and has given examples of what may be at stake if current practice continues. Giftedness researchers can learn from the mistakes made in other disciplines and can make changes to statistical practices now that will enhance our understanding and treatment of gifted children.

REFERENCES

American Psychological Association. (2001). *Publication manual of the American Psychological Association* (5th ed.). Washington, DC: Author.

Anderson, D. R., Burnham, K. P., & Thompson, W. L. (2000). Null hypothesis testing: Problems, prevalence and an alternative. *Journal of Wildlife Management, 64*, 912–923.

Asher, W. (1986). Conducting research with meta-analysis: A new direction for gifted education. *Gifted Child Quarterly, 30*, 7–10.

Bellini, S., & Akullian, J. (2007). A meta-analysis of video modelling and video self-modeling interventions for children and adolescents with autism spectrum disorder. *Exceptional Children, 73*, 264–288.

Burnham, K. P., & Anderson, D. R. (2002). *Model selection and multimodel inference: A practical information-theoretic approach* (2nd ed.). New York: Springer-Verlag.

Callahan, C. M., & Moon, T. R. (2007). Sorting the wheat from the chaff: What makes for good evidence of effectiveness in the literature in gifted education? *Gifted Child Quarterly, 51,* 305–319.

Carver, R. P. (1978). The case against statistical significance testing. *Harvard Educational Review, 48,* 378–399.

Cohen, J. (1962). The statistical power of abnormal–social psychological research: A review. *Journal of Abnormal and Social Psychology, 65,* 145–153.

Cohen, J. (1988). *Statistical power analysis for the behavioral sciences* (2nd ed.). Hillsdale, NJ: Erlbaum.

Cohen, J. (1994). The earth is round (*p* < .05). *American Psychologist, 49,* 997–1003.

Coulson, M., Healey, M., Fidler, F., & Cumming, G. (2009). *Confidence intervals permit, but don't guarantee, better inference than statistical significance testing.* Manuscript submitted for publication.

Cumming, G., Fidler, F., Leonard, M., Kalinowski, P., Christiansen, A., Kleinig, A., et al. (2007). Statistical reform in psychology: Is anything changing? *Psychological Science, 18,* 230–232.

Cumming, G., & Finch S. (2001). A primer on the understanding, use, and calculation of confidence intervals that are based on central and non-central distributions. *Educational and Psychological Measurement, 61,* 532–574.

Cumming G., & Finch, S. (2005). Inference by eye: Confidence intervals, and how to read pictures of data. *American Psychologist, 60,* 170–180.

Cutler, S. J., Greenhouse, S. W., Cornfield, J., & Schneiderman, M. A. (1966). The role of hypothesis testing in clinical trials. *Journal of Chronic Diseases, 19,* 857–882.

Fidler, F., Burgman, M., Cumming, G., Buttrose, R., & Thomason, N. (2006). Impact of criticism of null hypothesis significance testing on statistical reporting practices in conservation biology. *Conservation Biology, 20,* 1539–1544.

Fidler, F. (2005). *From statistical significance to effect estimation: Statistical reform in psychology, medicine and ecology.* Unpublished doctoral dissertation, University of Melbourne, Australia. Retrieved April 8, 2009, from http://www.latrobe.edu.au/psy/staff/fidler.html

Fidler, F., Cumming, G., Burgman, M., & Thomason, N. (2004). Statistical reform in medicine, psychology and ecology. *Journal of Socio-Economics, 33,* 615–630.

Fidler, F., Thomason, N., Cumming, G., Finch, S., & Leeman, J. (2004). Editors can lead researchers to confidence intervals but they can't make them think: Statistical reform lessons from medicine. *Psychological Science, 15,* 119–126.

Glass, G. V., McGaw, B., & Smith, M. L. (1981). *Meta-analysis in social research.* Beverly Hills, CA: Sage.

Hammill, D. D. (2004). What we know about correlates of reading. *Exceptional Children, 70,* 453–468.

Hill, C. R., & Thompson, B. (2004). Computing and interpreting effect sizes. In J. C. Smart (Ed.), *Higher education: Handbook of theory and research* (Vol. 19, pp. 175–196). New York: Kluwer.

Hubbard, R., & Ryan, P. A. (2000). The historical growth of statistical significance testing in psychology—and its future prospects. *Educational and Psychological Measurement, 60,* 661–681.

Huberty, C. J. (1993). Historical origins of statistical testing practices: The treatment of Fisher versus Neyman–Pearson views in textbooks. *Journal of Experimental Education, 61,* 317–333.

Hunt, M. (1997). *How science takes stock: The story of meta-analysis.* New York: Russell Sage Foundation.

Hunter, J. E. (1997). Needed: A ban on the significance test. *Psychological Science, 8,* 3–7.

Hunter, J. E., & Schmidt, F. L. (2004). *Methods of meta-analysis: Correcting error and bias in research findings* (2nd ed.). Thousand Oaks, CA: Sage.

International Committee of Medical Journal Editors. (1988). Uniform requirements for manuscripts submitted to biomedical journals. *Annals of Internal Medicine, 108,* 258–265.

Kirk, R. E. (1996). Practical significance: A concept whose time has come. *Educational and Psychological Measurement, 56,* 746–759.

Kline, R. B. (2004). *Beyond significance testing: Reforming data analysis methods in behavioral research.* Washington DC: American Psychological Association.

Lau, J., Antman, E. M., Jimenez-Silva, J., Kupelnick, B., Mosteller, F., & Chalmers, T. C. (1992). Cumulative meta-analysis of therapeutic trials for myocardial infarction. *New England Journal of Medicine, 327,* 248–254.

Marks, H. (1997). *The progress of experiment: Science and therapeutic reform in the United States, 1900–1990.* New York: Cambridge University Press.

Maxwell, S. E. (2004). The persistence of underpowered studies in psychological research: Causes, consequences, and remedies. *Psychological Methods, 9,* 147–163.

McCarthy, M. A. (2007). *Bayesian methods for ecology.* Cambridge, England: Cambridge University Press.

Meehl, P. E. (1978). Theoretical risks and tabular asterisks: Sir Karl, Sir Ronald, and the slow progress of soft psychology. *Journal of Consulting and Clinical Psychology, 46,* 806–834.

Morrison, D. E., & Henkel, R. E. (Eds.). (1970). *The significance test controversy.* Chicago: Aldine.

Mulkay, M., & Gilbert, G. N. (1981). Putting philosophy to work: Karl Popper's influence on scientific practice. *Philosophy of the Social Sciences, 11,* 389–407.

Popper, K. (1959). *The logic of scientific discovery.* London: Hutchinson.

Popper, K. (1963). *Conjectures and refutations.* London: Routledge and Kegan Paul.

Reid, R., Trout, A. L., & Schartz, M. (2005). Self-regulation interventions for children with attention deficit/hyperactivity disorder. *Exceptional Children, 71,* 361–378.

Rosenthal, R. (1994). Parametric measures of effect sizes. In H. Cooper & L. V. Hedges (Eds.), *The handbook of research synthesis* (pp. 231–260). New York: Russell Sage Foundation.

Rossi, J. (1990). Statistical power of psychological research: What have we gained in 20 years? *Journal of Consulting and Clinical Psychology, 58,* 646–656.

Rothman, K. J. (1998). Writing for epidemiology. *Epidemiology, 9,* 333–337.

Sabornie, E. J., Cullinan, D., Osborne, S. S., & Brock, L. B. (2005). Intellectual, academic, and behavioral functioning of students with high-incidence disabilities: A cross-categorical meta-analysis. *Exceptional Children, 72,* 47–64.

Salsburg, D. (2001). *The lady tasting tea: How statistics revolutionized science in the twentieth century.* New York: W. H. Freeman.

Schmidt, F. L. (1996). Statistical significance testing and cumulative knowledge in psychology: Implications for training of researchers. *Psychological Methods, 1,* 115–129.

Schmidt, F. L., & Hunter, J. E. (1981). Employment testing: Old theories and new research findings. *American Psychologist, 36,* 1128–1137.

Sedlmeier, P., & Gigerenzer, G. (1989). Do studies of statistical power have an effect on the power of studies? *Psychological Bulletin, 105,* 309–315.

Shrout, P. E. (1997). Should significance tests be banned? *Psychological Science, 8,* 1–2.

Spiegelhalter, D. J. (2004). On wasps and club dinners. *Significance, 1,* 183.

Sterling, T. D. (1959). Publication decisions and their possible effects on inferences drawn from tests of significance or vice versa. *Journal of the American Statistical Association, 54,* 30–34.

Thompson, B. (2001). Significance, effect sizes, stepwise methods, and other issues: Strong arguments move the field. *Journal of Experimental Education, 70,* 80–93.

Thompson, B. (2006a). *Foundations of behavioral statistics: An insight-based approach.* New York: Guilford Press.

Thompson, B. (2006b). Research synthesis: Effect sizes. In J. Green, G. Camilli, & P. B. Elmore (Eds.), *Handbook of complementary methods in education research* (pp. 583–603). Washington, DC: American Educational Research Association.

Vacha-Haase, T., & Thompson, B. (2004). How to estimate and interpret various effect sizes. *Journal of Counseling Psychology, 51,* 473–481.

Vaughn, V., & Feldhusen, J. F. (1991). Meta-analyses and review of research on pull-out programs in gifted education. *Gifted Child Quarterly, 35,* 92–98.

Xin, Y. P., Grasso, E., DiPipi-Hoy, C. M., & Jitendra, A. (2005). The effects of purchasing skill instruction for individuals with developmental disabilities: A meta-analysis. *Exceptional Children, 71,* 379–401.

5

RELIABILITY GENERALIZATION METHODS IN THE CONTEXT OF GIFTEDNESS RESEARCH

KEVIN M. KIEFFER, ROBERT J. REESE, AND TAMMI VACHA-HAASE

The process of defining and identifying exceptional or gifted children has been a delicate, controversial subject. Much of the controversy lies, in part, with the lack of agreement on what exactly constitutes the less than clear-cut constructs of *gifted*, *talented*, and *exceptional*. The conceptualizations of these constructs, much like theories of intelligence, have increased in scope and complexity over the years.

The ways in which children are being identified as gifted have broadened and moved beyond just traditional cognitive ability measures to include creativity, more specific academic domains (e.g., mathematics, music ability), and leadership abilities (Johnsen, 2004). Various models of giftedness have been developed, such as the Renzulli method (Renzulli, 2005), Tannenbaum's five factors (Tannenbaum, 1983), and Gagne's model (Gagne, 2005), and a federal definition for gifted and talented students has even been formulated (U.S. Department of Education, 1993) that attempts to bring order to the variety of ways in which a student could be identified as such. Further, the methods for identifying gifted students and tracking their progress within an enriched curriculum have become more varied and now include both quantitative (e.g., norm-based measures, rating scales) and qualitative (e.g., interviews, portfolios, free response formats) assessment means (Pierce et al., 2007).

Given that the construct of giftedness is conceptualized and measured in diverse and sophisticated ways, there is a great need to develop measurements that provide reliable and valid observations that advance both the understanding of giftedness and that pragmatically assist researchers and clinicians in identifying and evaluating such students "on the front lines." The consistency and accuracy of data generated from measuring instruments, however, is an area that is frequently overlooked in the social sciences, both in practice and in educating student researchers. For instance, Pedhazur and Schmelkin (1991) noted that

> measurement is the Achilles' heel of sociobehavioral research. Although most programs in sociobehavioral sciences . . . require a medium of exposure to statistics and research design, few seem to require the same where measurement is concerned. . . . It is, therefore, not surprising that little or no attention is given to the properties of measures used in many research studies. (pp. 2–3)

Generating accurate and reliable data is critical to strong scientific inquiry and essential to furthering giftedness research yet is often neglected by even the most attentive researchers.

From a measurement standpoint, much of the focus has been on the question of score validity (i.e., do assessments accurately identify gifted and talented students?) and test fairness (e.g., do assessments provide an unfair advantage based on socioeconomic status, race, ethnicity, culture, language, and other contextual factors that may affect assessment results?). Although valid and fair measurement is certainly a goal within the larger fields of both measurement and giftedness research, before score validity and test fairness can be addressed, instruments must first generate consistently repeatable and replicable scores. If a measure cannot generate reliable scores across the population for which the measure is intended, it will not be able to generate valid scores. The ability of a measure to generate repeatable, consistent scores is a psychometric concept known as *reliability*. This chapter's purpose is to explain the integral role of score reliability and reliability generalization across studies in advancing both the science of giftedness and the practice of identifying and measuring the progress of students that are gifted.

A PRIMER ON SCORE RELIABILITY AND CLASSICAL TEST THEORY

Reliability can be defined as "the degree to which scores are free from errors of measurement for a given group" (American Educational Research Association, American Psychological Association, & National Council on

Measurement in Education, 1999, p. 180). When measuring phenomena of interest, two types of variance can be generated: systematic or unsystematic. The former is associated with real differences and is likely to be replicated in future measurements. Systematic variance, therefore, is often referred to as "good variance." Unsystematic variance, however, represents variability that is likely to be indigenous only to the measurement or sample being investigated and will probably not replicate in future measurements or will vary in unpredictable ways. Thus, unsystematic variance, or error variance, is considered "bad variance" and is one of many random effects that psychometricians attempt to reduce or eliminate when collecting observations or measurements.

Classical Test Theory

The groundwork for what is often called *classical test theory* was originally articulated by Thorndike (1904). Thorndike argued that reliable information about individuals can be obtained by collecting measurements that have a maximum amount of systematic variance and a minimum amount of measurement error variance. This theoretical conception of reliability was operationalized in a mathematical formula offered by Spearman (1907) called the "true score" model of measurement.

Spearman (1907) extended the notion proffered by Thorndike (1904) to include the influences of both random and measurement error in explaining a score that a given respondent will exhibit on a given occasion. As noted by Crocker and Algina (1986), "The essence of Spearman's model was that any observed score could be envisioned as the composite of two hypothetical components—a true score and a random error component" (p. 107). Thus, the true score formula can be written in the equation

Observed Score = True Score + Random Error.

In the Spearman (1907) model, a *true score* refers to the average score that the same respondent will obtain over infinite administrations of the same version of a given test (Crocker & Algina, 1986). Thus, a true score indicates the actual performance of a particular respondent and is, by definition, a perfectly reliable score. An *observed score,* however, is the score that a respondent actually generates on a given administration of a test. This observed score may or may not be sufficiently reliable to be useful. *Random error* is composed of random measurement error that can accentuate or attenuate a given respondent's true score. Based on the positive or negative influences of the random error component, it is possible for a respondent's observed score to be higher or lower than the same respondent's true score.

Consider the following example: Suppose the respondent of interest is a sixth-grade mathematics student who is capable of correctly answering 16 out of 20 questions on a test (the student's true score). Now suppose the student is ill the day of the exam and fluctuates in cognitive functioning ability throughout the test, therefore randomly missing four questions that the student had the ability to answer correctly. This situation illustrates the negative influence of random error, as the student's true score is higher than the observed score. Suppose that on another occasion with the same exam, the respondent guessed correctly on two items that should have been missed. This condition represents the positive effect of random error, as the student's true score is lower than the observed score. Both positive and negative effects of random error lead to unreliable scores and potentially misleading estimates of the respondent's abilities.

Reliability Estimates in Classical Test Theory

The following cursory review of classical test theory reliability estimates presumes some knowledge of the subject matter and is not intended to be a thorough coverage of the material. Interested readers are referred to Arnold (1996), Eason (1991), and Thompson (2003) for more detailed explanations. As noted previously, classical test theory partitions observed score variance into only two components, true score variance and random error variance. Consequently, it is possible to examine only a single source of measurement error at any given time. This poses a serious dilemma for the researcher because, in reality, several types of measurement error can exist concurrently. In classical test theory, it is possible to consider estimates of measurement error due to inconsistency in forms (equivalence), observers (interrater agreement), sampling the item domain (internal consistency or split-half), or time (test–retest or stability; Arnold, 1996). However, only one measurement error influence can be considered in a given analysis.

Each type of reliability estimate (e.g., time, observers) can be used to determine the degree to which true scores deviate from observed scores. The problem, however, is that classical test theory is unable to examine inconsistencies in test forms, raters, items, or occasions simultaneously. That is, classical test theory renders the potentially erroneous assumption that the error observed in calculating a stability coefficient is the same error indicated by calculating an internal consistency alpha. As stated by Thompson and Crowley (1994),

> An embedded assumption of many researchers using the classical score approach is that sources of error substantially overlap each other (e.g., the 15% of error from a test–retest analysis is the [sic] essentially the *same* error as the 10% or 15% measurement error detected in an internal consistency

analysis) and that the sources of error do not interact to create additional error variance. (p. 3)

Much to the dismay of the researcher utilizing classical test theory reliability estimates, error components corresponding to items, occasions, and forms are actually distinct sources of variability and often are not equivalent. Further, in addition to examining only one source of error variance at a time, classical test theory also fails to examine the unique contribution of the interaction sources of measurement error variance (e.g., occasions with items, items with forms). As noted by Thompson (1991),

> a practitioner may do classical internal consistency, test–retest, and equivalent forms reliability analyses, and may find in all three that measurement error comprises 10% of score variance. Too many classicists would tend to assume that these 10 percents are the same and also tend to not realize that in addition to being unique and cumulative, the sources may also interact to define disastrously large interaction sources of measurement error not considered in classical theory. The effects of these assumptions are all the more pernicious because of their unconscious character. (p. 1072)

Thus, classical test theory does not consider sources of measurement error simultaneously, nor does it examine the effects of their unique interaction effects.

Estimates of reliability in classical test theory are represented in the form of reliability indexes or reliability coefficients (Arnold, 1996). A reliability index is simply the Pearson's product moment correlation coefficient (Pearson r) between observed scores and true scores (Crocker & Algina, 1986). To examine the amount of shared variance between observed scores and true scores, it is necessary to square the Pearson r between them. This statistic, termed a *reliability coefficient,* indicates the percentage of true score variance accounted for by the observed scores. Coefficient alpha, another type of reliability coefficient, also indicates the amount of shared variance between observed and true scores (Cronbach, 1951).

Estimates of score reliability are considered squared statistics because they involve the ratio of two variances (true score variance to total score variance), but they are not reported with an exponent of 2 like the variances themselves. Because estimates of reliability are squared statistics, their values typically range from zero to 1.0, with larger estimates indicating more reliable scores. However, even though reliability coefficients such as coefficient alpha are squared statistics, it is possible mathematically, although not theoretically, for their values to be negative and smaller than 1.0. Readers are referred to the first chapter in Thompson (2003) for an accessible understanding of how reliability coefficients can be as small as -7.1.

Properties of Reliable Data

The reliability of scores directly corresponds to the degree to which error is present or absent in a measurement. As such, reliability is a concept that inures to the scores generated by a particular measuring instrument and not to the instrument itself. Thus, Rowley (1976) noted that "an instrument itself is neither reliable nor unreliable. . . . A single instrument can produce scores which are reliable and other scores which are unreliable" (p. 53). Eason (1991) argued as follows:

> Though some practitioners of the classical measurement paradigm speak of reliability as a characteristic of tests, in fact reliability is a characteristic of data, albeit data generated on a given measure administered with a given protocol to given subjects on given occasions. (p. 84)

Thus, the scores of a particular group of individuals are reliable or unreliable, not the measuring instrument used to generate the scores. Unfortunately, based on the common and thoughtless use of the phrase "the test is reliable," many researchers have erroneously begun to believe that tests are reliable. As indicated previously, nothing could be more untrue.

Because it is the scores of a group of measured individuals that ultimately influence reliability, the consistency of the sample used to estimate reliability is critical. Like all statistics, reliability coefficients are affected by the variability of the scores in the sample of chosen individuals. Reliable data are generated by maximizing the systematic variance (e.g., real differences between people or groups) and minimizing the variance attributed to random sampling or measurement error (e.g., variance that will not replicate in future samples and is specific to only the sample under investigation).

Given the variety of academic environments, differing demographic variables of students, the uneven developmental shifts of students, and other contextual variables that may serve as sources of random sampling or measurement error, it is incumbent upon researchers to analyze and report score reliability estimates for the data in hand, rather than solely relying on previous research or a given testing manual's reported score reliability estimates. A measure that generates reliable scores in one setting is not guaranteed to do so in another.

As a group of individuals becomes more heterogeneous, the real or systematic differences among the individuals become more pronounced. This divergence in the systematic variance of the group typically leads to more variability in the set of scores (Wilkinson & APA Task Force on Statistical Inference, 1999). Consequently, the increased score variance for the set of individuals leads to higher reliability for the group. Because more heterogeneous groups of individuals tend to generate more variable scores than homogenized groups, the same measure administered to more heterogeneous or homogeneous groups will likely yield scores with differing reliabilities.

The lack of heterogeneity can be especially problematic with measuring children who are gifted; this problem is referred to as a *restriction of range* and has been a common lament among those measuring and tracking the progress of gifted and talented students (e.g., Sternberg, 2003). Gifted students are by definition at the upper end of the distribution of scores, which leads to a less heterogeneous group. The lack of heterogeneity, and subsequent reduced variability, can lead to attenuated reliability coefficients.

Heuristic Example of a Restriction in Range

To facilitate greater understanding of how a lack of heterogeneity can impact reliability, a heuristic example is provided. Suppose the data contained in Table 5.1 were generated by a Leadership Scale (LS), not unlike other measures used to help identify gifted students in both academic and social domains, that is focused on behaviors consistent with leadership abilities. The LS comprises five items, and each item is rated on a 6-point Likert-type scale (1 = *never* to 6 = *always*). The sample consisted of 5 gifted students and 5 students not identified as gifted (note that two students in the nonidentified group have

TABLE 5.1
Heuristic Data Set and Reliability Coefficients for Restriction
of Range Example

Student number	Time 1 items					Time 2 items				
	1	2	3	4	5	1	2	3	4	5
Gifted students										
1	5	6	5	5	6	6	6	6	6	6
2	6	5	5	5	6	6	6	6	6	6
3	5	6	6	6	6	5	6	6	6	6
4	5	4	5	6	5	5	5	6	6	6
5	5	5	4	5	5	5	6	6	6	5
Alpha	.59					.38				
Test–retest *r*	.64									
Nonidentified students										
1	2	4	3	4	4	4	5	4	5	5
2	1	2	1	3	2	3	3	3	3	2
3	3	2	3	4	3	4	4	3	5	4
4	5	4	5	6	5	5	5	6	6	6
5	5	5	4	5	5	5	6	6	6	5
Alpha	.96					.96				
Test–retest *r*	.98									

identical scores to those in the gifted group). Teachers rated the 10 students on leadership behaviors at the beginning and end of the school year to assess any changes in student behaviors over this span as part of an evaluation of the effectiveness of a leadership curriculum for the gifted students.

Based on the reliability estimates available from a classical test theory perspective and the given information, a researcher could examine two types of reliability: (a) stability over time (i.e., test–retest reliability) and (b) accurate sampling of the item domain (i.e., internal consistency reliability). Table 5.1 illustrates that readministering the same measure to track progress leaves little room for the gifted students to improve, thereby creating a ceiling effect and restricted range of test scores. This leads to an attenuated ability to generate reliable scores, as evidenced by the lower coefficient alpha and test–retest reliability coefficients generated by the gifted group.

A quick perusal would be disconcerting to the researcher. As a result of examining the reliability of the scores based on their stability and internal consistency, six different reliability coefficients were generated. The internal consistency alphas for the nonidentified students at both measurement times (.96 and .96, respectively) are exceptional, but the alphas for the gifted students are quite low (.59 and .38, respectively).

In examining the scores, there are not large rating differences within each of the individual student ratings, regardless of group (i.e., gifted or non-identified). However, the variability between the students across both groups is different, with the exception of identical data for the last two students in each group. With the gifted group, it is difficult to order the students based on scores but easier to do so with the nonidentified group because of differences in scores between students (i.e., their scores are not clustered together like those of the gifted group).

Just as with internal consistency alphas, the stability coefficients (i.e., the correlation of test scores between Time 1 and Time 2) are quite different as well—.64 (gifted group) and .98 (nonidentified group). The researcher has a major dilemma as both types of reliability estimates provide different results. If the researcher had simply examined the coefficient alpha or test–retest coefficient for nonidentified students, conclusions regarding the ability to generate reliable scores would be very different if only the gifted students were observed.

Classical test theory suggests that individuals can be ordered more reliably on a construct when the variability of scores increases. Henson, Kogan, and Vacha-Haase (2001) explained,

> In terms of classical measurement theory (holding the number of items on the test and the sum of the item variances constant), increased variability of total scores suggests that we can more reliably order people on the trait of interest and thus more accurately measure them. This assumption is made explicit in the test–retest reliability case, when consistent

ordering of people across time on the trait of interest is critical in obtaining high reliability estimates. (pp. 407–408)

A failure to apply this concept can have deleterious effects on interpreting data and studies when the results are based on measurements that are not interpreted in the context of the sample characteristics. By observing the influences on reliability, it becomes obvious why it is incorrect and inappropriate to use the statement "the test is reliable," as the same test can produce radically different results when administered to different groups of people. Giftedness researchers can circumvent problems associated with restriction of range by using measures that provide increased score variability or by ensuring that the measures they select have adequate ceilings to measure improvement over time.

RELIABILITY GENERALIZATION: GENERALIZING RELIABILITY ESTIMATES ACROSS SAMPLES

In the course of developing measuring instruments, researchers typically realize the importance of reporting both score reliability and validity information as evidence that an instrument measures a meaningful construct and generates scores with acceptable psychometric properties. However, few researchers report reliability coefficients in published research when the focus of empirical investigation does not involve instrument development. Such poor reporting practice was an issue addressed by the American Psychological Association (APA) Task Force on Statistical Inference (Wilkinson & APA Task Force on Statistical Inference, 1999):

> It is important to remember that a test is not reliable or unreliable. Reliability is a property of the scores on a test for a particular population of examinees. . . . Thus, authors should provide reliability coefficients of the scores for the data being analyzed even when the focus of their research is not psychometric. Interpreting the size of observed effects requires an assessment of the reliability of the scores. (p. 596)

Given the importance of reliability coefficients to the interpretation of statistical findings, it is imperative that authors report reliability coefficients in published research as demonstrable evidence that they were consulted before conducting substantive statistical analyses.

The Practice of Reliability Induction: Pervasive, but Inexcusable

Evaluating the psychometric properties of scores is essential to ensuring that analyses are not evaluating only measurement error variance. Evidence regarding score validity is particularly critical because valid scores inherently must be reliable, whereas the inverse does not have to be true (i.e., scores can be reliable but not valid). To explain the notion that scores can be reliable but not valid, it is useful to invoke an analogy using three darts and a standard dartboard where the intention of the dart thrower is to strike the bull's-eye with all three darts. On the first set of three throws, the three darts randomly strike the dartboard with none of the darts hitting the bull's-eye but all three landing somewhere on the dartboard. This set of darts is neither consistent (reliable) nor accurate (valid). On the second set of three throws, the darts land tightly clustered near the number 20 at the far edge of the dartboard. The throws were very consistent (reliable) but not at all accurate (valid) as the intention is to strike the bull's-eye with all three darts. In the final set of throws, the three darts all land within the bull's-eye. In this case, the set of darts is both consistent (reliable) and accurate (valid), paralleling the notion that scores generated by an instrument can be reliable (consistent) without being valid (actually measuring what the instrument purports to measure).

Why Authors May Not Report Reliability Estimates

Although it is possible that authors who chose not to report reliability coefficients in their published work actually did consult reliability analyses before analyzing their data, the practice of omitting these results in the published scientific literature is still problematic. One explanation posited in the literature for poor reliability reporting rates is the general notion that researchers continue to believe that tests, not samples, are reliable (Shields & Caruso, 2003; Vacha-Haase, 1998) because poor language patterns (i.e., using the phrase "the test is reliable") have unconsciously led them to believe that tests rather than scores are reliable (Thompson & Vacha-Haase, 2000). This is especially true for well-established instruments that have been widely researched and that may have accompanying comprehensive test manuals. However, it is important that researchers recognize that (a) reliability is a characteristic that applies to scores, not tests; (b) reliability magnitude is influenced by the heterogeneity of responses to a set of test items; (c) values reported in test manuals are useful only for comparative purposes, not for describing all other studies using a given instrument; and (d) there is a unique influence of the sample-specific participants on score consistency and stability.

Unfortunately, too many researchers continue to believe that reliability is a fixed and nascent quality of tests, and rather than reporting the reliability coefficients for the data in hand, they make either explicit (e.g., citing the magnitude of previous reliability estimates) or very vague (e.g., indicating the test has been reported to be reliable) citations to previously published reliability coefficients as evidence of acceptable reliability for their own studies. This procedure has been termed *reliability induction* by Vacha-Haase, Kogan, and Thompson (2001) and invokes a mind-set in which researchers are inductively generalizing from a specific instance (i.e., a single study) to a larger, more general conclusion (i.e., test scores are reliable across all administrations of the instrument). In deriving this terminology, Vacha-Haase et al. (2000) studied all articles using either of two selected measures in which authors invoked a reliability coefficient from a prior study; none of the articles in the two literatures compared either sample composition or variability with those in the original sample in an effort to justify the induction of the prior reliability to the current study.

Appropriate and Inappropriate Cases of Reliability Induction

Although not considered an acceptable practice, reliability induction may be minimally permissible when the current sample is similar or identical in composition and score variability to the former sample (Crocker & Algina, 1986). This can be particularly tempting for giftedness researchers when using intelligence measures that have large standardization samples with impressive reported psychometrics in the test manual. However, this enterprise can still be flawed, as Vacha-Haase et al. (2000) conclusively demonstrated. Reliability estimates can differ across studies even when the examined samples are very similar or identical in composition.

Although never a preferred method of reporting score reliability, reliability induction can be marginally permissible. At minimum, using reliability induction appropriately demonstrates that the authors have a requisite awareness that score reliability considerations are important to the integrity of statistical analyses and are based on the unique characteristics of a given sample.

Clearly, many authors do not appear to understand the importance of reporting reliability information for the data-in-hand and often resort to a reliability induction mindset when presenting the results of their studies. The implications for both practice and research are considerable. Those who develop and administer high-stakes tests must consider sources of error that influence score reliability. The sources of potential error variance are greater with children, from the developmental ability to focus on any given day to the cognitive shifts that occur in children that can impact measures taken over time. For example, the time interval for evaluating test–retest reliability may vary dramatically with children when evaluating cognitive processes (van den Burg & Kingma, 1999). Those researching and assessing giftedness have not only those issues of concern but also the issues of having enough sample heterogeneity and items that can adequately capture differences in ability at the upper end of the continuum.

Rigorous quantitative research requires consistent attention to the psychometric properties generated by a test, as knowledge is cumulated and science advanced only by the ability to replicate previous research findings. The assumption that a handful of studies (typically those first published) establish an instrument as reliable and valid is a questionable practice at best. Thus, evaluating score reliability in every study is critically important because poor reliability attenuates both power against Type II error and effect sizes (cf. Thompson, 1994). Attenuation of effect sizes is especially problematic given that various professional organizations (e.g., American Psychological Association) and many journal editorial policies require the reporting of effect size estimates in published research. This policy has come about as a result of problems noted in the professional literature with nil null statistical significance testing (Thompson, 1999a, 1999b).

Meta-analytic Examination of Measurement Error: Reliability Generalization

Concerted attention during the past several years has been focused on developing and expanding a meta-analytic method for examining sample influences on measured reliability coefficients, called *reliability generalization* (RG; Vacha-Haase, 1998). Poor score reliability reporting rates and confusion over reliability constructs were instrumental in Vacha-Haase's development of this meta-analytic method that permits the examination of sample-specific factors on score reliability estimates across studies. Given the tendency for test scores to vary as a function of sample characteristics, RG endeavors to provide the clarity for score reliability that Hunter and Schmidt (1990) provided for score validity generalizations across studies. RG can help identify (a) the typical score reliability for an instrument across studies, (b) factors that contribute to score variability across studies, and (c) upper and lower bounds of score reliability estimates in relation to measurement conditions and factors (Yin & Fan, 2000).

Increased attention to RG, the evaluation of typical reliability coefficients, and sample-specific influences on their magnitude was evidenced by the publication of a special issue of *Educational and Psychological Measurement* (August 2002) devoted to the topic, as well as the publication of more than 50 studies and at least one book (Thompson, 2003) using RG methodology during the past few years alone. RG, first articulated by Kennedy and Turnage (1991) but first operationalized as a meta-analytic method by Vacha-Haase (1998), invokes the logic that test scores, and not tests themselves, are reliable and that score reliability is a complex function influenced by a host of sample specific factors. Because score reliability is a function of variations present in a sample, the reliability induction logic previously described frequently leads to inaccurate result interpretation (Vacha-Haase et al., 2000). RG explicitly permits the examination of sample specific factors (that are therefore not completely replicable) on score reliability for the data in hand.

Comments on Conducting Reliability Generalization Studies

This section presents some basic guidelines for conducting RG studies as a guide for using the procedure. A useful first step in thoughtfully completing an RG study is to read the seminal RG study by Vacha-Haase (1998). Further, readers interested in exploring practical issues in conducting RG studies are referred to Henson and Thompson (2002).

Identification of an Appropriate Instrument

In a meta-analytic procedure such as RG, individual published studies become the data points under consideration. Given that the individual studies that use selected measures are the units of analysis, just as in the validity generalization studies described by Schmidt and Hunter (1977) and Hunter and Schmidt (1990), it is possible to compute means and standard deviations for reliability coefficients across studies in an effort to obtain an "average" reliability coefficient. As with validity generalization, the obtained reliability coefficients can serve as dependent variables in a host of statistical techniques with the sample-specific factors collected across studies operating as the predictor variables of the score reliability magnitude.

As with any meta-analysis, however, the entire study must commence with the selection of an appropriate educational or psychological instrument, in this case one that is typically used in the giftedness literature. Just about any measure that has been used in the giftedness research could be employed in a RG study, so long as the instrument generates scores that permit the computation of internal consistency reliability or test–retest reliability. It is also important to select measures that have been used in a number of published studies so that a sample of sufficient size to permit the use of inferential statistical analyses will be generated. Researchers conducting an RG study can expect that only 25% to 50% of all studies will report reliability coefficients for the data in hand, and thus they must select instruments with a large enough sample of published studies to account for this attrition. More important than just the sheer size of the sample, however, is the relative frequency with which those published studies report reliability coefficients for the data in hand. Only those studies that explicitly report reliability coefficients for the data used in the study are included in the meta-analysis, and all studies that invoked reliability by referencing previously reported reliability coefficients are omitted. The number of studies that report reliability for the data in hand also affects the types of statistical procedures that can be used to complete the meta-analysis.

Because many readers may not be familiar with the procedure typically used to complete an RG study, we use as an example an instrument commonly used in the giftedness literature in an effort to better explain the process. A popular measure of cognitive ability for children in Kindergarten through Grade 12 is the Cognitive Abilities Test, Form 6 (CogAT; Lohman & Hagen, 2001). The CogAT is purported to measure abilities in reasoning and problem solving using verbal (V), quantitative (Q), and spatial or nonverbal (N) symbols, and respondents complete two to three subtests in each of the three domains to generate the three overall scores associated with the measure. Because the tests used in the batteries vary according to age level, it would be necessary to make a decision early in the RG study whether to examine subtests and batteries only of one age group or of all age groups. Also, the researchers would have to decide whether to examine (a) only reported score reliabilities for the three main batteries, (b) only score reliabilities for the subtests used to generate battery scores, or (c) both battery score reliabilities and subtest score reliabilities. The latter option offers the greatest amount of information about typical score reliability generated by the CogAT and also increases the likelihood of locating studies in the professional literature that report score reliability for either subtests or batteries.

Developing a Coding Form

Because the data being collected in an RG meta-analysis will involve selected sample characteristics from previously published studies, it is necessary to develop a form that will allow the researchers to capture all relevant data. Based on the collective experience of the authors in completing RG studies, it is useful to code as much data about the studies as possible while also not exceeding one single-sided page of the coding form. Creating a well-constructed form will enable the trained raters to quickly and accurately code all necessary information.

The form must include the type of reliability assessed, internal consistency (Cronbach's alpha or split-half), and/or test–retest methods. Next, the researchers must decide which sample specific variables may be likely to influence the magnitude of reliability coefficients. It is important to note that the choice of these variables will vary from study to study and is largely determined by those variables the researchers believe are likely to influence the magnitude of reliability coefficients generated by a particular instrument. Common predictors of reliability magnitude include the number of items on the instrument or subscales (when there are multiple versions of given instruments), overall sample size, translation of the instrument (when evaluating a measure that has been translated into multiple languages), gender homogeneity (proportion of sample size that is male or female; this variable can literally be expressed as a ratio of one gender to the total sample size, thus generating a continuous variable that ranges from 0 to 1.0), racial/ethnic homogeneity (similar to gender homogeneity, except this is a ratio of one racial/ethnic group to the entire sample), sample age and standard deviation, mean scale or subscale score and standard deviation, and sample type (e.g., elementary students vs. high school students), among others. If the information presents in continuous form (e.g., sample size), the data can be directly analyzed, whereas information that is categorical in nature (e.g., type of sample—high school students, gifted students, middle school children) will need to be transformed prior to analysis (e.g., dummy coded).

Organization of the Study and the Literature Review

Once the instrument has been selected, the researchers can search the relevant scholarly literature for studies that used the measure under evaluation. Depending on the measure, it may be necessary to search any number of databases, including PsycINFO, PSYCHLIT, ERIC, Medline, or other commonly used electronic databases. When searching the databases, it is important to use precise search strings to avoid the inclusion of articles unrelated to the RG study. Also, it is important to search for both the name of the test (e.g., in our example case, "cognitive abilities test, form 6") and any acronyms for the measure (e.g., in our example case, "CogAT").

We recommend that researchers focus their attention on published research reports as the units of analysis. In locating these published research reports, researchers can use any delimiters that make intuitive sense, but it is common to limit the years of the search to the first year the instrument was published through present year and to limit the search to peer-reviewed scholarly research articles written in language(s) understandable to the researchers.

To provide a concrete example of a literature review search in an RG study, we searched both PsycINFO and ERIC for peer-reviewed journal articles in the English language published between 2000 (the year the CogAT was released) and November 2007. Using the words "cognitive abilities test," the search resulted in a total of 385 hits in PsycINFO and 138 hits in ERIC. To ensure that we had obtained all available studies using the CogAT, we also searched with the acronym, resulting in eight hits in PsycINFO and 138 hits in ERIC. Researchers wishing to conduct this RG study on the CogAT would then need to sort through the articles, remove duplicates from the two samples, and retain only those articles that empirically used the CogAT.

Collecting Data

Once the literature research has been completed, a master list has been generated, and a coding form has been developed, each article must be obtained, read, and coded. After the articles are coded, it is then possible to divide the larger group of articles into categories. For instructional purposes, we interjected the name of our example instrument into these three categories: (a) articles that used the CogAT and reported reliability information for the data in hand, (b) articles that used the CogAT but reported score reliability information only from the original test manual or previous studies, and (c) articles that used the CogAT but failed to report any information about score reliability, past or present.

Don't Forget to Examine the Reliability of Ratings

Although the reason we conduct RG studies is to examine typical score reliability across studies and those factors that affect it, a by-product of publishing RG research is to increase awareness that score reliability is a sample-specific, not test-specific, factor. That also means that researchers completing RG studies must examine the reliability of their own observations. This can be accomplished in a variety of ways, depending on the number of raters. When there is only one rater, it is possible for the rater to simply select a random sample of the articles examined and recode those articles. How many articles the rater needs to recode is a function of both sample size and ambition, but a reasonable number used in past RG studies has ranged from 5% to 20% of the total articles in the study. Once the articles have been recoded, it is possible to employ bivariate correlation (either Pearson's product–moment correlation coefficient or Spearman rho) to generate a measure of observational reliability.

With two or more raters, more options are available. These include simple bivariate correlation (in which all possible combinations between pairs of *n* raters are computed using either the Pearson *r* or Spearman rho and then are averaged), Cohen's kappa (Cohen, 1960; two rater case), Fleiss's kappa (Fleiss, 1971; more than two rater case), intraclass correlation coefficient (Shrout & Fleiss, 1979), and mean difference between ratings with a confidence interval around the mean (Bland & Altman, 1986). Regardless of the method employed, it is incumbent upon RG researchers to demonstrate that their observations are reliable.

Data Analysis in RG Studies

Entering the Data

Once all data have been coded, the coded information must be entered into a statistical software program for analysis. Any statistical software can be used, but the approach used by the authors is to first enter all of the data into a Microsoft Excel file, then import the data directly into the Statistical Software Package for the Social Sciences (SPSS). This approach is particularly useful when working with multiple raters, as most individuals have access to Excel, thus easing the data entry process. All smaller Excel data files can be combined into a final data set through simple cut and paste techniques. To aid the speed of data entry, it is useful to title the columns of the Excel file in the exact order that items appear from top to bottom on the coding sheet. It is not necessary to develop eight-character titles for the columns in Excel (as required by some statistical software packages), as programs like SPSS will generate unique eight-character names and use the Excel column headings as variable labels when the data are imported.

Cleaning, Dummy Coding, and Recoding Data

Once the data file has been imported into a suitable statistical software package, it is possible to begin the data analysis process. Prior to actually conducting any analyses, however, it is necessary to clean the data by running frequencies on all variables and ensuring all values are within range for a given item. In the event that data entry errors have been committed, it is necessary to consult the coding sheets or the original study to resolve the discrepancy.

After the data have been cleaned, it is possible to recode or dummy code variables. Variables that are coded in continuous or interval-level data typically do not need to be recoded. However, when using many analytic techniques, it is not possible to use variables that are nominally scaled and have more than two levels (e.g., racial/ethnic origin may have as many as eight or more categories within the larger variable). In the case of these polychotomous variables, dummy coding the variables with a 1 (for the main category of interest) and 0 (for all other categories) permits analysis of the data. In the case where the relative contribution of multiple categories within a larger variable is to be examined (e.g., perhaps researchers seek to examine the contributions of White, Black, and Hispanic students on CogAT score reliability), several new variables will need to be created, each with the target variable of interest compared with all other groups.

Statistical Analysis of RG Data

The initial task in a reliability generalization study is to characterize the variability in the reliability coefficients across the various studies (Vacha-Haase, 1998). This is typically accomplished through a box-and-whisker plot, a method of graphically displaying the variability present in a data set, or the degree to which it is spread out, that can be particularly useful in visually evaluating the degree of consistency (or lack thereof) in reliability coefficients across studies. It is also important for RG researchers to compute means, standard deviations, and 95% confidence intervals (see Henson, 2004, for details on computing confidence intervals in RG studies) for the various subscales (and/or total scale) of the measure as well. These analyses provide an overview of the typical reliability generated across all of the various studies examined.

The next task in an RG study involves examining the relationship between coded sample characteristics and reported reliability coefficients.

Statistical analysis of RG data can employ a wide array of statistical methods, including multiple linear regression (Vacha-Haase, 1998), bivariate correlation (Henson et al., 2000), canonical correlation analysis (Vacha-Haase, 1998), analysis of variance (Caruso, 2000), and mixed effects hierarchical linear modeling (Beretvas & Pastor, 2003). The approach used in a given study will be dependent upon the number of reliability coefficients published in the literature and the comfort level of researchers with certain statistical techniques.

Estimation of Score Reliability

In the case that researchers are examining a dichotomously scored instrument (i.e., the answer to each question is either yes or no or correct or incorrect), it is possible to provide a lower-bound estimate of reliability for each study that did not report a reliability coefficient for the data in hand but that did provide a scale mean and standard deviation by using the Kuder–Richardson formula 21 (KR-21; Kuder & Richardson, 1937). The KR-21 estimate of reliability, in contrast to KR-20, presumes that all item difficulties are equal, thus circumventing the need to calculate individual item variances (Crocker & Algina, 1986). As such, all that is needed to calculate KR-21 is the scale mean, scale standard deviation, and the number of items on the test. Using the KR-21 method will result in a lower-bound estimate of reliability because all of the individual item difficulties are assumed equal (Henson et al., 2001; Kuder & Richardson, 1937).

Computation of KR-21 involves obtaining the uncorrected total score variance of the test. To use the standard deviation of the sample versus the uncorrected total score variance, the latter can be estimated with the formula

$$\sigma^2 = \left[SD^2 * (n-1)\right]/n$$

where *SD* is the standard deviation of the scale and *n* is the size of the sample used in the study (Henson et al., 2001). An example of using KR-21 to estimate lower-bound score reliability can be found in Henson et al. (2001) and Kieffer and Reese (2002).

SUMMARY AND CONCLUSIONS

Reliability generalization is an analytic method that permits the examination of score reliability across studies in an effort to identify sample specific factors that influence the magnitude of reliability coefficients generated by an instrument of interest. Henson and Thompson (2002) also noted uses of RG beyond simple examination of sample specific factors affecting reliability magnitude:

> ... RG is also an important tool to change thinking regarding reliability issues. RG forces us to see that reliability is not an immutable unchanging property of tests stamped indelibly into booklets during the printing process. Instead, RG helps us to see that score reliability for a given measure may fluctuate across samples that differ in their variability or their composition or across variations in the measurement protocol. RG studies help us determine which of these protocol features are relevant to obtaining higher score quality. (p. 124)

Thus, it is important to reiterate that reliability is a function of myriad sample-specific factors, many of which will not replicate in future studies with very similar or even identical samples. Giftedness researchers can improve their analytical practices by (a) using precision in their language and using the terminology *score reliability*, not *test reliability*; (b) reporting reliability coefficients for all measures used in all studies, even when the focus of a given study is not psychometric in nature; and (c) making explicit comparisons between the sample used in the original study in which an instrument was developed and the current study if the researchers engage in reliability induction practices. Understanding the critical role that score reliability plays in the integrity of statistical findings and the validity of test scores may result in increased rates at which researchers report reliability information for the data in hand.

Appropriately using reliability information in the context of giftedness research is critical, but it can prove challenging for a variety of reasons. The terms *gifted* and *talented* are used in varying ways throughout the research literature, often resulting in confusion about the intended use of the concepts. Also, the different ways in which these concepts are measured can significantly impact the reliability of scores generated. For example, there may be a desire to take shortcuts in identifying gifted students given time constraints (e.g., using a shorter measure or using a measure that lacks empirical support). Just because a measure is named "The Creativity Scale" does not mean it is necessarily a useful instrument for a given population or that it is even measuring creativity. Lastly, educators and researchers must acknowledge that tests scores do not occur in a vacuum; the social context in which tests are administered must be considered. They must remain mindful of this issue and of how such variables can influence the psychometrics of an instrument, and subsequently the utility of a test. A test may be useful for one group under certain conditions but useless with another group under different conditions.

Regardless of the difficulties with accurately measuring complex concepts, and given that students' academic lives are at stake when interpreting the consistency and stability of test scores, it is incumbent upon educators, clinicians, and researchers to develop a firm understanding of what factors influence score reliability and, ultimately, test validity. Only through concerted attention to the constellation of factors affecting the accuracy and consistency of test scores will giftedness research be advanced. Tests for selection and placement in the educational arena have been criticized for being unfair and biased and having too much influence. Some criticism is apt, as no test is perfect. Our discussion here has suggested that all tests have error; therefore, the scores generated by our attempts to measure constructs will never be perfect. However, if appropriate care is taken to utilize research techniques as described in this chapter, researchers and educators can be better informed of the utility as well as the limits of the tests they use. Such information can lead to better decision making and recognition that tests can be an efficient, meaningful component of accurately identifying gifted children.

REFERENCES

American Educational Research Association, American Psychological Association, & National Council of Measurement in Education. (1999). *Standards for educational and psychological testing.* Washington, DC: American Educational Research Association.

Arnold, M. E. (1996). Influences on and limitations of classical test theory reliability estimates. *Research in the Schools, 3,* 61–74.

Beretvas, S. N., & Pastor, D. A. (2003). Using mixed-effects models in reliability generalization studies. *Educational and Psychological Measurement, 63,* 75–95.

Bland, J. M., & Altman, D. G. (1986). Statistical methods for assessing agreement between two methods of clinical measurement. *Lancet, i,* 307–310.

Caruso, J. C. (2000). Reliability generalization of the NEO personality scales. *Educational and Psychological Measurement, 60,* 236–254.

Cohen, J. (1960). A coefficient for agreement for nominal scales. *Educational and Psychological Measurement, 20,* 37–46.

Crocker, L., & Algina, J. (1986). *Introduction to classical and modern test theory.* Fort Worth, TX: Harcourt Brace Jovanovich.

Cronbach, L. J. (1951). Coefficient alpha and the internal structure of tests. *Psychometrika, 16,* 297–334.

Eason, S. (1991). Why generalizability theory yields better results than classical test theory: A primer with concrete examples. In B. Thompson (Ed.), *Advances in educational research: Substantive findings, methodological developments* (Vol. 1, pp. 83–98). Greenwich, CT: JAI Press.

Fleiss, J. L. (1971). Measuring nominal scale agreement among many raters. *Psychological Bulletin, 76,* 378–382.

Gagne, F. (2005). From gifts to talents: The DMGT as a developmental model. In R. J. Sternberg & J. E. Davidson (Eds.), *Conceptions of giftedness and talent* (2nd ed., pp. 98–119). New York: Cambridge University Press.

Henson, R. K. (2004). Expanding reliability generalization: Confidence intervals and Charter's combined reliability coefficient. *Perceptual and Motor Skills, 99*(3, Part 1), 818–820.

Henson, R. K., Kogan, L. R., & Vacha-Haase, T. (2001). A reliability generalization study of the Teacher Efficacy Scale and related instruments. *Educational and Psychological Measurement, 61,* 404–420.

Henson, R. K., & Thompson, B. (2002). Characterizing measurement error in scores across studies: Some recommendations for conducting "reliability generalization" studies. *Measurement and Evaluation in Counseling and Development, 35,* 113–127.

Hunter, J. E., & Schmidt, F. L. (1990). *Methods of meta-analysis: Correcting error and bias in research findings.* Newbury Park, CA: Sage.

Johnsen, S. K. (2004). Definitions, models, and characteristics of gifted students. In S. K. Johnsen (Ed.), *Identifying gifted students: A practical guide* (pp. 1–22). Waco, TX: Prufrock Press.

Kennedy, R. S., & Turnage, J. J. (1991). Reliability generalization: A viable key for establishing validity generalization. *Perceptual and Motor Skills, 72,* 297–298.

Kieffer, K. M., & Reese, R. J. (2002). A reliability generalization study of the Geriatric Depression Scale (GDS). *Educational and Psychological Measurement, 62,* 969–994.

Kuder, G. F., & Richardson, M. W. (1937). The theory of the estimation of test reliability. *Psychometrika, 2,* 151–160.

Lohman, D. F., & Hagen, E. P. (2001). *Cognitive Abilities Test, Form 6.* Rolling Meadows, IL: Riverside Publishing.

Pedhazur, E. J., & Schmelkin, L. P. (1991). *Measurement, design, and analysis: An integrated approach.* Hillsdale, NJ: Erlbaum.

Pierce, R. L., Adams, C. M., Neumeister, K. L. S., Cassady, J. C., Dixon, F. A., & Cross, T. L. (2007). Development of an identification procedure for a large urban school corporation: Identifying culturally diverse and academically gifted elementary students. *Roeper Review, 29,* 113–118.

Renzulli, J. S. (2005). The three-ring conception of giftedness: A developmental model for promoting creative productivity. In R. J. Sternberg & J. E. Davidson (Eds.), *Conceptions of giftedness and talent* (2nd ed., pp. 246–279). New York: Cambridge University Press.

Rowley, G. L. (1976). The reliability of observational measures. *American Educational Research Journal, 13,* 51–59.

Schmidt, F. L., & Hunter, J. E. (1977). Development of a general solution to the problem of validity generalization. *Journal of Applied Psychology, 62,* 529–540.

Shields, A. L., & Caruso, J. C. (2003). Reliability generalization of the Alcohol Use Disorders Identification Test. *Educational and Psychological Measurement, 63,* 404–413.

Shrout, P., & Fleiss, J. L. (1979). Intraclass correlation: Uses in assessing rater reliability. *Psychological Bulletin, 86,* 420–428.

Spearman, C. (1907). Demonstration of formulae for true measurement of correlation. *American Journal of Psychology, 18,* 161–169.

Sternberg, R. J. (2003). Issues in the theory and measurement of successful intelligence: A reply to Brody. *Intelligence, 31,* 331–337.

Tannenbaum, A. J. (1983). *Gifted children: Psychological and educational perspectives.* New York: Macmillan.

Thompson, B. (1991). Review of generalizability theory: A primer by R. J. Shavelson & N. W. Webb. *Educational and Psychological Measurement, 51,* 1069–1075.

Thompson, B. (1994). Guidelines for authors. *Educational and Psychological Measurement, 54,* 837–847.

Thompson, B. (1999a). If statistical significance tests are broken/misused, what practices should supplement or replace them? *Theory & Psychology, 9,* 165–181.

Thompson, B. (1999b). Statistical significance tests, effect size reporting, and the vain pursuit of pseudo-objectivity. *Theory & Psychology, 9,* 191–196.

Thompson, B. (Ed.). (2003). *Score reliability: Contemporary thinking on reliability issues.* Thousand Oaks, CA: Sage.

Thompson, B., & Crowley, S. (1994). *When classical measurement theory is insufficient and generalizability theory is essential.* Paper presented at the annual meeting of the Western Psychological Association, Kailua-Kona, Hawaii. (ERIC Document Reproduction Service No. ED 377 218)

Thompson, B., & Vacha-Haase, T. (2000). Psychometrics is datametrics: The test is not reliable. *Educational and Psychological Measurement, 60,* 174–195.

Thorndike, E. L. (1904). *An introduction to the theory of mental and social measurements.* New York: Wiley.

U.S. Department of Education, Office of Educational Research and Improvement. (1993). *National excellence: A case for developing America's talent.* Washington, DC: Author.

Vacha-Haase, T. (1998). Reliability generalization: Exploring variance in measurement error affecting score reliability across studies. *Educational and Psychological Measurement, 58,* 6–20.

Vacha-Haase, T., Kogan, L. R., & Thompson, B. (2000). Sample compositions and variabilities in published studies versus those in test manuals: Validity of score reliability inductions. *Educational and Psychological Measurement, 60,* 509–522.

van den Burg, W., & Kingma, A. (1999). Performance of 225 Dutch school children on Rey's Auditory Verbal Learning Test (AVLT): Parallel test–retest reliabilities with an interval of 3 months and normative data. *Archives of Clinical Neuropsychology, 14,* 545–559.

Wilkinson, L., & APA Task Force on Statistical Inference. (1999). Statistical methods in psychology journals: Guidelines and explanations. *American Psychologist, 54,* 594–604. (Available from http://www.apa.org/journals/amp/amp548594.html)

Yin, P., & Fan, X. (2000). Assessing the reliability of Beck Depression Inventory scores: Reliability generalization across studies. *Educational and Psychological Measurement, 60,* 201–223.

6

MIXED DATA COLLECTION AND ANALYSIS FOR CONDUCTING RESEARCH ON GIFTEDNESS AND BEYOND

ANTHONY J. ONWUEGBUZIE, KATHLEEN M. T. COLLINS,
NANCY L. LEECH, AND QUN G. JIAO

In this chapter, our purpose is to present mixed research as an alternative approach toward addressing five challenges characterizing the field of gifted education research. First, we provide a critique of the dominant types of monomethods—quantitative and qualitative research—utilized in the field of gifted education. In so doing, we contend that mixed research, which involves the mixing or embedding of quantitative and qualitative research approaches within the same framework, offers a better potential to address the five challenges than do monomethod studies. Second, we present a formal definition of mixed research, followed by a discussion of the mixed research process. Third, we present a mixed data collection model applicable for identifying various rationales and purposes for conducting mixed data collection techniques within a single study or a gifted program of research. This discussion is followed by a presentation of mixed analytical techniques (i.e., techniques involving combining quantitative and qualitative analyses). Additionally, we contextualize our discussion of mixed data collection and analytical techniques with illustrative examples addressing the five gifted education research challenges. Our chapter concludes with a call for researchers to conduct more mixed studies in gifted education.

FIVE CHALLENGES IN GIFTED EDUCATION
RESEARCH—AN OVERVIEW

The field of contemporary gifted education research is characterized by distinct challenges, five of which will be addressed here. The first challenge is to address ceiling effects in standardized scores obtained from gifted samples in an attempt to measure progress or growth. A second challenge is to locate suitable comparison groups to assess the effects of the curricula of gifted programs on the performance levels of gifted students and to infer appropriate generalizations about program effects (Swiatek, 2007). A third challenge is to address participant attrition in longitudinal research conducted to document developmental processes of gifted students' abilities and achievements (Swiatek, 2002). Definitions of *gifted* and *talented* vary widely. Therefore, a fourth challenge in gifted education is to position giftedness within a domain-specific definition of giftedness (e.g., giftedness in mathematics). The fifth challenge is to utilize, within a research design, the high levels of verbal skill and articulation that are characteristic of gifted samples in general.

MIXED RESEARCH—AN ALTERNATIVE APPROACH

Because of the weaknesses inherent in both quantitative and qualitative research in the field of social sciences, in recent years, an increasing number of researchers are advocating that studies be conducted that utilize both quantitative and qualitative techniques within the same inquiry. Such investigations represent what is often termed *mixed methods,* although other terms have been used, such as *multimethods, blended methods,* and *integrated methods* (Johnson, Onwuegbuzie, & Turner, 2007). However, the term *mixed research* has intuitive appeal because this class of research involves more than just mixing methods. Moreover, mixed research can involve the mixing of quantitative and qualitative paradigms, worldviews, techniques, methods, concepts, and/or language (Johnson & Onwuegbuzie, 2004; Johnson et al., 2007). As noted by Johnson et al. (2007), use of the phrase *mixed research* represents a deliberate decision designed to de-emphasize methods alone as a definition and focus more emphasis upon a methodological approach in defining the mixed research process. Indeed, mixing of different research approaches—representing both quantitative and qualitative research—allows the researcher to address an important type of research legitimation, termed *weakness minimization* (Onwuegbuzie & Johnson, 2006).

Johnson et al. (2007) have developed a recent definition of mixed research. According to Johnson et al.,

Mixed methods research is an intellectual and practical synthesis based on qualitative and quantitative research; it is the third methodological or research paradigm (along with qualitative and quantitative research). . . . Mixed research is the research paradigm that (a) partners with the philosophy of pragmatism in one of its forms (left, right, middle); (b) follows the logic of mixed methods research (including the logic of fundamental principle and any other useful logics imported from qualitative or quantitative research that are helpful for producing defensible and useable research findings); (c) relies on qualitative and quantitative viewpoints, data collection, analysis, and inference techniques combined according to the logic of mixed methods research to address one's research question(s); and (d) is cognizant, appreciative, and inclusive of local and broader sociopolitical realities, resources, and needs. (p. 129)

In accordance with this definition, mixed research is interpreted broadly as representing a methodology encompassing philosophical stances and assumptions and strategies and techniques associated with designing mixed research (e.g., quantitative experiments and qualitative interviews), collecting mixed types of data (e.g., numbers in terms of frequencies and descriptive and/or nonnumerical narratives), and analyzing mixed data (e.g., quantitative descriptive and inferential analyses and qualitative content and domain analyses; Greene, 2006, 2008; Johnson et al., 2007; Onwuegbuzie, Johnson, & Collins, 2009).

Collins, Onwuegbuzie, and Sutton (2006) subdivided the mixed research process into the formulation stage, the planning stage, and the implementation stage. These three stages comprise 13 distinct, interactive, and recursive steps. The three stages and the accompanying 13 steps defining each stage are illustrated in Figure 6.1.

Research Formulation Stage

The *mixed research formulation stage* is represented by a linear completion of Steps 1 through 5 (illustrated by rectangles in Figure 6.1). Step 1 involves determining the goal of the study, which entails making a decision about what the overall, long-term aim of the mixed research is. We recommend utilizing Newman, Ridenour, Newman, and DeMarco's (2003) framework. These authors identified the following nine goals: (a) add to the knowledge base; (b) predict; (c) measure change; (d) have a personal, social, institutional, and/or organizational impact; (e) understand complex phenomena; (f) generate new ideas; (g) test new ideas; (h) inform constituencies; and (i) examine the past. In the area of gifted education research, all of these goals are viable. In mixed research studies, researchers often have two or more goals, one or more goals each for the quantitative and qualitative phases.

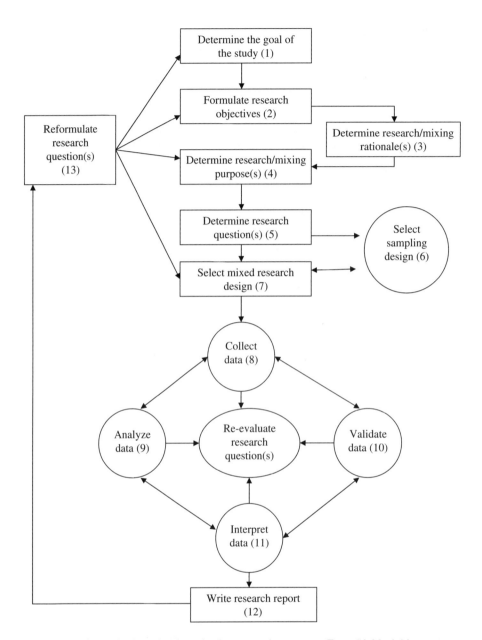

Figure 6.1. Steps in the mixed methods research process. From "A Model Incorporating the Rationale and Purpose for Conducting Mixed Methods Research in Special Education and Beyond," by K. M. T. Collins, A. J. Onwuegbuzie, and I. L. Sutton, 2006, *Learning Disabilities: A Contemporary Journal, 4,* p. 71. Copyright 2006 by *Learning Disabilities: A Contemporary Journal.* Reprinted with permission.

The research goal leads directly to the research objective (Step 2). In this step, the researcher should determine which of the following five major standard research objectives are pertinent for the quantitative and qualitative phases of the study: (a) exploration, (b) description, (c) explanation, (d) prediction, and/or (e) influence (Johnson & Christensen, 2008). Both the qualitative and quantitative phases of each mixed research study can be linked to one or more of these five research objectives. As part of determining the research goal and objective, the mixed researcher would conduct an in-depth, comprehensive, and rigorous review of the extant literature. An in-depth, comprehensive, and rigorous review of the extant literature is not necessary and might even be inappropriate for what are termed *qualitative-dominant mixed research studies* that are driven by grounded theory research designs in which the researcher needs to set aside all prejudgments and assumptions about social reality—a process known as *bracketing* (Schwandt, 1997). Onwuegbuzie, Collins, Leech, Dellinger, and Jiao (2009) have provided a 13-step model for conducting a literature review using mixed research techniques called *mixed research synthesis* (Sandelowski, Voils, & Barroso, 2006).

Once the research goal, objective(s), and relevant literature have been identified, the next step in the mixed research process is to determine the research mixing/rationale (Step 3). This step involves not only determining the rationale of the study but also identifying the rationale for mixing quantitative and qualitative approaches. Collins et al. (2006) identified the following four major rationales for mixing quantitative and qualitative approaches: (a) participant enrichment (i.e., mixing quantitative and qualitative techniques in an attempt to optimize the sample, such as increasing the number of participants), (b) instrument fidelity (i.e., maximizing the appropriateness and/or utility of the instruments used in the study, whether quantitative or qualitative—e.g., via a pilot study), (c) treatment integrity (i.e., mixing quantitative and qualitative procedures in order to assess the fidelity of interventions, programs, or treatments), and (d) significance enhancement (i.e., mixing quantitative and qualitative techniques in order to optimize data interpretations).

Alongside determining the research/mixing rationale, the researcher should identify the research/mixing purpose (Step 4). Collins et al. (2006) identified 65 purposes for mixing quantitative and qualitative approaches. Each of these purposes falls under one of the four major rationales (see Figure 6.2). Another useful framework for identifying the purpose for mixing is Greene, Caracelli, and Graham's (1989) typology. These authors identified the following five general purposes of mixed research studies: (a) triangulation, (b) complementarity, (c) initiation, (d) development, and (e) expansion.

Identifying the mixing rationale and purpose helps the researcher to develop appropriate research questions (Step 5). As can be seen from Figure 6.1,

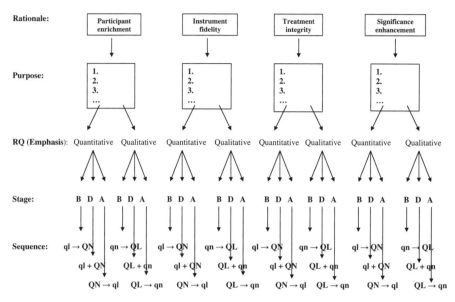

Figure 6.2. Visual representation of the rationale and purpose model. B = before study; D = during study; A = after study; QN/qn = quantitative; QL/ql = qualitative; uppercase = dominant; lowercase = less dominant; → = sequential; + = concurrent. From "A Model Incorporating the Rationale and Purpose for Conducting Mixed Methods Research in Special Education and Beyond," by K. M. T. Collins, A. J. Onwuegbuzie, and I. L. Sutton, 2006, *Learning Disabilities: A Contemporary Journal,* *4,* p. 90. Copyright 2006 by *Learning Disabilities: A Contemporary Journal.* Reprinted with permission.

research questions play a central role in the mixed research process, a role that is interactive, emergent, fluid, and evolving (Onwuegbuzie & Leech, 2006). In addition to the development of research questions occurring at the fifth step of the mixed research process, these questions are reevaluated during the data collection (i.e., Step 8), data analysis (i.e., Step 9), data legitimation (i.e., Step 10), and/or data interpretation (i.e., Step 11) phases. Any of these latter steps might lead to the research questions being modified and/or to additional research questions being addressed (i.e., Step 13).

Onwuegbuzie and Leech (2006) introduced the concept of mixed research questions by indicating that the questions embed both a quantitative question and a qualitative research question that lead to collection of both qualitative and quantitative data. Gifted education researchers can benefit from developing and addressing mixed research questions by addressing the five aforementioned challenges for gifted education research to a greater extent.

Tashakkori and Creswell (2007) have provided a typology for classifying mixed research questions. This typology makes explicit three ways that research questions are constructed in mixed research. The first way of constructing research questions in mixed research involves writing separate quantitative and qualitative questions, followed by an explicit mixed research question. The second method of constructing research questions in mixed research involves writing an overarching mixed or integrated research question, subsequently broken down into separate qualitative and quantitative subquestions to address in each phase or component of the investigation. According to Tashakkori and Creswell, this type of research question is more common in parallel or concurrent studies than in sequential studies. Although this overarching question might be implicitly present, sometimes it is not explicitly stated.

The third method of constructing research questions in mixed research involves writing research questions for each phase of a study as the study evolves. If the first phase is a quantitative phase, the question would be framed as a quantitative research question. If the second phase is qualitative, the question for that phase would be framed as a qualitative research question. As such, this method of constructing research questions is more relevant to sequential studies than to concurrent or parallel studies. Consistent with the recommendation of Onwuegbuzie and Leech (2006), Tashakkori and Creswell (2007) recommended the development of a single mixed research question that addresses the nature of mixing and integration or a single mixed research question that transcends any subsequent qualitative and quantitative subquestions.

Research Planning Stage

The research planning stage involves selecting the sampling design (Step 6) and the mixed research design (Step 7). These steps are interactive because choice of sampling design affects the selection of mixed research design and vice versa. With regard to the sampling design, we suggest the use of Onwuegbuzie and Collins's (2007) model. This model provides a typology for classifying mixed sampling designs according to (a) the time orientation of the components or phases and (b) the relationship of the qualitative and quantitative samples—namely, identical (i.e., same participants are involved in both the qualitative and quantitative phases), parallel (i.e., samples for the qualitative and quantitative components of the research are different but are drawn from the same population of interest), nested (i.e., participants selected for one phase of the study represent a subset of those sample members selected for the other phase), or multilevel (i.e., two or more sets of samples are extracted from different levels of the population of interest—e.g., students vs. special education teachers). The two criteria, time orientation (two levels) and sample relationship (four levels), yield eight different types of major sampling designs that mixed researchers have at their disposal.

Another useful typology of sampling schemes is that developed by Teddlie and Yu (2007), who subdivided sampling schemes into the following four types: (a) probability sampling, (b) purposive sampling, (c) convenience sampling, and (d) mixed methods sampling. Further, Onwuegbuzie and Leech (2007a) identified 24 sampling schemes that can be used in mixed research. For gifted education research, the most common sampling schemes include homogeneous sampling, critical case sampling, criterion sampling, confirming/disconfirming sampling, extreme case sampling, snowball/chain sampling, quota sampling, and multistage purposeful sampling.

For the research design step (i.e., Step 7), several useful typologies and frameworks have been designed. A particularly useful typology is that developed by Teddlie and Tashakkori (2006). These authors conceptualized what they termed the *methods–strands matrix* by crossing number of methods used by the number of research components or strands. The multistrand, mixed methods cell in the matrix comprises four families of mixed research designs: sequential, concurrent, conversion, and fully integrated. Teddlie and Tashakkori also described what they referred to as *quasi-mixed designs*, wherein qualitative and quantitative data are collected, but there is no true integration of the findings or inferences for the overall study. The authors also presented a seven-step process for selecting the most appropriate mixed research design.

Leech and Onwuegbuzie (2009) presented a three-dimensional typology in which mixed designs can be represented as a function of the following three dimensions: (a) level of mixing (i.e., fully mixed [mixing of quantitative and qualitative approaches occurring within or across the data collection, analysis, and interpretation stages] vs. partially mixed [mixing occurring only at the data interpretation stage]), (b) time orientation (i.e., concurrent [quantitative and qualitative phases occur at approximately the same point in time] vs. sequential [first phase informs or drives second phase]), and (c) emphasis of approaches (i.e., equal status [quantitative and qualitative components have approximately equal emphasis] vs. dominant status [one component has higher priority than does the other]). Leech and Onwuegbuzie's typology thus can be characterized by a 2 (fully mixed vs. partially mixed) × 2 (concurrent vs. sequential) × 3 (equal status vs. dominant status–quantitative vs. dominant status–qualitative), which yields 12 types of mixed research designs that gifted education researchers can utilize.

Research Implementation Stage

The research implementation stage consists of the following four steps: (a) data collection, (b) data analysis, (c) data validation, and (d) data interpretation. These four steps are cyclical and interactive. For the data collection stage (Step 8), we recommend the use of Johnson and Turner's (2003) typology. Johnson and Turner identified two dimensions guiding data collection within an inquiry. The first dimension requires the researcher to select a research approach, and the second dimension requires the researcher to select a method of data collection. A research approach lies on a continuum anchored by pure qualitative research approach and pure quantitative research approach. According to Johnson and Turner, descriptors identifying a pure qualitative approach culminate in data that can be described as open ended, inductive, exploratory, and free flowing and that are obtained in a naturalistic setting. In contrast, descriptors identifying a pure quantitative approach result in data that can be described as closed ended, deductive, confirmatory, and linear and that are obtained in a controlled setting. A mixed approach is centered on the continuum, and it represents data reflecting a mixing of approaches or a less extreme version of the pure quantitative or qualitative strands of data collected (Johnson & Turner, 2003). Additionally, these authors identified the following six specific data collection strategies in mixed research: (a) mixture of open- and closed-ended items on one or more questionnaires, (b) mixture of depth and breadth interviewing, (c) mixture of a priori and emergent/flowing focus group strategies, (d) mixture of standardized open- and closed-ended predesigned tests, (e) mixture of standardized/confirmatory and less structured/exploratory observations, and (f) mixture of nonnumeric and numeric archival-based documents.

The data collection step is followed by the data analysis step (Step 9). Onwuegbuzie and Teddlie (2003) identified the following seven stages of the mixed analysis process:

1. data reduction (i.e., reducing the dimensionality of the qualitative data [e.g., via exploratory thematic analysis, memoing] and quantitative data [e.g., via descriptive statistics, exploratory factor analysis, cluster analysis])

2. data display (i.e., describing pictorially the qualitative data [e.g., graphs, charts, networks, matrices, checklists, rubrics, Venn diagrams, photographs] and quantitative data [e.g., tables, graphs])

3. data transformation (i.e., quantitizing data by converting qualitative data into numerical codes that can be analyzed statistically and/or qualitizing data by converting quantitative data into narrative representations that can be analyzed qualitatively; Tashakkori & Teddlie, 1998)

4. data correlation (i.e., correlating qualitative data with quantitized data or quantitative data with qualitized data)

5. data consolidation (i.e., combining qualitative and quantitative data to create new or consolidated variables, codes, or data sets)

6. data comparison (i.e., comparing data extracted from the qualitative and quantitative components)

7. data integration (i.e., integrating qualitative and quantitative data into either a coherent whole or separate qualitative and quantitative sets of coherent wholes).

The data analysis step is followed by data legitimation (Step 10). We recommend Onwuegbuzie and Johnson's (2006) typology of legitimation types pertaining to the overall mixed research process, which contains nine legitimation types. Each of these types is summarized in Table 6.1. Gifted education researchers also can use frameworks for examining validity/legitimation pertaining to the individual quantitative (e.g., Campbell & Stanley, 1963; Onwuegbuzie, 2003b) and qualitative (e.g., Maxwell, 1992; Onwuegbuzie & Leech, 2007b) components of their mixed research studies.

TABLE 6.1
Typology of Mixed Methods Legitimation Types

Legitimation type	Description
Sample integration	The extent to which the relationship between the quantitative and qualitative sampling designs yields quality metainferences
Inside–outside	The extent to which the researcher accurately presents and appropriately utilizes the insider's view and the observer's views for purposes such as description and explanation
Weakness minimization	The extent to which the weakness from one approach is compensated by the strengths from the other approach
Sequential	The extent to which one has minimized the potential problem wherein the metainferences could be affected by reversing the sequence of the quantitative and qualitative phases
Conversion	The extent to which the quantitizing or qualitizing yields quality metainferences
Paradigmatic mixing	The extent to which the researcher's epistemological, ontological, axiological, methodological, and rhetorical beliefs that underlie the quantitative and qualitative approaches are successfully (a) combined or (b) blended into a usable package
Commensurability	The extent to which the metainferences made reflect a mixed worldview based on the cognitive process of Gestalt switching and integration
Multiple validities	The extent to which addressing legitimation of the quantitative and qualitative components of the study results from the use of quantitative, qualitative, and mixed validity types, yielding high-quality metainferences
Political	The extent to which the consumers of mixed methods research value the metainferences stemming from both the quantitative and qualitative components of a study

Note. From "The Validity Issue in Mixed Research," by A. J. Onwuegbuzie and R. B. Johnson, 2006, *Research in the Schools, 13*(1), p. 57. Copyright 2006 by the Mid-South Educational Research Association and *Research in the Schools.* Reprinted with permission.

Once validated/legitimated, these data then are interpreted (Step 11). In making inferences, gifted education researchers likely will find useful Tashakkori and Teddlie's (2006) integrative model of quality that comprises design quality (i.e., standards used for the evaluation of the methodological rigor of the mixed research study) and interpretive rigor (i.e., standards for evaluating the validity of conclusions). Specifically, design quality contains the following four elements: (a) within-design consistency, (b) design suitability, (c) design fidelity, and (d) analytic adequacy. Tashakkori and Teddlie conceptualized interpretive rigor as involving the following five elements: (a) interpretive agreement (i.e., "consistency of interpretations across people"; p. 40), (b) interpretive distinctiveness (i.e., the "degree to which the inferences are distinctively different from other possible interpretations of the results and rival explanations are ruled out"; p. 40), (c) interpretive consistency (i.e., whether the inferences adequately stem from the results in terms of type, intensity, and scope and the multiple inferences made on the basis of the findings are consistent with each other), (d) theoretical consistency (i.e., whether the inferences are consistent with the extant theory and the state of knowledge in the field), and (e) integrative efficacy (i.e., whether the metainference adequately incorporates the inferences stemming from both quantitative and qualitative phases of the study).

Writing the research report (Step 12), as is the case in quantitative and qualitative research, is the last step in the research process of a single study. Several guidelines exist for writing mixed research reports (e.g., Onwuegbuzie, Collins, & Leech, in press). As contended by Onwuegbuzie, Jiao, and Collins (2007), a well-written mixed research report should be highly descriptive of all steps of the mixed research process and should describe the context in which the mixed research study took place. Such contextualization not only helps the gifted education researcher evaluate how the quantitative and qualitative results are connected but also provides information regarding the extent to which metainferences can be made.

Once the research report has been written (i.e., Step 12), the role of the research question(s) does not end. Rather, this step leads to the research question(s) being reformulated (Step 13), which, in turn, might lead to a reformulation of the research goal (i.e., Step 1), research objective (i.e., Step 2), research/mixing rationale (i.e., Step 3), and/or research/mixing purpose (i.e., Step 4) in subsequent studies. Alternatively, the research goal, research objective, and research purpose can stay intact, in which case the reformulation of the research question directly leads to a reformulation of the mixed sampling design (i.e., Step 6) and research design (i.e., Step 7). Thus, in subsequent studies, Steps 6 through 11 are repeated until all research goals, objectives, purposes, and questions are adequately addressed.

ROLE OF MIXED RESEARCH FOR ADDRESSING FIVE CHALLENGES IN GIFTED EDUCATION RESEARCH

Mixed Research Model for Data Collection

To facilitate gifted education researchers' data collection decisions, we recommend application of a model developed by Collins et al. (2006) that was presented in the previous section. Additionally, when planning the data collection stage of the mixed research process, the mixed researcher must decide the time orientation—specifically, whether the quantitative data collection phase and qualitative data collection phase of the study will be implemented concurrently or sequentially. Utilizing a concurrent data collection design, data obtained from one phase of the study are collected separately or at approximately the same point in time, and the data collected at one phase do not inform or drive data collection obtained from the other phase of the study. Furthermore, integration in terms of analyses does not occur until after data collection ends. In contrast, a sequential data collection design involves using data collected for one phase of the study to inform decisions and or drive data interpretation and, subsequently, the type of data collected for the other phase of the study. Finally, the researcher must decide the degree of emphasis or weight that he or she will place upon data collected from one phase in terms of design and drawing inferences from the findings.

Mixed Research Applications to the Five Challenges

Eliminating Ceiling Effects in Standardized Tests

The mixing rationale of instrument fidelity could be applicable for addressing the first challenge, which is to eliminate ceiling effects in standardized tests. As a recap, *instrument fidelity* refers to the steps undertaken by the researcher to maximize the utilization of instruments within a study. Validity and trustworthiness of data are crucial when designing above-level tests for gifted students (Swiatek, 2007). Utilizing the rationale of participant enrichment, the researcher collects pilot data to assess test item difficulty on gifted samples for the purpose of developing items for an above-level instrument. Pilot data might be in the form of individually based interviews or group-based interviews or focus groups. Using a mixed sequential approach, these pilot data would be analyzed to inform subsequent data collection, such as refining and administering a revised above-level test. Alternatively, qualitative interview data can be obtained after the test has been administered to facilitate explanations of between-participant variations in outcomes. Instrument fidelity in this context leads to a mixed research design if the approach used in whole or in part for data collection (e.g., qualitative) that is implemented as a prestudy study or as a poststudy data point is different from the approach used for data collection (e.g., quantitative) during the main study.

Obtaining Equitable Comparative Groups

A second challenge is the difficulty obtaining a comparative sample or comparison group for gifted samples. In response to this challenge, researchers could optimize a comparative sample (e.g., participant enrichment rationale) by employing interview techniques and content analysis of curriculum artifacts. Specifically, researchers could conduct interviews of teachers, parents, and other stakeholders, via pilot studies, to identify potential nominees for the comparative group. Potential participants could be interviewed to establish further potentiality as a participant of the comparative group. Quantitative data collection measures also could be implemented to collect descriptive data in terms of students' standardized test scores and curriculum-based measures in order to identify potential participants.

Limiting Sample Attrition in Longitudinal Studies

Sample attrition is a challenge in longitudinal research conducted for the purpose of documenting the developmental processes (e.g., ability, achievement, attitude, motivation, perceptions) of gifted students over a long period of time, especially into adulthood. Utilizing mixed data collection techniques can provide data useful for addressing this challenge. Specifically, the researcher could obtain interview data at various points within the longitudinal study. These data could be collected in the forms of individually conducted interviews or group-conducted focus groups. The collection of interview data could be accompanied by the collection of artifacts, such as inventories documenting the study sample's interests, employment histories, and educational pursuits. Observational data also could be collected to monitor behaviors, actions, and the like. Analyses of all data sources would be used to document the sample's longitudinal progression.

Developing Domain-Specific Definitions of Giftedness

Debriefing interviews also could be useful to obtain a gifted sample's reaction to the content of tests, as well as to provide a forum for students to present their individual stories. Collecting these stories in the form of case studies could provide a compelling form of data collection for noting patterns across individuals in terms of documenting domain-specific giftedness. These qualitative data can be collected to augment quantitative measured performances on standardized tests administered across various domains.

Capturing the Voice of Gifted Participants

As noted above, responses to these four challenges often reflect a collection of verbal data obtained in interview and focus group contexts. Thus, gifted samples' characteristics of high verbal abilities and high levels of articulation play an important part toward expanding mixed data collection techniques. Additionally, these characteristics suggest that gifted students are excellent candidates to participate in mixed research studies that focus upon obtaining verbal data as one form of data. Indeed, because of the gifted students' high levels of articulation, researchers should engage them in in-depth semistructured and unstructured interviews as part of their mixed research designs. Such mixed research studies are more likely to represent *qualitative-dominant mixed research*, in which the researcher takes a qualitative, constructivist–poststructuralist (i.e., the belief that language is "an unstable system of referents, thus it is impossible ever to capture completely the meaning of an action, text, or intention"; Denzin & Lincoln, 2005, p. 27)–postmodernist (i.e., having a contemporary sense that "privileges no single authority, method, or paradigm"; Denzin & Lincoln, p. 27)–critical stance with respect to the research process while, at the same time, deeming the inclusion of quantitative data and approaches to help provide thicker, richer data and interpretations (Johnson et al., 2007).

In sum, utilizing mixed data collection techniques to address the five aforementioned challenges leads to enhancement of findings because multiple techniques accompanied by multiple criteria improve the quality of data interpretation and, ultimately, lead the researcher to formulate metainferences. Traditionally, utilization of quantitative and qualitative data collection techniques has been associated with confirming interpretation of one set of findings (e.g., quantitative) with findings obtained from a second data source (e.g., qualitative). However, divergent findings obtained from both data collection sources might lead the researcher to develop a different interpretive perspective, leading to a different form of data collection or a different research question and/or research focus.

Mixed Data Analytical Techniques

The recent typologies of Onwuegbuzie, Slate, Leech, and Collins (2007, 2009) provide frameworks that gifted education researchers might find useful for conducting mixed analyses, especially analyses that help to address the five aforementioned challenges. Each of these frameworks is described below.

Mixed Analysis Matrix

According to Onwuegbuzie, Slate, et al. (2007), before conducting a mixed analysis, the researcher needs to make four decisions. First, the researcher must determine the number of data types that will be analyzed. These data types can be represented by quantitative and/or qualitative data. Either one data type (i.e., *monotype* data—quantitative data only or qualitative data only) or multiple data types (i.e., *multitype* data—quantitative data and qualitative data) can be analyzed. This decision is based on the number of data types obtained during the data collection stage of the mixed research process, which, in turn, might be based on which of the five aforementioned challenges, if any, is being addressed. Second, the researcher should determine which data analysis types should be utilized. The data analysis types can be either quantitative or qualitative. Either one data analysis type (i.e., *monoanalysis*—quantitative analysis only or qualitative analysis only) or multiple data analysis (i.e., *multianalysis*—quantitative data analysis and qualitative data analysis) can be used. Third, the researcher should decide whether the qualitative and quantitative analyses will be carried out concurrently or sequentially. Fourth, the researcher should decide whether the qualitative or quantitative analyses will be given priority or whether they will be assigned equal status in the mixed analysis.

These four decisions help to generate what Onwuegbuzie, Slate, et al. (2007) referred to as the *mixed analysis matrix*, which is presented in Table 6.2. It can be seen from this table that the first two decisions are the backbone of the mixed analysis matrix, wherein the number of data types and the number of data analysis types are crossed, which yields a 2×2 representation that contains four cells. The mixed analysis matrix incorporates analyses involved in all three research paradigms. Cell 1 represents an analysis of one data type using one analysis type. As such, this cell represents traditional monotype monoanalyses. Cell 2 represents analysis of two data types using only one data analysis type—that is, multitype monoanalyses. Because only one type of analytical technique is used, the analysis is not mixed. Indeed, one data type will not be analyzed, leading to an incomplete analysis. As noted by Onwuegbuzie, Slate, et al., these types of analyses should be avoided. Thus, we will focus on the cells—namely, Cell 3 and Cell 4—that lead to analyses that involve a combination of quantitative and qualitative analyses, or what Onwuegbuzie, Slate, et al. referred to as a *mixed analysis*.

Cell 3

Cell 3 represents analysis of one data type using both data analysis types. This class of analysis is called a *monotype mixed analysis*. The analysis is mixed because both quantitative and qualitative analytical techniques are used. The first analysis utilized in this cell should directly match the data type. Data that stem from the initial analysis then are converted or transformed into the other data type. In other words, the qualitative data are transformed into numerical codes that can be analyzed statistically—what is known as *quantitizing* data (Tashakkori & Teddlie, 1998)—or,

TABLE 6.2
The Mixed Analysis Matrix: A Typology of Analyses
Involving Mixed Methods

Number of analysis types[a]	Number of data types[b]	
	1	2
1	**Cell 1** Monotype monoanalysis: 1. Complete QUAN 2. Complete QUAL	**Cell 2** Multitype monoanalysis: 1. Incomplete QUAN 2. Incomplete QUAL
2	**Cell 3** Monotype mixed analysis: 1. Quantitative-dominant mono- type mixed analysis: a. QUAN → Qual b. Qual → QUAN 2. Qualitative-dominant mono- type mixed analysis: a. QUAL → Quantitize b. Quan → QUALITIZE 3. Equal-status monotype mixed analysis: a. QUAN→QUAL b. QUAL→QUAN	**Cell 4** Multitype mixed analysis: 1. Quantitative-dominant sequen- tial multitype mixed analysis: a. QUAN → Qual b. Qual → QUAN 2. Qualitative-dominant sequen- tial multitype mixed analysis: a. Quan → QUAL b. QUAL → Quan 3. Equal-status sequential multi- type mixed analysis: a. QUAN → QUAL b. QUAL → QUAN 4. Quantitative-dominant concur- rent multitype mixed analysis: a. QUAN + Qual 5. Qualitative-dominant concur- rent multitype mixed analysis: a. QUAL + Quan 6. Equal-status concurrent multi- type mixed analysis: a. QUAN + QUAL

Note. Qual = qualitative analysis, Quan = quantitative analysis, + = concurrent, → = sequential, capital letters = high priority or weight, and lowercase letters = lower priority or weight (cf. Morse, 1991, 2003). From "Conducting Mixed Analyses: A General Typology," by A. J. Onwuegbuzie, J. R. Slate, N. L. Leech, and K. M. T. Collins, 2007, *International Journal of Multiple Research Approaches, 1,* p. 8. Copyright 2007 by *International Journal of Multiple Research Approaches.* Reprinted with permission.
[a]An analysis type is either quantitative (i.e., statistical) or qualitative. [b]A data type is either quantitative or qualitative.

alternatively, the quantitative data are transformed into data that can be analyzed qualitatively—what is known as *qualitizing* data (Tashakkori & Teddlie, 1998).

Quantitizing Data. Quantitizing often involves reporting effect sizes associated with qualitative observations (Onwuegbuzie, 2003a; Sandelowski & Barroso, 2003), which can range from manifest effect sizes (i.e., counting qualitative data to determine the prevalence rates of codes, observations, words, or themes) to latent effect sizes (i.e., quantifying nonobservable content, for example, by factor analyzing emergent themes or correlating emergent themes with quantitative data; cf. Onwuegbuzie, 2003a).

Qualitizing Data. One way of qualitizing data is via the formation of narrative profiles, wherein narrative descriptions are constructed from statistical data. For example, a researcher could conduct a longitudinal study of two sets of students—namely, gifted and nongifted elementary students—with regard to baseline data. At some point during their high school years, these researchers can use quantitative criteria to reclassify these students' levels of giftedness/ nongiftedness. These quantitative data could then be converted (i.e., qualitized) into qualitatively defined student profiles that reflect levels of giftedness/ nongiftedness (e.g., gifted across several domains, gifted in one domain alone [e.g., mathematics], not gifted in any specific domain). These school profiles then could be used to add greater understanding to the researchers' longitudinal, evolving perspectives on domain-specific definitions of giftedness (cf. Challenge 5).

In Cell 3, the researcher also has to decide whether the qualitative or quantitative analyses will be given priority or whether they will be given equal status in the mixed analysis. This decision, which stems from the goals and objectives of the mixed research as well as from the rationale and purpose for mixing, is important because it allows the investigator to determine the level of sophistication of one analysis relative to the other analysis.

Cell 4

Cell 4 represents analysis of both data types using both analysis types. This class of analysis is called a *multitype mixed analysis*. The multitype mixed analysis might be concurrent or sequential in nature, and either the quantitative or qualitative analyses can be dominant or these analyses can share equal status.

Although not presented in the mixed analysis matrix, Cell 4 can accommodate much more complex analytical designs. For instance, any of the nine analytical designs in Cell 4 could include quantitizing and/or qualitizing data. Also, both Cell 3 and Cell 4 can be expanded to incorporate iterative data analysis techniques. Table 6.3 illustrates which of the seven stages of the mixed analysis process can occur for each of the four cells of the mixed analysis matrix. In particular, in Cell 3 (i.e., monotype mixed analysis), in addition to the data reduction and data display stages, data transformation can occur. Indeed, data transformation is a trademark of Cell 3 because there is only one type of data collected, which necessitates what Onwuegbuzie, Slate, et al. (2007) referred to as a *between-paradigm analysis*, whereby an analysis technique is used that is more associated with one traditional paradigm to analyze data that originally represented the type of data collected that are more often associated with the other traditional paradigm. In Cell 4, all seven stages of

TABLE 6.3
Linking Mixed Analysis Stage to the Mixed Analysis Matrix

No. of analysis types	No. of data types	
	1	2
1	**Cell 1**	**Cell 2**
	Monotype monoanalysis:	Multitype monoanalysis:
	Data reduction	Data reduction
	Data display	Data display
2	**Cell 3**	**Cell 4**
	Monotype mixed analysis:	Multitype mixed analysis:
	Data reduction	Data reduction
	Data display	Data display
	Data transformation	Data transformation
		Data correlation
		Data consolidation
		Data comparison
		Data integration

Note. From "Conducting Mixed Analyses: A General Typology," by A. J. Onwuegbuzie, J. R. Slate, N. L. Leech, and K. M. T. Collins, 2007, *International Journal of Multiple Research Approaches, 1,* p. 13. Copyright 2007 by *International Journal of Multiple Research Approaches.* Reprinted with permission.

the mixed analysis process are possible because it involves both data types and both classes of analysis. Thus, depending on the research goal(s), research objective(s), rationale(s) and purpose(s) for mixing, and research question(s) underlying the mixed study, Cell 4 has the greatest potential to yield the most in-depth and rigorous analysis possible.

As noted by Collins et al. (2006), the five purposes/rationales of Greene et al. (1989) (i.e., triangulation, complementarity, initiation, expansion, and development) actually pertain to the data analysis step of the mixed research process. Thus, Table 6.4 illustrates which of Greene et al.'s purposes/rationales are pertinent for each of the four cells of the mixed analysis matrix. Because Cell 1 and Cell 2 do not involve any form of mixed analysis, none of these purposes are pertinent. In Cell 3, the purposes/rationales for mixing can be complementarity, expansion, and/or development. In Cell 4, all five purposes/ rationales are pertinent.

Two-Dimensional Framework for Classifying and Organizing Quantitative and Qualitative Analyses

Case-Oriented Analyses Versus Variable-Oriented Analyses

According to Onwuegbuzie et al. (2009), any specific quantitative analysis or qualitative analysis technique can be operationalized as representing either a case-oriented analysis or a variable-oriented analysis. A *case-oriented*

TABLE 6.4
Linking Significance Enhancement Rationale Type
to the Mixed Analysis Matrix

No. of analysis types	No. of data types	
	1	2
1	**Cell 1** Monotype monoanalysis: N/A	**Cell 2** Multitype monoanalysis: N/A
2	**Cell 3** Monotype mixed analysis: Complementarity Expansion Development	**Cell 4** Multitype mixed analysis: Triangulation Complementarity Development Initiation Expansion

Note. N/A = not applicable. From "Conducting Mixed Analyses: A General Typology," by A. J. Onwuegbuzie,
J. R. Slate, N. L. Leech, and K. M. T. Collins, 2007, *International Journal of Multiple Research Approaches, 1,*
p. 14. Copyright 2007 by *International Journal of Multiple Research Approaches.* Reprinted with permission.

analysis is an analysis that focuses primarily or exclusively on the selected case(s) (Miles & Huberman, 1994). The goal of such analyses is to analyze and interpret the perceptions, attitudes, opinions, experiences, or the like of one or more individuals. That is, in a case-oriented analysis, the researcher treats the case as a whole entity or unit such that the focus of the analysis tends toward particularizing and analytic generalizations (i.e., "applied to wider theory on the basis of how selected cases 'fit' with general constructs"; Curtis, Gesler, Smith, & Washburn, 2000, p. 1002). This class of analysis is most useful for identifying patterns common to one or a relatively small number of cases. Therefore, a case-oriented analysis is best suited to qualitative analytical techniques. However, because case-oriented analyses can be used for any number of cases (Miles & Huberman, 1994), it is also relevant for quantitative analysis techniques, such as single-subject analyses, descriptive analyses, and profile analyses (Onwuegbuzie et al., 2009).

On the other hand, variable-oriented analyses involve identifying relationships—typically probabilistic in nature—among entities that are conceptualized as variables. This class of analysis, whose " 'building blocks' are variables and their intercorrelations, rather than cases" (Miles & Huberman, 1994, p. 174), tends to be conceptual and theory centered in nature and, thus, has a proclivity toward external statistical generalizations (i.e., making generalizations, predictions, or inferences on data obtained from a representative [optimally random] statistical sample to the population from which the sample was drawn). As such, a variable-oriented analysis is more apt for quantitative analyses. However, although the use of large and representative samples often facilitates the identification of relationships among variables, small samples also can serve this purpose (i.e., especially for making analytic generalizations). Thus, variable-oriented analyses also are relevant for qualitative analyses.

Case-Oriented Analyses and Variable-Oriented Analyses

The fact that case-oriented analyses and variable-oriented analyses are pertinent to both qualitative and quantitative analyses suggests that mixed analyses involve the use of case-oriented analyses and variable-oriented analyses in some meaningful combination. Because case-oriented analyses are more associated with qualitative analyses and variable-oriented analyses are more characteristic of quantitative analyses, the way the case-oriented analyses and variable-oriented analyses are combined in a mixed research study plays an important role in determining the research emphasis—that is, whether the study represents *qualitative-dominant mixed research*, *quantitative-dominant mixed research*, or *equal-status mixed research*.

THREE-DIMENSIONAL FRAMEWORK FOR CLASSIFYING AND ORGANIZING QUANTITATIVE AND QUALITATIVE ANALYSES

In some studies, data are collected over time (cf. Challenge 1 and Challenge 3). For example, a mixed researcher might collect quantitative and/or qualitative over a period of months or even years, making the data set longitudinal in nature. Alternatively, in some investigations, data are collected of experiences or processes that have occurred over a significant period of time. For instance, a researcher might collect data from participants (e.g., via an interview) involving their public school experiences. In either type of study (i.e., longitudinal or long-term experience or process), time is an important consideration when analyzing these data. Thus, in Figure 6.3, in addition to case-oriented and variable-oriented analyses, Onwuegbuzie et al. (2009) included a third class of analyses—namely, process/experience-oriented analyses. *Process/experience-oriented analyses* involve evaluating processes or experiences pertaining to one or more cases within a specific context over time. According to these authors, an important difference between processes and experiences is that the former tends to be associated with variables and the latter tends to be associated with cases.

Table 6.5 illustrates how the analyses undertaken in quantitative and qualitative research can represent case-oriented, variable-oriented, and process/experience-oriented analyses. This list is by no means exhaustive. However, this table captures most of the major qualitative and quantitative analyses. Some of these techniques are discussed in detail in other chapters of this

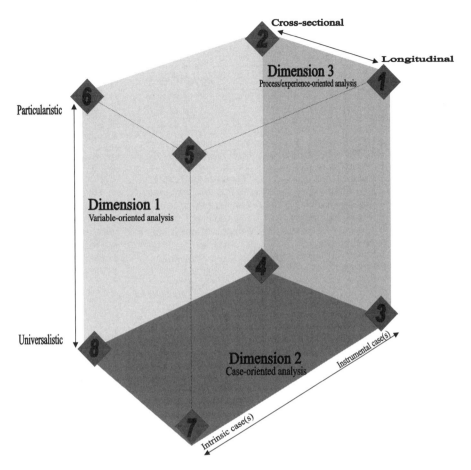

Figure 6.3. A three-dimensional model for categorizing and organizing orientations for mixed analyses. Directionality of the continua across each dimension is arbitrary. There is no intentionality of suggesting superiority of one continuum point or extreme over another. Rather, the appropriateness of the continuum point depends on the research goal, research objectives(s), mixing rationale and purpose, mixed research question(s), mixed sampling design, and mixed research design. Numbers at each corner represent eight possible combinations of the extreme points on the three dimensions of case-oriented, variable-oriented, and process/experience-oriented analyses. From "Mixed Data Analysis: Advanced Integration Techniques," by A. J. Onwuegbuzie, J. R. Slate, N. L. Leech, and K. M. T. Collins, 2009, *International Journal of Multiple Research Approaches, 3,* p. 28. Copyright 2009 by *International Journal of Multiple Research Approaches.* Reprinted with permission.

TABLE 6.5
Two-Dimensional Representation Indicating Analytical Techniques
as a Function of Approach and Analysis Emphasis

	Analysis emphasis		
Approach	Case oriented	Variable oriented	Process/ experience oriented
Quantitative	Descriptive analyses (e.g., measures of central tendency, variability, position) Cluster analysis Q methodology Time series analysis Profile analysis Panel data analysis Single-subject analysis Classical test theory Item response theory Multidimensional scaling Hazard/proportional hazards models	Descriptive analyses Correlation analysis Independent t tests Dependent t tests Analysis of variance Analysis of covariance Multiple analysis of variance Multiple analysis of covariance Multiple regression (Multivariate) logistic regression Descriptive/predictive discriminant analysis Log-linear analysis Canonical correlation analysis Path analysis Structural equation modeling Hierarchical linear modeling Correspondence analysis Multidimensional scaling Exploratory/ confirmatory factor analysis Time series analysis Classical test theory Item response theory	Descriptive analyses (e.g., measures of central tendency, variability, position) Dependent t tests Time series analysis Profile analysis Panel data analysis Single-subject analysis Classical test theory Item response theory Repeated measures analysis of variance Repeated measures analysis of covariance Survival analysis Path analysis Structural equation modeling Hierarchical linear modeling
Qualitative	Method of constant comparison Word count Keywords in context Classical content analysis Domain analysis Taxonomic analysis Componential analysis	Word count Keywords in context Classical content analysis Secondary data analysis Taxonomic analysis Componential analysis Text mining	Method of constant comparison Word count Keywords in context Classical content analysis Domain analysis Taxonomic analysis Componential analysis

TABLE 6.5
Two-Dimensional Representation Indicating Analytical Techniques
as a Function of Approach and Analysis Emphasis   *(Continued)*

	Analysis emphasis		
Approach	Case oriented	Variable oriented	Process/ experience oriented
	Conversation analysis	Qualitative comparative analysis	Conversation analysis
	Discourse analysis	Semantic network analysis	Discourse analysis
	Secondary data analysis	Cognitive map analysis	Secondary data analysis
	Membership categorization analysis	Causal network analysis	Text mining
	Narrative analysis	Conceptually ordered matrix analysis	Narrative analysis
	Semiotics		Manifest content analysis
	Manifest content analysis	Case-ordered matrix/network analysis	Latent content analysis
	Latent content analysis	Time-ordered matrix/network analysis	Qualitative comparative analysis
	Text mining		Semantic network analysis
	Qualitative comparative analysis	Variable-by-variable matrix analysis	Cognitive map analysis
	Microinterlocutor analysis	Predictor–outcome matrix analysis	Causal network analysis
	Partially ordered matrix analysis	Explanatory effect matrix analysis	Time-ordered matrix/network analysis
	Time-ordered matrix/network analysis		

Note. All quantitative analyses above include nonparametric counterparts. From "Mixed Data Analysis: Advanced Integration Techniques," by A. J. Onwuegbuzie, J. R. Slate, N. L. Leech, and K. M. T. Collins, 2009, *International Journal of Multiple Research Approaches, 3,* p. 27. Copyright 2009 by *International Journal of Multiple Research Approaches.* Reprinted with permission.

volume. It can be seen from Table 6.5 that, with respect to quantitative analyses, some of the analyses (i.e., descriptive analyses, time series analysis, classical test theory, item response theory) can be used to conduct both case-oriented and variable-oriented analyses. For instance, descriptive statistics can be used to describe characteristics (e.g., mathematics ability) of one or more individuals on a case-by-case basis or as a single group of cases. Alternatively, descriptive statistics can be utilized to determine characteristics of variables (e.g., proportion of gifted students who later become eminent as adults) on a variable-by-variable basis or as a set of variables (e.g., each variable representing a distinguished accomplishment at adulthood). Similarly, classical test theory techniques can be employed to describe characteristics (e.g., test score) of one or more individuals on a case-by-case basis or as a single group of cases. Alternatively, descriptive statistics can be used to determine characteristics of variables (e.g., score reliability, score validity) on a variable-by-variable basis or as a set of variables. With respect to qualitative analyses, several of the analyses (i.e., word count, keywords in context, classical content analysis, text mining, taxonomic analysis, componential analysis, qualitative comparative analysis, secondary data analysis, time-ordered matrix/network analysis) can be used to conduct both case-oriented and variable-oriented analyses. For example, as noted by Miles and Huberman (1994), a time-ordered matrix/network analysis often can "produce 'generic narratives' that retain the 'plot line' of individual cases [i.e., case-oriented analysis], but show us principles that cut across them [i.e., variable-oriented analysis]" (p. 206).

As seen in Table 6.5, many of the qualitative analyses that are pertinent for case-oriented analyses and variable-oriented analyses also are appropriate for process/experience-oriented analyses. However, time-ordered displays (Miles & Huberman, 1994) represent the class of qualitative analyses that lends itself to conducting process/experience-oriented analyses. As conceptualized by Miles and Huberman (1994), time-ordered displays are visual depictions that order data by time and sequence, thereby preserving the historical chronological order of events and assisting an analysis of when the processes or experiences occurred and their antecedents. According to Miles and Huberman, for within-case analyses (i.e., those bounded within a single case), time-ordered displays include event listing (i.e., matrix or flowchart that organizes a series of concrete events by chronological time periods and sorts them into multiple categories), critical incident chart (i.e., maps a few critical events, processes, or experiences), event–state network (i.e., maps general states that are not as time limited as events and might represent moderators or mediators that link specific processes or experiences of interest), activity record (i.e., displays a specific recurring activity that is limited narrowly in time and space), decision modeling flowchart (i.e., maps thoughts, plans, and decisions made during a flow of activity that is bounded by specific conditions), growth gradient (i.e., network that maps events that are conceptualized as being linked to an underlying variable that changes over time), and time-ordered matrix (i.e., maps when particular events, experiences, or phenomena occurred). For cross-case analyses (i.e., analyses that examine simultaneously two or more cases), time-ordered displays include time-ordered meta-matrix (i.e., table in which columns are organized sequentially by time period and the rows are not necessarily ordered), time-ordered scatter plots (i.e., display similar variables in cases over two or more time periods), and composite sequence analysis (i.e., permits extraction of typical stories that two or more cases share, without eliminating meaningful sequences). (See also Onwuegbuzie & Dickinson, 2008.)

Thus, the qualitative and quantitative analyses in Table 6.5 can be used in an almost unlimited number of combinations, depending on the combination of case-oriented, variable-oriented, and process/experience-oriented analyses needed to obtain interpretive consistency between the ensuing metainferences and the elements that characterize the study (i.e., the research goal, objective(s), mixing rationale and purpose, mixed research question(s), mixed sampling design, and mixed research design). This implies that mixed research opens up more possibilities for analyzing data in gifted education research than does quantitative or qualitative research alone.

THREE-DIMENSIONAL MODEL FOR CATEGORIZING AND ORGANIZING ORIENTATIONS FOR MIXED ANALYSES

Figure 6.3 presents Onwuegbuzie et al.'s (2009) three-dimensional model for categorizing and organizing orientations for mixed analyses. This model illustrates several important concepts related to mixed analyses. In particular, as can be seen, the model includes three dimensions, each focused upon a given set of strategies for analyzing quantitative and qualitative data, and each positioned at 90-degree angles to the other two. Using this model, a given mixed analysis can be positioned anywhere within the three-dimensional space as a way of indicating the multidimensional complexity or sophistication of the analytical design.

The model's first dimension (variable-oriented analyses) can be conceptualized as falling on a particularistic–universalistic continuum classifying the extent to which the metainferences stemming from the variable-oriented analysis can be generalized. At one end of the continuum (i.e., particularistic) are variable-oriented analyses that yield metainferences that are utilized to describe a specific set of variables, factors, concepts, or constructs that occur in a specific context, whereas at the other end of the continuum (i.e., universalistic) are variable-oriented analyses that yield metainferences that are utilized to describe a specific set of variables, factors, concepts, or constructs that can be applied to broad contexts (whether the context represents people other than the study participants or represents different settings, situations, locations, or time periods for the same study participants). Thus, for instance, a sample of, say, 200 randomly or purposively selected participants probably would motivate variable-oriented analyses that lie further along the universalistic end of the particularistic–universalistic continuum than would a sample of, say, 20 randomly or purposively selected participants, regardless of whether the sample is selected intrinsically (i.e., each case is selected because in all its particularity and ordinariness, each case itself is of interest; Stake, 2005) or instrumentally (i.e., one or more cases are of secondary interest and are selected primarily to provide insight into an issue or to redraw a generalization; Stake, 2005) (Dimension 2) and whether the data were collected cross-sectionally or longitudinally (Dimension 3). Further, a study of multiple contexts probably would generate variable-oriented analyses that lie further along the universalistic end of the particularistic–universalistic continuum than would a study of one context, regardless of whether the participants are selected intrinsically or instrumentally (Dimension 2) and whether the data were collected cross-sectionally or longitudinally (Dimension 3). The midpoint of the continuum represents variable-oriented analyses that yield metainferences that are used to describe a specific set of variables, factors, concepts, or constructs that operate in a specific context and can be applied to broad contexts within the same framework.

Dimension 2, case-oriented analyses, ranges across an intrinsic–instrumental continuum categorizing the purpose for selecting cases. At one extreme are mixed research studies in which all participants in the quantitative and qualitative phases are selected intrinsically. At the other extreme are mixed research investigations wherein all participants in the quantitative and qualitative phases are selected instrumentally. Thus, for instance, a sample of, say, 1,000 randomly selected participants probably would facilitate case-oriented analyses that lie further along the instrumental end of the intrinsic–instrumental continuum than a sample of, say, 100 participants who were selected randomly, and even further along the instrumental end of the intrinsic–instrumental continuum than a sample of, say, 10 participants who were selected purposively, regardless of how many variables were analyzed (i.e., Dimension 1) and whether the data were collected cross-sectionally or longitudinally (Dimension 3). All other points of the continuum support Stake's (2005) contention that because the researcher simultaneously can pursue several interests, there is no clear line separating intrinsic case studies from instrumental case studies. Instead, a "zone of combined purpose separates them" (p. 437).

Dimension 3, process/experience-oriented analyses, categorizes the degree to which the study has a temporal element. At one extreme of the continuum (i.e., cross-sectional) are mixed research studies in which data collected in both the quantitative and qualitative phases are from a single point in time or during a single, relatively short time frame (Johnson & Christensen, 2008). At the other extreme are mixed research investigations in which data collected in both the quantitative and qualitative phases represent multiple time points or data collection periods (Johnson & Christensen, 2008) or represent one or more accounts of events or processes that occurred over time. All other points of the continuum represent some combination of cross-sectional and longitudinal mixed research study. For example, a mixed research study might involve a longitudinal qualitative phase and a cross-sectional quantitative phase. Alternatively, the qualitative and/or quantitative phases might involve a trend study, in which samples composed of different persons (i.e., independent samples) are selected from the same population over time and the same data are collected from each sample (Johnson & Christensen, 2008). Moreover, data collected, say, over a few months probably would facilitate process/experience-oriented analyses that lie further along the longitudinal end of the cross-sectional–longitudinal continuum than the same data collected, say, over several years regardless of how many variables were analyzed (i.e., Dimension 1) and how the sample was selected (Dimension 2).

A mixed research study can be situated anywhere on the three-dimensional representation, demonstrating that quantitative and qualitative analyses can be mixed or embedded in numerous ways. As such, the three-dimensional representation is consistent with Johnson and Onwuegbuzie's (2004) assertion that

> Ultimately, the possible number of ways that studies can involve mixing is very large because of the many potential classification dimensions. It is a key point that mixed methods research truly opens up an exciting and almost unlimited potential for future research. (p. 20)

This three-dimensional representation can be used to design each qualitative phase and each quantitative analytical phase of a mixed research study. However, according to Onwuegbuzie et al. (2009), its greatest utility lies in its potential to help researchers—including gifted education researchers—rigorously design their mixed research studies in general and their mixed analyses in particular, where *rigor* is defined as the attainment of interpretive consistency when making metainferences by aligning generalizations that stem from their data analyses as much as possible with the design elements of the study, especially the sampling design (e.g., sampling scheme, sample size). Further, this model provides a framework for helping gifted education researchers make their decisions pertaining to mixed analyses explicit. As noted by Onwuegbuzie et al. (2009), this framework has the potential to serve as

> (a) a means for thinking about the complexity of mixed analyses; (b) a starting point for discussion about the distinctions among "variable-oriented analyses," "case-oriented analyses," and process/experience-oriented analyses; (c) a visual representation of the extent to which specific qualitative and quantitative analyses are linked to analysis orientation (i.e., variable-oriented analyses, case-oriented analyses, and process/experience-oriented analyses); and (d) a means for initiating discussions about design issues in mixed research. (p. 31)

Moreover, with respect to gifted education research, Onwuegbuzie et al.'s (2009) framework can help researchers design their analyses such that it helps them address one or more of the five aforementioned challenges.

CONCLUSION

Combining quantitative and qualitative research enables gifted educa-tion researchers to be more flexible, integrative, holistic, and rigorous in their investigative techniques as they attempt to address a range of complex research questions. More specifically, mixed research helps gifted education researchers to attain participant enrichment, instrument fidelity, treatment integrity, and significance enhancement (Collins et al., 2006). Additionally, by utilizing mixed research approaches, researchers are in a better position to combine empirical precision with descriptive precision (Onwuegbuzie, 2003a). As such, mixed research studies afford gifted education researchers the opportunity to combine micro and macro levels of an investigation (Onwuegbuzie & Leech, 2005).

As documented by Leech, Collins, Jiao, and Onwuegbuzie (2009), to date, only a few gifted education researchers are utilizing mixed research tech-niques. Yet, neither quantitative nor qualitative research alone has been able to address the five challenges in gifted education research. Thus, it is clear that a new direction is needed for the field of gifted education research. We believe that mixed research should be this new direction.

REFERENCES

Campbell, D. T., & Stanley, J. C. (1963). *Experimental and quasi-experimental designs for research.* Chicago: Rand McNally.

Collins, K. M. T., Onwuegbuzie, A. J., & Sutton, I. L. (2006). A model incorporat-ing the rationale and purpose for conducting mixed methods research in special education and beyond. *Learning Disabilities: A Contemporary Journal, 4,* 67–100.

Curtis, S., Gesler, W., Smith, G., & Washburn, S. (2000). Approaches to sampling and case selection in qualitative research: Examples in the geography of health. *Social Science and Medicine, 50,* 1001–1014.

Denzin, N. K., & Lincoln, Y. S. (2005). *The Sage handbook of qualitative research* (3rd ed.). Thousand Oaks, CA: Sage.

Greene, J. C. (2006). Toward a methodology of mixed methods social inquiry. *Research in the Schools, 13*(1), 93–98.

Greene, J. C. (2008). Is mixed methods social inquiry a distinctive methodology? *Journal of Mixed Methods Research, 2,* 7–22.

Greene, J. C., Caracelli, V. J., & Graham, W. F. (1989). Toward a conceptual frame-work for mixed-method evaluation designs. *Educational Evaluation and Policy Analysis, 11,* 255–274.

Johnson, R. B., & Christensen, L. B. (2008). *Educational research: Quantitative, qual-itative, and mixed approaches* (3rd ed.). Thousand Oaks, CA: Sage.

Johnson, R. B., & Onwuegbuzie, A. J. (2004). Mixed methods research: A research paradigm whose time has come. *Educational Researcher, 33*(7), 14–26.

Johnson, R. B., Onwuegbuzie, A. J., & Turner, L. A. (2007). Toward a definition of mixed methods research. *Journal of Mixed Methods Research, 1,* 112–133.

Johnson, R. B., & Turner, L. A. (2003). Data collection strategies in mixed methods research. In A. Tashakkori & C. Teddlie (Eds.), *Handbook of mixed methods research in social and behavioral research* (pp. 297–319). Thousand Oaks, CA: Sage.

Leech, N. L., Collins, K. M. T., Jiao, Q. G., & Onwuegbuzie, A. J. (2009). *Mixed research in gifted education research: A mixed research investigation of trends in the literature.* Manuscript submitted for publication.

Leech, N. L., & Onwuegbuzie, A. J. (2009). A typology of mixed methods research designs. *Quality & Quantity: International Journal of Methodology, 43,* 265–275.

Maxwell, J. A. (1992). Understanding and validity in qualitative research. *Harvard Educational Review, 62,* 279–299.

Miles, M. B., & Huberman, A. M. (1994). *Qualitative data analysis: An expanded sourcebook* (2nd ed.). Thousand Oaks, CA: Sage.

Morse, J. M. (1991). Approaches to qualitative–quantitative methodological triangulation. *Nursing Research, 40,* 120–123.

Morse, J. M. (2003). Principles of mixed methods and multimethod research design. In A. Tashakkori & C. Teddlie (Eds.), *Handbook of mixed methods in social and behavioral research* (pp. 189–208). Thousand Oaks, CA: Sage.

Newman, I., Ridenour, C. S., Newman, C., & DeMarco, G. M. P. (2003). A typology of research purposes and its relationship to mixed methods. In A. Tashakkori & C. Teddlie (Eds.), *Handbook of mixed methods in social and behavioral research* (pp. 167–188). Thousand Oaks, CA: Sage.

Onwuegbuzie, A. J. (2003a). Effect sizes in qualitative research: A prolegomenon. *Quality & Quantity: International Journal of Methodology, 37,* 393–409.

Onwuegbuzie, A. J. (2003b). Expanding the framework of internal and external validity in quantitative research. *Research in the Schools, 10*(1), 71–90.

Onwuegbuzie, A. J., & Collins, K. M. T. (2007). A typology of mixed methods sampling designs in social science research. *The Qualitative Report, 12,* 281–316. Retrieved April 15, 2008, from http://www.nova.edu/ssss/QR/QR12-2/onwuegbuzie2.pdf

Onwuegbuzie, A. J., Collins, K. M. T., Leech, N. L., Dellinger, A. B., Jiao, Q. G. (2009). A meta-framework for conducting mixed research syntheses for stress and coping and beyond. In G. S. Gates, W. H. Gmelch, & M. Wolverton (Series Eds.) & K. M. T. Collins, A. J. Onwuegbuzie, & Q. G. Jiao (Vol. Eds.), *Toward a broader understanding of stress and coping: Mixed methods approaches: Vol. 5. The research on stress and coping in education* (pp. 169–211). Charlotte, NC: Information Age Publishing.

Onwuegbuzie, A. J., Collins, K. M. T., & Leech, N. L. (in press). *Mixed research: A step-by-step guide.* New York: Taylor & Francis.

Onwuegbuzie, A. J., & Dickinson, W. B. (2008). Mixed methods analysis and information visualization: Graphical display for effective communication of research results. *The Qualitative Report, 13*, 204–225. Retrieved January 16, 2009, from http://www.nova.edu/ssss/QR/QR13-2/onwuegbuzie.pdf

Onwuegbuzie, A. J., Jiao, Q. G., & Collins, K. M. T. (2007). Mixed methods research: A new direction for the study of stress and coping. In G. Gates (Ed.), *Emerging thought and research on students, teacher, and administrator stress and coping* (Research on Stress and Coping in Education, Vol. 4, pp. 215–243). Greenway, CT: Information Age.

Onwuegbuzie, A. J., & Johnson, R. B. (2006). The validity issue in mixed research. *Research in the Schools, 13*(1), 48–63.

Onwuegbuzie, A. J., Johnson, R. B., & Collins, K. M. T. (2009). *A call for mixed analysis: A philosophical framework for combining qualitative and quantitative.* International Journal of Multiple Research Approches, 3, 114–139.

Onwuegbuzie, A. J., & Leech, N. L. (2005). On becoming a pragmatist researcher: The importance of combining quantitative and qualitative research methodologies. *International Journal of Social Research Methodology: Theory & Practice, 8*, 375–387.

Onwuegbuzie, A. J., & Leech, N. L. (2006). Linking research questions to mixed methods data analysis procedures. *The Qualitative Report, 11*, 474–498. Retrieved January 16, 2009, from http://www.nova.edu/ssss/QR/QR11-3/onwuegbuzie.pdf

Onwuegbuzie, A. J., & Leech, N. L. (2007a). A call for qualitative power analyses. *Quality and Quantity: International Journal of Methodology, 41*, 105–121.

Onwuegbuzie, A. J., & Leech, N. L. (2007b). Validity and qualitative research: An oxymoron? *Quality & Quantity: International Journal of Methodology, 41*, 233–249.

Onwuegbuzie, A. J., Slate, J. R., Leech, N. L., & Collins, K. M. T. (2007). Conducting mixed analyses: A general typology. *International Journal of Multiple Research Approaches, 1*, 4–17.

Onwuegbuzie, A. J., Slate, J. R., Leech, N. L., & Collins, K. M. T. (2009). Mixed data analysis: Advanced integration techniques. *International Journal of Multiple Research Approaches, 3*, 13–33.

Onwuegbuzie, A. J., & Teddlie, C. (2003). A framework for analyzing data in mixed methods research. In A. Tashakkori & C. Teddlie (Eds.), *Handbook of mixed methods in social and behavioral research* (pp. 351–383). Thousand Oaks, CA: Sage.

Sandelowski, M., & Barroso, J. (2003). Creating metasummaries of qualitative findings. *Nursing Research, 52*, 226–233.

Sandelowski, M., Voils, C. I., & Barroso, J. (2006). Defining and designing mixed research synthesis studies. *Research in the Schools, 13*(1), 29–40.

Schwandt, T. A. (1997). *Qualitative inquiry: A dictionary of terms.* Thousand Oaks, CA: Sage.

Stake, R. E. (2005). Qualitative case studies. In N. K. Denzin & Y. S. Lincoln (Eds.), *The Sage handbook of qualitative research* (3rd ed., pp. 443–466). Thousand Oaks, CA: Sage.

Swiatek, M. A. (2002). A decade of longitudinal research on academic acceleration through the study of mathematically precocious youth. *Roeper Review, 24,* 141–144.

Swiatek, M. A. (2007). The talent search model: Past, present, and future. *Gifted Child Quarterly, 51,* 320–329.

Tashakkori, A., & Creswell, J. W. (2007). Editorial: Exploring the nature of research questions in mixed methods research. *Journal of Mixed Methods Research, 1,* 207–211.

Tashakkori, A., & Teddlie, C. (1998). *Mixed methodology: Combining qualitative and quantitative approaches* (Applied Social Research Methods Series, Vol. 46). Thousand Oaks, CA: Sage.

Tashakkori, A., & Teddlie, C. (2006, April). *Validity issues in mixed methods research: Calling for an integrative framework.* Paper presented at the annual meeting of the American Educational Research Association, San Francisco, CA.

Teddlie, C., & Tashakkori, A. (2006). A general typology of research designs featuring mixed methods. *Research in the Schools, 13*(1), 12–28.

Teddlie, C., & Yu, F. (2007). Mixed methods sampling: A typology with examples. *Journal of Mixed Methods Research, 1,* 77–100.

II

COMPLEX ANALYSES

7

PROMISE AND PITFALLS OF STRUCTURAL EQUATION MODELING IN GIFTED RESEARCH

REX B. KLINE

The family of statistical techniques that make up structural equation modeling (SEM) offers many potential advantages in education research, including studies about gifted students. These techniques are highly versatile and permit the evaluation of a wide range of hypotheses, including those about direct or indirect effects, measurement, or mean differences on either observed or latent variables. They have also become quite popular among researchers. Indeed, it is increasingly difficult to look through an issue of an education research journal and not find at least one article in which results of SEM analyses are reported. In gifted research, SEM has been used less often, but there are more and more such studies in this area, too. However, there are some potential pitfalls of using SEM in gifted research that are inherent to the study of a special population, including range restriction, regression effects, and the need for large samples. Accordingly, the goals of this chapter are to (a) review the general characteristics of SEM with special consideration of possible advantages in educational research and (b) consider specific potential pitfalls of using SEM in gifted research.

Outlined next are important issues in basically all applications of SEM. Later sections deal with problems specific to the use of SEM in education research in general and in gifted research in particular.

Terms and Hypotheses

Other terms for SEM include *covariance structure analysis* and *covariance structure modeling*, but both of these labels are restrictive. This is because although covariances are analyzed in all applications of SEM, it is also possible to analyze means (and mean differences), too. That is, all models estimated in SEM have a covariance structure, but depending on the data and hypotheses, the model may have an optional mean structure, too. Most structural equation models described in the literature do not involve the analysis of means, but the possibility to analyze both means and covariances gives SEM much flexibility.

A *covariance structure* concerns a specific pattern of relations, or covariances, among a set of observed or latent variables. For observed variables X and Y, the sample covariance is calculated as the product $r_{XY} SD_X SD_Y$. In SEM, the researcher specifies a statistical model of the covariance structure that he or she presumes reflects the population structure. This structure often includes latent variables that correspond to hypothetical constructs and the observed variables that are presumed to measure those constructs. Observed variables in SEM can be categorical, ordinal, or continuous (i.e., quantitative), but all latent variables analyzed in SEM are continuous. There are other statistical techniques for analyzing categorical latent variables, which are also referred to as *classes,* but classes are not analyzed in SEM. The covariance structure specified by the researcher provides a "map," or a set of hypotheses, about how the observed and latent variables should covary. All applications of SEM involve the analysis of covariance structures.

It is also possible in SEM to analyze means. This is accomplished through the specification of a mean structure in addition to a covariance structure. A *mean structure* is basically a set of instructions for the computer to estimate the means of variables included in that structure. These variables may include observed variables or latent variables that correspond to hypothetical constructs. Other statistical techniques, such as the analysis of variance (ANOVA), analyze means of observed variables but not also of latent variables. Although means are not analyzed in most SEM studies, the possibility to do so lends much flexibility to the analysis. For example, sometimes we want to test hypotheses about hypothetical constructs (i.e., latent variables) by examining relations (i.e., usually covariances) among the observed variables, but we also want to test whether estimated means on these latent variables are equal across constructs or on a given construct across different groups. That is, the hypotheses to be tested concern both covariances and means. At other times, we are not interested in means on the latent variables and focus only on trying to discern (interpret) latent variables, based on investigation of the covariances among the measured variables. For example, in one case we might only want to know, "How many factors or latent variables underlie the responses of gifted students to IQ test items?" In another instance, we might want to know both, such as "How many factors or latent variables underlie the responses of gifted students to IQ test items?" and "Do boys and girls have different means on each of the given IQ factors?"

Specification and Respecification

Perhaps the single most important step in SEM occurs at the very beginning when the researcher specifies the model to be analyzed. This specification includes information about things such as which variables are presumed to affect other variables (i.e., directionalities of effects) and also about the correspondence between observed and latent variables (e.g., measurement). These a priori specifications reflect the researcher's hypotheses, and together they comprise the model to be evaluated. Model specification is the single most important step in SEM. This is because the scientific merit of all that follows depends much on the ability of the researcher to specify a reasonably accurate model, one that stands at least some chance of being true in the population. That is, the adage "garbage in, garbage out" applies to SEM—and to any other statistical modeling technique.

The requirement that the researcher specify an entire model before the analysis can begin makes SEM more confirmatory than exploratory. But as often happens in SEM, the data may not be consistent with the model, which means that analysis typically takes a more exploratory turn as revised models are tested with the same data. This is *respecification*, also referred to as a *specification search*. Just as in more conventional statistical methods, respecification should be guided much more by substantive considerations than by purely statistical ones. For example, stepwise methods in multiple regression select predictors for entry into or removal from the equation based solely on the statistical significance of regression coefficients. However, stepwise regression is generally unacceptable due to extreme capitalization on chance (i.e., the results are unlikely to replicate; see Thompson, 1995).

The parallel to stepwise regression in SEM concerns the use of *modification indexes*, which are tests of whether adding a particular parameter to the model would result in a statistically significant improvement in model fit. Some SEM computer programs even offer an "automatic modification" option where parameters are automatically added to the model if their associated modification indexes are statistically significant. However, such procedures represent extreme capitalization on chance, just as do stepwise methods regression. Also, the results of some computer simulation studies indicate that respecification based solely on modification indexes is unlikely to lead to discovery of the true model (e.g., Silvia & MacCallum, 1988). Instead, respecification should be guided by the researcher's knowledge of extant theory and empirical results (i.e., base specification and respecification on the same grounds).

Note that the cautions about respecification just mentioned presume the analysis of a model in a single data set. These cautions may not apply when the researcher has a very large data set that is randomly split into two or more subsamples, an empirically based specification search is conducted in the first subsample, and the fit of the resulting model in the other subsamples is evaluated. This strategy is known as *internal replication*, and results that replicate across two or more subsamples may be more stable than ones found in a single data set. Internal replication in SEM would require a very large sample size, and probably for this reason there are relatively few examples of internal replication in the SEM literature. Even rarer still is *external replication*, where a structural equation model specified by one researcher is tested in a different sample collected by a different researcher in a different setting. External replication is a gold standard in science, but, unfortunately, it is rare in SEM.

Sample Size

Large samples are generally required in SEM. Although there have been attempts to develop ways to apply SEM in smaller samples (e.g., Marsh & Hau, 1999), such methods are not widely used and can be more difficult to apply. Problems in the analysis are more likely to occur, parameter estimates may not be very precise, and the power of statistical tests may be low, all due to the absence of a large sample size. In general, a sample size of less than 100 cases may be too small to analyze even a very basic model. Between 150 and 200 cases is a better minimum, but perhaps even 200 cases is an insufficient amount to analyze more complex models, which require the estimation of more parameters. A suggestion for models with latent variables that correspond to constructs (i.e., they have a measurement model) is to think about minimum sample size relative to model complexity. Ideally, one should have at least 20 cases for every estimated parameter (i.e., a 20:1 ratio); a 10:1 ratio is less ideal but may suffice (Jackson, 2003).

Data Screening

It is necessary to thoroughly "clean and screen" the data before analyzing them in SEM. This is because data-related problems can make such computer tools yield an illogical solution or even crash. It is also true that the default estimation method in most SEM computer tools, maximum likelihood (ML), requires certain assumptions about the distributional characteristics of the data. One is multivariate normality for outcome (dependent) variables. This requirement is critical and cannot be violated with impunity; otherwise, the values of parameter estimates or statistical indexes of model fit may be inaccurate. If obvious skew or kurtosis is apparent, then corrective action, such as applying transformations in order to normalize the scores, is necessary when using ML estimation. There are other, more specialized estimation methods for nonnormal distributions, but they may be more difficult to apply or require even larger sample sizes.

Another critical issue is that of missing data. Not all SEM computer programs can process raw data files where some cases have missing observations. Thus, it may be necessary to address this problem first in a general program for statistics before conducting SEM. But just how missing data are handled in SEM can adversely affect the results. For example, the use of pairwise deletion of incomplete cases can result in a data matrix, such as a covariance matrix, that cannot be analyzed. This happens when the matrix contains values that would be mathematically impossible to obtain in a sample with no missing data. Unfortunately, there are no free lunches concerning data integrity in SEM—see Kline (2005, chap. 3) for more information. Along the same lines, McCoach (2003) noted that although "structural equation models may look impressive, SEM cannot salvage studies that contain badly measured constructs, inappropriate samples, or faulty designs" (p. 43).

Ease of Use Should Not Mean Suspension of Judgment

Virtually all computer tools for SEM allow data and model specification with a series of equations written in the native syntax of each individual program. Of course, specification in syntax requires knowledge of that syntax. As an alternative, some SEM computer tools, such as Amos, EQS, LISREL, and mxGraph, also permit the user to specify the model by drawing it on the screen. The user is typically provided with a palette of drawing tools in a graphical editor for drawing the model. Also, some drawing editors prevent the user from making "illegal" specifications with the drawing tools. The capability to draw a model on the screen helps beginners to be productive right away because it is not necessary to learn program syntax.

A possible drawback is that such ease of use could encourage the application of SEM in uninformed or careless ways. Steiger (2000) made the related point that the emphasis on ease of use in advertisements for some computer tools (e.g., SEM made easy!) can give beginners the false impression that SEM itself is easy. However, nothing could be further from the truth. Things can and do go wrong in SEM analyses, and this is more likely to happen when analyzing more complex models. When (not *if*) problems crop up, a researcher will need all of his or her expertise about the data and model in order to "help" the computer with the analysis. This is in part why Pedhazur and Schmelkin (1991) advised concerning statistical analyses in general that "no amount of technical proficiency will do you any good, if you do not think" (p. 2).

Proper Reporting

There are some serious shortcomings in the way that results of SEM analyses are often reported. For example, MacCallum and Austin (2000) reviewed 500 SEM analyses published in 16 different research journals. In about 50% of these analyses, the reporting of parameter estimates was incomplete. The most common mistake was to report the standardized solution only. This is a problem because the default estimation method in most SEM computer programs, maximum likelihood, calculates standard errors for unstandardized estimates only. These standard errors are the denominators of statistical tests of individual parameter estimates. Many researchers do not realize that results of these tests may not apply in the standardized solution. This means that if an unstandardized estimate is statistically significant, then its standardized counterpart is not guaranteed to be statistically significant, too. There is a special method known as *constrained estimation* (*optimization*) that can calculate correct standard errors for standardized estimates, but it is not available in all SEM computer programs.

In about 25% of the published studies reviewed by MacCallum and Austin (2000), it was not specified whether the raw data, a covariance matrix, or a correlation matrix was analyzed. Probably most researchers input raw data files, but another option is to submit a matrix summary of the data. If a raw data file is submitted, an SEM computer program will create its own matrix, which is then analyzed. If means are not analyzed, a covariance matrix—or a correlation matrix and the standard deviations—is generally required when submitting a matrix summary. This is because ML estimation assumes that the variables are unstandardized. If a correlation matrix is analyzed instead of a covariance matrix, then the results—including values of standard errors and model fit statistics—may be wrong. The method of constrained estimation can be used to correctly analyze a correlation matrix.

In about 10% of the studies reviewed by MacCallum and Austin (2000), the model specified was not described in enough detail to replicate the analysis. An example of this kind of problem is the failure to describe the association between observed and latent variables. All of the shortcomings just described are serious. They are also surprising considering that there are published guidelines for the reporting of results in SEM (e.g., McDonald & Ho, 2002).

Assessing Model Fit

A related issue concerns the reporting of values of statistical indexes of model fit. Literally dozens of alternative fit statistics exist, and the output of SEM computer programs often lists the values of many more such statistics than a researcher would ever report. This embarrassment of statistical riches means that it can be difficult to decide which subset of fit indexes to report. It also increases the temptation for selective reporting—that is, for the researcher to report only those fit indexes with favorable values. Elsewhere I recommended that a minimal set of fit indexes to report include the model chi-square statistic with its degrees of freedom, the Steiger–Lind root mean square error of approximation (RMSEA) with its 90% confidence interval, the Bentler comparative fit index (CFI), and the standardized root mean squared residual (SRMR; Kline, 2005, pp. 133–145).

The fit statistics just mentioned measure somewhat different aspects of model fit. Briefly, the RMSEA measures the degree of approximate fit of the model taking account of sample size and model complexity, and values less than .05 may indicate good approximate fit. Another favorable result is when the value of the upper limit of the 90% confidence interval for the RMSEA is less than .10. The CFI ranges from 0 to 1.00, where 1.00 indicates perfect fit. Its value indicates the relative improvement in fit of the researcher's model over a baseline model that usually assumes zero covariances between all pairs of observed variables. Values of the CFI greater than .90 suggest good fit. The SRMR is a standardized summary of the difference between sample and model-implied covariances, and values less than .10 are considered favorable. Note that even higher (e.g., CFI) or lower (e.g., RMSEA, SRMR) values are expected by many researchers, and over time, informed by Monte Carlo research, the trend has been to set increasingly demanding cutoffs for describing model fit as adequate (e.g., Fan, Thompson, & Wang, 1999; Hu & Bentler, 1999).

It is unacceptable to report the value of a single fit index. This is because no single fit statistic captures all aspects of model fit. Also, the guidelines just suggested for cutting values of fit statistics that indicate good fit of the model to the data (e.g., RMSEA < .05) are just that. This means that such cutting values should not be blindly applied without considering other aspects of the model, such as whether the individual parameter estimates make theoretical sense or whether most differences between observed and model-implied covariances or correlations are in fact small. As noted by Robert and Pashler (2000), good statistical fit of a model indicates little about (a) theory flexibility (e.g., what it cannot explain), (b) variability of the data (e.g., whether the data can rule out what the theory cannot explain), and (c) the likelihoods of other outcomes. These are all matters of rational, not statistical, analysis.

Consider Equivalent Models

For most structural equation models, it is possible to generate at least one equivalent version that fits the data just as well but with a different configuration of effects among the same variables. Some of these equivalent versions may include effects in the reverse direction compared with the original model. For example, if variable Y_1 is presumed to affect Y_2 in the original model (i.e., $Y_1 \rightarrow Y_2$), there may be an equivalent version in which the direction of that effect is reversed (i.e., $Y_2 \rightarrow Y_1$), but both models will have equal fit to the data. Specifically, equivalent models have equal values of fit statistics, including the model chi-square, the RMSEA, and the other indexes described earlier. For any structural equation model, there may be many equivalent versions; thus, the researcher is obliged to explain why his or her preferred model is superior over mathematically equivalent ones. Equivalent versions of structural equation models are generated by applying rule described in Kline (2005, pp. 153–156, 192–194, 229); see also Hershberger (2006). Unfortunately, it seems that authors of articles in which SEM results are reported rarely acknowledge the existence of equivalent models (MacCallum & Austin, 2000).

Causality It Ain't

Pardon the poor diction, but sometimes a little everyday language, plainly spoken, gets the point across. And the point is that certain regression coefficients in structural equation models that estimate directional effects can be interpreted as indicating causality only if the model is correctly specified in the first place. That is, if the causal structure is known in advance, then SEM could be used to estimate the magnitudes of the direct effects implied by that structure. However, this is certainly not how most researchers use SEM. Instead, they specify a hypothetical model of causality, and then they evaluate how well that model fits the data. If a satisfactory model is found after respecification, then about all that can be concluded is that the data are consistent with the causal structure represented in the model. This is especially true in nonexperimental studies with no design elements that directly support causal inference, such as random assignment, control groups, and the measurement of presumed causes before presumed effects. This is in part why Wilkinson and APA Task Force on Statistical Inference (1999) emphasized that the use of SEM computer programs "rarely yields any results that have any interpretation as causal effects" (p. 600).

It also seems that, in general, too many education researchers are not as cautious as they should be when inferring causality from correlational data. For example, Robinson, Levin, Thomas, Pituch, and Vaughn (2007) reviewed

EXHIBIT 7.1
Summary of Thompson's (2000) Ten Commandments of Structural Equation Modeling

1. Do not estimate models in small samples.
2. Do not standardize variables or analyze a correlation except when using a special method for standardized variables; otherwise, analyze the raw data or a covariance matrix.
3. Given roughly equal fit, more parsimonious models are preferred over more complex models.
4. Verify distributional assumptions, such as multivariate normality, of the estimation method used.
5. Apply rational considerations—including practical and theoretical significance—when evaluating model adequacy.
6. Use multiple statistical criteria (fit indexes) to evaluate different aspects of the correspondence between the model and the data.
7. In structural regression models, evaluate the measurement model by itself before estimating the whole model.
8. Test plausible alternative models, when they exist.
9. Do not respecify a model without a priori theoretical justification.
10. Remember that infinitely many models—including equivalent models based on the same variables and numbers of paths—can fit the same data.

Note. Adapted from Thompson, 2000, "Ten Commandments of Structural Equation Modeling," in *Reading and Understanding More Multivariate Statistics* (p. 277), by L. G. Grimm and P. R. Yarnold (Eds.), 2000, Washington, DC: American Psychological Association. Copyright 2000 by American Psychological Association. Adapted with permission.

about 275 articles published in five different journals in the area of teaching and learning. They found that (a) the proportion of studies based on experimental or quasi-experimental designs (i.e., with researcher-manipulated variables) declined from 45% in 1994 to 33% in 2004. Nevertheless, (b) the proportion of nonexperimental studies containing claims for causality increased from 34% in 1994 to 43% in 2004. Robinson et al. suggested that an increased but uncritical use of SEM in education research may be a factor behind these results.

Listed in Exhibit 7.1 is a summary of Thompson's (2000) "10 commandments" of SEM. Each point deals with a critical issue in SEM, and most were mentioned earlier. However, it helps to see them all in one place. See also Kline (2005, pp. 313–324) for a discussion of 44 different ways to fool yourself with SEM and McCoach, Black, and O'Connell (2007) for an outline of common misinterpretations of SEM in school psychology research.

TYPES OF SEM ANALYSES WITH EDUCATION RESEARCH EXAMPLES

Described next are major types of structural equation models with specific examples from the education research literature. These examples illustrate some of the potential promise of various types of analyses in SEM.

Path Models

There are two characteristics of a path model: (a) there is a single measure (indicator) of each hypothetical variable (construct), and (b) the only latent variables are the error (residual) terms of outcome variables. The latter are called *endogenous variables* in SEM, and these variables in path models are represented as the consequences of other variables. The error term for an endogenous variable is called a *disturbance*, which represents all omitted causes of the corresponding endogenous variable. In contrast, *exogenous variables* are represented as having effects on other variables, but whatever causes exogenous variables is not represented in a path model. It is assumed in path analysis that every exogenous variable is measured without error (i.e., there is perfect score reliability). This requirement is unrealistic in practice. Measurement error in endogenous variables is reflected in their disturbances, but this implies that estimation of the proportion of unexplained variance is confounded with that of measurement error.

For an analysis described by Cramond, Matthews-Morgan, and Bandalos (2005), an IQ test and the Figural form of the Torrance Tests of Creative Thinking (TTCT; Torrance, 1966) were administered in 1959 to a sample of high school students. The version of the TTCT studied by Cramond et al. generated four scale scores, including Fluency, Flexibility, Originality, and Elaboration, but the IQ test yielded a single score. The lifetime creative achievements of the participants 40 years later were classified by expert raters in terms of quality and quantity.

A path model of the 40-year predictive validity of IQ and the TTAC is presented in Figure 7.1(a). The TTAC is represented in this model with a single total score across the four scale scores; likewise, creative achievement is represented by the sum of the quality and quantity scores. Observed variables are represented in diagrams of path models by squares or rectangles and latent variables by circles or ellipses. The IQ variable is exogenous because its cause is not represented in the model. In contrast, the TTAC and creative achievement variables are specified as endogenous. Every endogenous variable has a disturbance, which is also considered exogenous. The two-headed curved arrows that exit and reenter the same variable in the figure represent the variances of the exogenous variables, which are free to vary. The numbers (1) that appear in the figure are scaling constants for latent variables. In Figure 7.1(a), general intelligence and creative thinking are each specified as direct causes of later creative achievement. Creative thinking is also specified as a mediator of the effect of general intelligence on creative achievement. A mediator variable is part of an indirect effect, and here it reflects the hypothesis that creative thinking "passes on" some of the prior effect of general intelligence to creative achievement.

(a) Path model

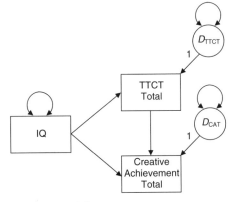

(b) Structural regression model

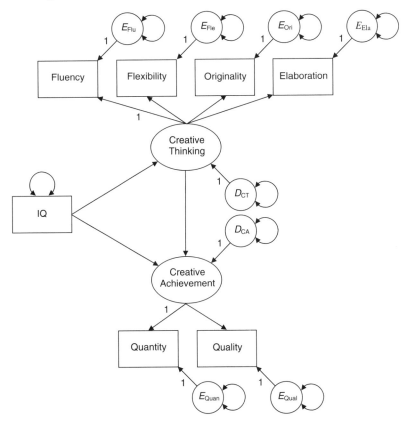

Figure 7.1. (a) A path model of the predictive validity of IQ and creative thinking. (b) A structural regression model for the same basic research question. CAT = creative achievement total; D = disturbance; E = error; TTCT = Torrance Tests of Creative Thinking (Torrance, 1966).

Structural Regression Models

An alternative kind of model similar to the one actually analyzed by Cramond et al. (2005) is presented in Figure 7.1(b). This is a *structural regression* (SR) *model*, which has both a structural part and a measurement part. As with path models, SR models permit the specification of presumed direct and indirect effects. Specifically, the SR model in Figure 7.1(b) contains the same basic structural relations among the general intelligence, creative thinking, and creative achievement variables as the path model in Figure 7.1(a). However, these effects in SR models can involve latent variables represented as measured by multiple indicators. For example, the four scale scores of the TTAC are specified as the indicators of a creative thinking factor in Figure 7.1(b), and the quantity and quality variables are represented as the indicators of a creative achievement factor. The paths from the factors to the indicators are direct effects, and here they reflect the presumed influence of the factors on their respective indicators. In contrast, there is only one measure of general intelligence (IQ scores), so no explicit measurement model for this indicator is represented in the SR model of Figure 7.1(b). This specification reflects the reality that there are times when a researcher has only one measure of some construct.

Each indicator in the measurement part of the model in Figure 7.1(b) has its own error term, which reflects systematic variance not explained by the corresponding factor and measurement error. Also, each of two endogenous factors in the structural part of the model has its own disturbance. This combination in an SR model means that the proportion of unexplained variance in endogenous factors (e.g., creative thinking) is estimated controlling for measurement error in its indicators (e.g., E_{Flu}, E_{Fle}, E_{Ori}, E_{Ela}). However, because there is no measurement error term for the single indicator of general intelligence in Figure 7.1(b), it is assumed that IQ scores are perfectly reliable, which is just as unrealistic as for the path model in Figure 7.1(a). Cramond et al. (2005) reported acceptable fit of this basic SR model to the data. They also found that general intelligence explained about 9% of the variance in the creative thinking and that IQ and creative thinking together explained about 50% of the variance in creative achievement. Considering the time span in this longitudinal study (40 years), the latter result is impressive.

Confirmatory Factor Analysis Models

When analyzing an SR model, it is often important to first verify its measurement model—that is, to test the hypotheses about the correspondence between the indicators and the factors they are supposed to measure. If these hypotheses are wrong, then knowing relations among the factors specified in the structural part of the model may be of little value (Thompson, 2000). For example, if the two-factor measurement model implied by the SR model in Figure 7.1(b) did not explain covariance patterns among the six indicators, then the fit of the whole SR model may be poor and the path coefficients may have little interpretive value. This is why many researchers use a two-step method to analyze SR models described by Anderson and Gerbing (1988), as follows: In the first step, researchers evaluate the measurement model implied by the original SR model. If this model is rejected, then it must be respecified. Given a satisfactory measurement model, the second step involves the testing of hypotheses about direct and indirect effects; that is, the structural part of the SR model is now analyzed. In this way, effects of misspecification of the measurement model are isolated from those of the structural model.

Confirmatory factor analysis (CFA) is the SEM technique for evaluating pure measurement models. Of all SEM techniques, it is probably CFA that has been applied most often in education research, especially in studies of construct validity. There are three characteristics of standard CFA models: (a) Each indicator is represented as having two causes, a single underlying factor it is supposed to measure and all other sources of variation represented by its error term. (b) These measurement errors are independent of each other. (c) Finally, all associations between every pair of factors are unanalyzed. That is, there are no direct effects between factors in CFA models, but such effects are a part of SR models (e.g., Figure 7.1(a)). Presented in Figure 7.2(a) is a standard CFA measurement model for the Mental Processing scale of the first edition Kaufman Assessment Battery for Children (KABC–I) (Kaufman & Kaufman, 1983), an individually administered cognitive ability test for children ages 2½ to 12½ years old. The test's authors claimed that the eight subtests represented in Figure 7.2(a) measure two factors, sequential processing and simultaneous processing. The three tasks believed to reflect sequential processing all require the correct recall of auditory or visual stimuli in a particular order, but more holistic, less order dependent reasoning is required for the five tasks thought to reflect simultaneous processing. The curved line with two arrowheads that connects the two factors in Figure 7.2(a) represents the covariance between them. This symbol also designates an unanalyzed association between two exogenous variables. If this symbol were replaced with a direct effect (e.g., Sequential → Simultaneous), then the whole model would be an SR model, not a CFA model.

The results of several CFA analyses of the KABC–I conducted in the 1980s and 1990s—including some with gifted students (Cameron et al., 1997)—generally supported the two-factor model presented in Figure 7.2(a). However, other results indicated that some subtests, such as Hand Movements, may actually measure both factors and that some of the measurement errors

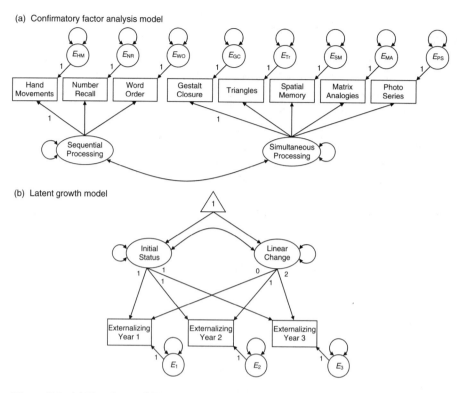

(a) Confirmatory factor analysis model

(b) Latent growth model

Figure 7.2. (a) Two-factor CFA measurement model of the first edition of the Kaufman Assessment Battery for Children (Kaufman & Kaufman, 1983). (b) Latent growth model of change in level of externalization over 3 years. E = error.

may covary (e.g., Kline, 2005, pp. 185–189). It may be possible to include both types of effects just mentioned in CFA measurement models. For example, the assumption that an indicator is multidimensional in that it reflects more than one domain corresponds to the specification that it loads on more one factor. The specification of error covariances, or unanalyzed associations between pairs of error terms, reflects the assumption that the two corresponding indicators share something in common that is not explicitly represented in the model. This "something" could be a common method of measurement, such as self-report, or autocorrelated error in the case of repeated measures variables. See Reynolds, Keith, Fine, Fisher, and Low (2007) for results of CFA analyses about the construct validity of the second edition of the Kaufman Assessment Battery for Children (KABC–II; Kaufman & Kaufman, 2004).

It is crucial to not commit the *naming fallacy:* Just because a factor is named does not mean that it is understood or even correctly labeled. Factors require some sort of designation, however, if for no reason other than communication of the results, especially in a diagram. Although verbal labels are clearer than more abstract symbols (e.g., A, ξ_1), they should be viewed as conveniences and not as explanations. For example, just because a two-factor model of the KABC–I may fit the data does not prove that one factor is sequential processing and the other factor is simultaneous processing (see Figure 7.2a). Based on their CFA results, Keith and Dunbar (1984) suggested that an alternative label for the "sequential processing" factor of the KABC–I is "short-term memory," and for the "simultaneous processing" factor, an alternative label is "nonverbal reasoning." Which among a set of alternative labels for the same factor is correct is a matter of rational analysis.

Latent Growth Models

If a sample is tested on at least three occasions and all cases are tested at the same intervals, then it may be possible to analyze in SEM a latent growth model (LGM). Besides its covariance structure, an LGM has a mean structure, too. Presented in Figure 7.2(b) is an example of an LGM similar to one analyzed by Deković, Buist, and Reitz (2004). In a longitudinal study, Deković et al. collected annual measures of externalization over a 3-year period in a sample of adolescents. The mean structure in the figure is represented in part by the graphic symbol △, which stands for a constant that equals 1.0 for every case. In SEM, this constant is treated as an exogenous variable (even though its variance is zero) that has direct or indirect effects on other variables in the model except for residual terms. The unstandardized coefficients for effects of the constant are interpreted as either means or intercepts. This is the same basic method carried out "behind the scenes" when a modern computer program for regression calculates an intercept.

In the covariance structure of the LGM in Figure 7.2(b), each annual measurement of externalization is represented as an indicator of two latent growth factors, Initial Status (IS) and Linear Change (LC). The IS factor represents the baseline level of externalization, adjusted for measurement error. Because the IS factor is analogous to an intercept in a regression equation, the unstandardized loadings of all indicators on this factor are fixed to 1. In contrast, loadings on the LC factor are fixed to constants that correspond to the times of measurement, beginning with zero for the first measurement and ending with 2 for the last. Because these constants (0, 1, 2) are positive and evenly spaced, they specify a positive linear trend, but one that is adjusted for measurement error when the model is estimated. The IS and LC factors are specified to covary, and the estimate of this covariance indicates the degree to which initial levels of externalization predict rates of subsequent linear change, again corrected for measurement error. A positive estimated covariance would indicate that adolescents with higher initial levels of externalization show greater rates of linear increase over time, and a negative estimated covariance would indicate just the opposite.

There are no error covariances in the LGM of Figure 7.2(b). In models with at least four measurement occasions, it may be possible to specify that the measurement errors of adjacent assessments are assumed to covary, among other possibilities. Error covariances reflect dependencies among scores from the same cases across different measurement occasions.

In their sample, Deković et al. (2004) found that the levels of externalization increased in a positive linear way from year to year, but levels of initial externalization were not related to the rate of linear change. That is, adolescents with lower versus higher levels of externalization at the first observation did not differ appreciably in their subsequent rates of change. In follow-up analyses, Deković et al. added to the model three predictors of latent growth factors—adolescent gender, quality of parent relationships, and quality of peer relationships. All three predictors together explained about 30% of variance in the initial status factor but only about 3% of the variance in linear change factor. The single best predictor of initial level of externalization was quality of parent relationships, but it did not tell much about the rate of change over time in behavior problems.

Multiple-Sample SEM

Essentially any type of structural equation model can be analyzed across multiple samples. The main question addressed in a multiple-sample SEM is whether values of estimated model parameters vary appreciably across the groups. If so, then (a) group membership moderates the relations specified in the model (i.e., there is a group × model interaction), and (b) separate estimates of some model parameters may be needed for each group. There are many examples in the education research literature of multiple-sample SEM. For instance, Willett and Sayer (1996) analyzed latent growth models of change in reading and arithmetic at three ages (7, 11, and 16 years) across samples of children who differed in health status (healthy, chronic asthma, seizure disorder). They found that healthy children and those with chronic asthma had generally similar growth curves for academic skills, but children with a seizure disorder showed declining trajectories over time, a result that could be due to side effects of anticonvulsant medication. In a series of multiple-sample confirmatory factor analyses, Reynolds et al. (2007) concluded that the KABC–II seems to measure the same basic constructs across the age range 3 to 18 years. In multiple-sample SEM, it is possible to evaluate models across basically any grouping variable, including age, gender, diagnosis, placement in regular versus special education, and so on.

POTENTIAL PITFALLS OF SEM IN GIFTED RESEARCH

Three different potential problems of using SEM in gifted research are described next. One is the requirement for large sample sizes. Because gifted students make up a relatively small proportion of all schoolchildren (1% to 5%), it can be difficult for researchers in this area to collect samples large enough for proper analysis in SEM. The sample size problem is an issue in the study of special populations in general, so it is not unique to gifted research. Also, there are now published reports, two of which are described later in this chapter, of the use of SEM in large samples of gifted students, so the sample size problem is not insurmountable. Two other serious challenges are considered next—range restriction and regression artifacts.

Range Restriction

Gifted students are selected because their scores on measures including classroom grades, nomination reports, verbal or nonverbal cognitive ability scales, or standardized achievement tests are relatively high. There is ongoing debate about optimal ways to apply such measures in order to identify and select gifted students, especially in minority or underrepresented populations; for example, see the special issue of the journal *Theory Into Practice* (Ford & Moore, 2005). However, there is no doubt that variability on many cognitive or scholastic variables is restricted within samples of gifted students. Assuming linear associations, absolute values of bivariate correlations tend to be reduced through range restriction on either variable, and the amount of the difference between population and restricted sample correlations can be substantial. The use of measures that generate unreliable scores can also truncate sample correlations. Because covariances are made up of correlations and variances, their values for cognitive and scholastic variables may be restricted in gifted samples, too. Covariances are the basic statistic analyzed in SEM, so effects of range restriction could affect the results when models are tested with data from gifted students. An example follows.

Suppose that the XYZ test is a measure of general cognitive ability for students in elementary school. It is standardized for use across the whole range of student ability. The subtests of the XYZ test are placed on four different scales according to a theoretical measurement model. Reported in the test's manual are results of confirmatory factor analyses conducted within the standardization sample, and these results support the measurement model. A researcher administers the XYZ test within a large sample of gifted students. He or she specifies and tests the same model in a CFA but finds that the model's fit to the data is poor. Inspection of the parameter estimates indicates that the estimated factor correlations are much lower and that indicator error variances are much higher than the corresponding values reported in the test manual. Based on these results, the researcher concludes that the XYZ test does not measure the same cognitive abilities among gifted students as it does in the general population. This conclusion may be unsound, however, and the reason is that this pattern of results is expected due to range restriction. In this case, it would safer to conclude that the construct validity of the XYZ tests holds across the whole range of ability, given the results reported in the test's manual.

There are various statistical methods that correct sample statistics for effects of range restriction, but they generally assume that (a) the unrestricted population variance is known and (b) the researcher wishes to generalize the corrected results to the unrestricted population (Sackett & Yang, 2000). The former requirement is not generally a problem with standardized tests, for which the population variance may be known. For example, the standardized score metric $\mu = 100.0$, $\sigma = 15.0$ (i.e., $\sigma^2 = 225.0$) is widely used for cognitive ability or achievement tests. However, if there is no interest in generalizing from a restricted sample to an unrestricted population, then statistical corrections for range restriction are of little use. In SEM analyses of cognitive or achievement variables measured in gifted samples, the possibility that the results are the consequences of range restriction is quite strong. Range restriction would present less of a problem when other kinds of variables are analyzed, specifically those weakly correlated with IQ or grades. These kinds of variables include self-esteem, personality traits, general psychological adjustment, family characteristics, and so on. Ranges of individual differences among gifted students on such variables may not differ substantially from those expected in the general population of students.

Regression Artifacts

This issue concerns the phenomenon of statistical regression to the mean, which refers to the tendency for cases with extreme scores to obtain less extreme scores when retested on the same or similar measures. Regression artifacts are a concern whenever cases are selected because they had scores either lower or higher than average and in studies where cases with extreme scores are matched across different conditions. Regression to the mean is caused by imperfect correlations (i.e., $|r| < 1.00$) between two sets of scores, and anything that lowers the correlation, such as score unreliability, increases it.

Regression effects should be expected in gifted research due to how gifted students are selected (i.e., because they have extreme high scores). Lohman (2006) reminded us that about half of students with scores in the top 3% of the distribution in one year will not obtain scores in the top 3% in the next year due to regression to the mean, and this is true even for very reliable scores. If we forget about regression effects, then we could fool ourselves into thinking that many, or perhaps most, students identified as gifted in one year are no longer so the next. However, this result is exactly what we expect given that test scores basically never have perfect predictive validity, especially over one year. Regression effects can be reduced by measuring status on selection variables more than once and then averaging the scores together before classifying students as gifted or not. This reduces error in selection in part because effects of individual outlier scores tend to cancel out when scores are summed. It may also detect students who attain high scores on selection variables at a later point in time.

Although latent variables in structural equation models are continuous variables only, it is possible to test models with categorical latent variables in other types of statistical techniques. Using such techniques, it would be silly to test a model with predictors of whether students' classification as gifted or not remains stable over time when such stability is not expected even when working with very reliable scores, given regression effects. In SEM, it would be possible to specify and test a structural model of the predictive validity of variables used to select gifted students, but effects due to range restriction may compromise the results (i.e., underestimation of predictive power is expected).

SELECTED EXAMPLES OF SEM IN GIFTED RESEARCH

Considered next are two recent examples of SEM analyses conducted in large samples of gifted or high-ability students. An SR model with both measurement and structural components was analyzed in the first example, and a path model was estimated across separate samples by gender in the second example. These examples illustrate some of the kinds of hypotheses that can be evaluated in SEM when just covariance structures are estimated (i.e., means were not analyzed in these studies) in gifted research.

Within a sample of 624 gifted students in Hong Kong between the ages of 9 and 19 years (age $M = 13.0$ years, $SD = 2.3$ years; 49% boys, 51% girls), Chan (2006) administered measures of emotional intelligence (EI), social coping (SC), and psychological distress (PD). Variances on psychological or social variables among gifted students may be less affected by range restriction compared with cognitive or achievement variables. This may be true in part because, as noted by Chan, high ability does not make one immune from emotional, or social, or other kinds of personal problems. Two types of emotional intelligence were each assessed with two indicators, including self-relevant EI (self-management, utilization) and other-relevant EI (empathy, social skills). Likewise, two separate factors of SC were each assessed by two indicators, including avoidant SC (denial, avoidance) and self-interaction SC (helping others, peer acceptance). The PD factor was measured by a total of five indicators (health concern, sleep problems, anxiety, dysphoria, suicidal thoughts). In a two-step analysis, Chan first verified that the measurement model just described had acceptable fit to the data before testing alternative SR models. In one SR model, effects of EI on PD were represented as entirely indirect through SC (i.e., a mediation-effect model). In another, direct effects of EI on PD were added (i.e., a mediation-direct-effect model). The latter model, although more complex than the former model, did not fit the data appreciably better than the simpler model. That is, the final results were consistent with the view that enhancement of EI alone may be insufficient to enhance psychological well-being or reduce distress among gifted students. Instead, an approach that recognizes the need to enhance the EI of gifted students relevant to SC by reducing avoidant coping and increasing empathy and social skills is consistent with the final mediation-effect model. Chan acknowledged that (a) these results only failed to disconfirm the final mediation-effect model, and (b) there are competitive models that could be found to be equally viable given similar testing methods.

A path model tested by Speirs Neumeister and Finch (2006) represented the hypothesis that parenting style affects the quality of a sense of attachment among children, which in turn predicts the degree of two different kinds of perfectionism. One is self-oriented perfectionism, where individuals impose high standards on themselves and evaluate their performance against these standards. The other type of perfectionism is socially prescribed, where individuals believe that high standards are established by others and that they are obliged to meet these standards. Speirs Neumeister and Finch speculated that self-oriented perfectionism would be associated more with motivation for mastery or performance approach compared with socially prescribed perfectionism, which would be associated more with a fear of failure due to the belief that self-worth depends on meeting the high standards of others. In a sample of 265 first-year university honor students (125 men, 140 women; total SAT score M = 1396.1), Speirs Neumeister and Finch administered separate measures of the parenting styles of mothers versus fathers, quality of attachment, self-oriented perfectionism and socially prescribed perfectionism, and achievement motivation (approach, avoidance, mastery). In a multiple-sample SEM, a path model with direct effects from parenting style variables to attachment, from attachment to perfectionism, and then from perfectionism to motivation was tested across samples of female versus male students. The results indicated that less-supportive parenting styles predicted less-secure attachment, but the effect of mother's style was stronger than that of father's style. Also, the general relation just described was even stronger for female students than for male students. For both women and men, it was found that (a) less-secure attachment predicted higher levels of perfectionism, and (b) the relation of perfectionism to achievement motivation was consistent with the hypotheses described earlier. This issue of equivalent or alternative path models was not addressed by the authors.

CONCLUSION

The price of the great diversity of research hypotheses that can be evaluated in SEM is that these techniques make several requirements, including the need to carefully specify the model in the first place, select measures that generate reliable scores, screen the data and check distributional assumptions before analyzing them, base model respecification on substantive grounds, and properly and accurately interpret and report the results. In education research, SEM is already widely used, but as noted, there are some serious shortcomings with its application in too many studies. Probably due to the need for large sample sizes, SEM has been used less often in gifted research, but its flexibility offers researchers in this area many potential advantages. However, these same researchers should be prepared to address the potential pitfalls of range restriction and regression effects, depending on the variables included in the model and the hypotheses tested about gifted students.

REFERENCES

Anderson, J. C., & Gerbing, D. W. (1988). Structural equation modeling in practice: A review and recommended two-step approach. *Psychological Bulletin, 103,* 411–423.

Cameron, L. C., Ittenbach R. F., McGrew, K. S., Harrison, P., Taylor, L. R., & Hwang, Y. R. (1997). Confirmatory factor analysis of the K–ABC with gifted referrals. *Educational and Psychological Measurement, 57,* 823–840.

Chan, D. W. (2006). Emotional intelligence, social coping, and psychological distress among Chinese gifted students in Hong Kong. *High Ability Studies, 16,* 163–178.

Cramond, B., Matthews-Morgan, J., & Bandalos, D. (2005). A report on the 40-year follow-up of the Torrance Tests of Creative Thinking: Alive and well in the new millennium. *Gifted Child Quarterly, 49,* 283–291.

Deković, M., Buist, K. L., & Reitz, E. (2004). Stability and changes in problem behavior during adolescence: Latent growth analysis. *Journal of Youth and Adolescence, 33,* 1–12.

Fan, X., Thompson, B., & Wang, L. (1999). The effects of sample size, estimation methods, and model specification on SEM fit indices. *Structural Equation Modeling, 6,* 56–83.

Ford, D. Y., & Moore, J. L. (2005). This issue: Gifted education. [Special issue]. *Theory Into Practice, 44*(2).

Hershberger, S. L. (2006). The problem of equivalent models. In G. R. Hancock & R. O. Mueller (Eds.), *Structural equation modeling: A second course* (pp. 13–41). Greenwich, CT: Information Age Publishing.

Hu, L., & Bentler, P. M. (1999). Cutoff criteria for fit indexes in covariance structure analysis: Conventional criteria versus new alternatives. *Structural Equation Modeling, 6*, 1–55.

Jackson, D. L. (2003). Revisiting sample size and number of parameter estimates: Some support for the *N:q* hypothesis. *Structural Equation Modeling, 10*, 128–141.

Kaufman, A. S., & Kaufman, N. L. (1983). *K–ABC administration and scoring manual.* Circle Pines, MN: American Guidance Service.

Kaufman, A. S., & Kaufman, N. L. (2004). *Kaufman Assessment Battery for Children— Second Edition.* Circle Pines, MN: AGS Publishing.

Keith, T. Z., & Dunbar, S. B. (1984). Hierarchical factor analysis of the K–ABC: Testing alternate models. *Journal of Special Education, 18*, 367–375.

Kline, R. B. (2005). *Principle and practice of structural equation modeling* (2nd ed.). New York: Guilford Press.

Lohman, D. F. (2006, April). *Understanding and predicting regression effects in the identification of academically gifted children.* Paper presented at the annual meeting of the American Educational Research Association, San Francisco. Retrieved March 13, 2007, from http://faculty.education.uiowa.edu/dlohman/pdf/Understanding_and_predicting_regression.pdf

MacCallum, R. C., & Austin, J. T. (2000). Applications of structural equation modeling in psychological research. *Annual Review of Psychology, 51*, 201–236.

Marsh, H. W., & Hau, K.-T. (1999). Confirmatory factor analysis: Strategies for small sample sizes. In R. H. Hoyle (Ed.), *Statistical strategies for small sample research* (pp. 252–284). Thousand Oaks, CA: Sage.

McCoach, D. B. (2003). SEM isn't just the schoolwide enrichment model anymore: Structural equation modeling (SEM) in gifted education. *Journal for the Education of the Gifted, 27*, 36–61.

McCoach, D. B., Black, A. C., & O'Connell, A. A. (2007). Errors of inference in structural equation modeling. *Psychology in the Schools, 44*, 461–470.

McDonald, R. P., & Ho, M.-H. R. (2002). Principles and practice in reporting structural equation analyses. *Psychological Methods, 7*, 64–82.

Pedhazur, E. J., & Schmelkin, L. P. (1991). *Measurement, design, and analysis: An integrated approach.* Hillsdale, NJ: Erlbaum.

Reynolds, M. R., Keith, T. Z., Fine, J. G., Fisher, M. E., & Low, J. A. (2007). Confirmatory factor structure of the Kaufman Assessment Battery for Children—Second Edition: Consistency with Cattell–Horn–Carroll theory. *School Psychology Quarterly, 22*, 511–539.

Robert, S., & Pashler, H. (2000). How persuasive is a good fit? A comment on theory testing in psychology. *Psychological Review, 15,* 351–357.

Robinson, D. H., Levin, J. R., Thomas, G. D., Pituch, K. A., & Vaughn, S. (2007). The incidence of "causal" statements in teaching-and-learning research journals. *American Educational Research Journal, 44,* 400–413.

Sackett, P. R., & Yang, H. (2000). Correction for range restriction: An expanded typology. *Journal of Applied Psychology, 85,* 112–118.

Silvia, E. S. M., & MacCallum, R. C. (1988). Some factors affecting the success of specification searches in covariance structure modeling. *Multivariate Behavioral Research, 23,* 297–326.

Speirs Neumeister, K. L., & Finch, H. (2006). Perfectionism in high-ability students: Relational precursors and influences on achievement motivation. *Gifted Child Quarterly, 50,* 238–251.

Steiger, J. H. (2001). Driving fast in reverse: The relationship between software development, theory, and education in structural equation modeling. *Journal of the American Statistical Association, 96,* 331–338.

Thompson, B. (1995). Stepwise regression and stepwise discriminant analysis need not apply here: A guidelines editorial. *Educational and Psychological Measurement, 55,* 525–534.

Thompson, B. (2000). Ten commandments of structural equation modeling. In L. G. Grimm & P. R. Yarnold (Eds.), *Reading and understanding more multivariate statistics* (pp. 261–283). Washington, DC: American Psychological Association Books.

Torrance, E. P. (1966). *Torrance Tests of Creative Thinking: Norms—technical manual* (Research ed.). Princeton, NJ: Personnel Press.

Wilkinson, L., & APA Task Force on Statistical Inference. (1999). Statistical methods in psychology journals: Guidelines and explanations. *American Psychologist, 54,* 594–604.

Willett, J. B., & Sayer, A. G. (1996). Cross-domain analyses of change over time: Combining growth modeling and covariance structure analysis. In G. A. Marcoulides & R. E. Schumacker (Eds.), *Advanced structural equation modeling* (pp. 125–157). Mahwah, NJ: Erlbaum.

8

HIERARCHICAL LINEAR MODELING APPLICATIONS IN THE CONTEXT OF GIFTEDNESS RESEARCH

J. KYLE ROBERTS, KIM NIMON, AND LINDSEY MARTIN

The history of hierarchical linear models generally traces its roots back to the work of Robinson (1950) in recognizing contextual effects. The discovery that Robinson made is sometimes thought of as the "frog pond" theory and is fairly simple to relate. Suppose that a researcher was conducting an analysis on environmental factors affecting the weight of frogs. And also suppose that two of the frogs being analyzed both weighed 500 grams. However, the first frog that weighed 500 grams was drawn from a pond where it was the largest frog in the pond. The second frog that weighed 500 grams was drawn from a lake where 500 grams was the weight of the average frog for that pond. In a typical ordinary least squares (OLS) analysis, the researcher would have no way of honoring the pond nesting structure for these two frogs and would then erroneously assume that the environmental factors affecting frog growth were the same regardless of which pond was home to the frog.

This same problem often presents itself when researchers are analyzing data obtained from school research. For example, suppose that a researcher were to try to run a regression analysis in which student grade point average (GPA) scores were used to predict performance on the Stanford Achievement Test (SAT). It stands to reason that, within a given school, GPAs might be good predictors of SAT scores where higher GPAs correlate with higher scores on the SAT. However, across schools, the relationship between GPA and SAT may be dramatically different. Whereas in a low-performing school, a student with a 4.0 GPA might score only a 1,000 on the SAT, a student with a 4.0 GPA in an elite, high-performing private school might score a 1,600 on the SAT. This happens because GPA scores are not independent of the school from which they are drawn. This problem of independence of observations is often a factor when collecting data in schools, yet until the development of hierarchical linear modeling (HLM), no methods for dealing appropriately with such data existed.

WHAT ARE HIERARCHICAL LINEAR MODELS?

Although the popularity and awareness of multilevel and hierarchical linear models have increased dramatically in the last few years, it is still a field that is in the early stages of development. Two volumes that laid the groundwork for the proliferation of these models were Goldstein (1995) and Raudenbush and Bryk (2002; now in the second edition). The advantage of HLM over OLS regression or analysis of variance (ANOVA) is that it allows the researcher to look at hierarchically structured data while not violating the independence of observation assumption (the assumption that when an observation is drawn from a nested structure like a school, that structure has no bearing on the outcome of the observation).

A typical multilevel or hierarchically structured data set includes some Level 1 units (e.g., students or measurement occasions) nested inside Level 2 units (e.g., schools or years). Although three-, four- and even five-level structures are plausible, multilevel models are typically easier to interpret when they are limited to two levels. Consider the following multilevel data sets:

- students nested within classrooms,
- students nested within schools,
- students nested within classrooms nested within schools (three levels),
- people nested within districts,
- measurement occasions nested within subjects (repeated measures),
- students cross-classified by school and neighborhood, and
- students having multiple membership within schools across time (longitudinal data).

Although not an exhaustive list of the model types that can be run in a multilevel framework, the list does provide several examples of the utility of these types of models. More recently, the application of HLM has been applied to those doing work in Rasch modeling (Beretvas & Kamata, 2005) and latent variable modeling (Skrondal & Rabe-Hesketh, 2004).

As mentioned above, the assumption of independence of observations is often a problem for the researcher working on school data. In addition to being able to overcome this problem, hierarchical linear models have several advantages over their OLS counterparts (e.g., ANOVA, analysis of covariance [ANCOVA], multiple regression, descriptive discriminant analysis, canonical correlation analysis). First, statistical models that are not hierarchical typically ignore complex data structures and as a result report underestimated standard errors (no between-unit variation). This could lead to increased Type I error rates. This means that we could be interpreting p values from our analysis as statistically significant when in fact that difference is due solely to chance or does not actually present itself in the population (Goldstein et al., 1998).

Second, multilevel techniques are statistically efficient, whereas the OLS counterparts are not. For example, suppose that a researcher in gifted education wanted to explore the relationship between IQ scores and advanced mathematics testing among 200 gifted students in 20 schools. In order to look at the different school effects, the researcher would be forced to run 20 different OLS regression analyses (one for each school) and then attempt to interpret results based on these regressions. While this may not seem that daunting of a task, consider if the researcher wanted to run the same analysis for 10,000 gifted students in 1,000 schools. Now the limitations of OLS regression really present themselves. Further, the OLS analysis would not provide useful estimation of school variability and the school effect of IQ on advanced mathematics testing.

Third, multilevel techniques assume a general linear model framework and, therefore, can perform multiple types of analyses while honoring the nesting structure of the data. For example, HLM can perform analyses including ANCOVA, regression, maximum likelihood estimation, repeated measures analysis, meta-analysis, multivariate response, Bayesian modeling, binary response, bootstrap estimation, Rasch modeling, factor analysis, and multiple membership models (where students may go to more than one school in a given year).

FIXED VERSUS RANDOM COEFFICIENTS

Probably the most basic of concepts to multilevel modeling is that of fixed and random coefficients. For random coefficient models, we allow either the intercepts or slopes (or both) to vary across the Level 2 units. For example, in a random coefficients model, we might assume and want to model that the relationship between student grade point average and SAT scores is different from school to school; hence, we would model a random coefficient for the slope of grade point average on SAT scores. This is fairly easy to relate and can be best understood graphically (see Figure 8.1). The panel in the top left corner of Figure 8.1 represents a typical OLS analysis where the fixed effects of an analysis are modeled with no random effects. The top right panel shows a model in which each of the Level 2 units (i.e., schools) are allowed to have a random estimate for their slope in addition to the fixed estimate, but no random estimate for the intercept. In this case, the fixed effect for the slope would represent the maximum likelihood estimate of the average slope across all Level 2 units. Adding the random effect to the slope coefficient for this model means that we will estimate a unique slope coefficient for each of the Level 2 units (or schools in school-effects research).

The panel in the bottom left corner represents a model in which each of the Level 2 units are fixed to all have the same slope but are allowed to have different intercept values, or random effects for the intercept. Lastly, the panel in the bottom right corner represents a model in which both the intercept and slope coefficients are allowed to have random estimates for each of the Level 2 units.

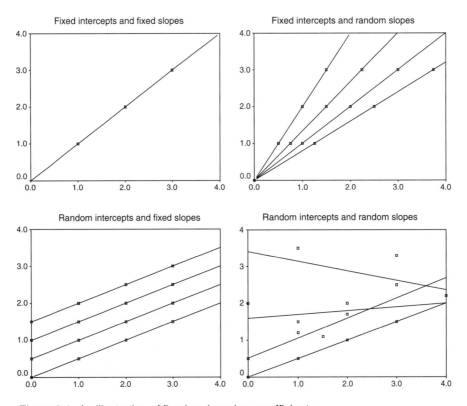

Figure 8.1. An illustration of fixed and random coefficients.

THE MULTILEVEL MODEL

We typically notate the one-level OLS regression model with one explanatory variable as follows:

$$y = a + bx + e, \qquad (1)$$

where y is the response variable, a is the intercept, b is the slope, x is the explanatory variable, and e is each individual's distance between the predicted score and the observed score (or residual). We assume an error term in the regression equation because we know in social science research that we will typically never have perfect prediction. The multilevel model is a slight variation on the single-predictor regression model and is notated as follows:

$$y_{ij} = \gamma_{00} + \gamma_{10}x_{ij} + u_{0j} + e_{ij} \qquad (2)$$

where γ_{00} represents an estimate of the grand intercept and γ_{10} represents the fixed effect for the slope of x_{ij} (a Level 1 explanatory variable), u_{0j} is the random variation of each Level 2 unit's intercept around the grand intercept γ_{00}, and e_{ij} is the residual score, or each person's deviation from the predicted score.

One of the strengths of HLM is that Equation 2 can actually be broken down into models representing each level of the hierarchy. For example, Equation 2 can also be written as the combination of a Level 1 model

$$y_{ij} = \beta_{0j} + \beta_{1j}x_{ij} + e_{ij} \qquad (3)$$

and a Level 2 model

$$\beta_{0j} = \gamma_{00} + u_{0j} \qquad (4)$$

with the variance $u_{0j} = \sigma_{u0}^2$ and the variance $e_{ij} = \sigma_e^2$. Thus, Equations 3 and 4 are simply a deconstruction of Equation 2. This model is also referred to as a *random intercept model* because of the random estimate u_{0j} for each Level 2 intercept around the grand intercept γ_{00}.

For the purposes of this chapter, we are going to talk specifically about the two-level repeated measures model as it applies to gifted education. It is often the case that there are so few gifted students in a school or classroom that comparing them to the general population of students violates a number of model assumptions. The multilevel repeated measures model uses slightly different notation than the original model presented in Equation 2. This chapter illustrates three separate models. The first model is

$$y_{ti} = \beta_{00} + \beta_{10}T_{ti} + u_{0i} + u_{1i} + e_{ti} \qquad (5)$$

where y_{ti} is the response of student i at time point t, β_{00} is the grand intercept, β_{10} is the grand slope for the time variable T_{ti}, u_{0i} is the random variation of each student's intercept around the grand intercept β_{00}, u_{1i} is the random variation of each student's slope for the time variable around the grand slope β_{10}, and e_{ti} is the residual score or each person's deviation from their predicted score at time point t. In this example, measurement occasions (Level 1) are nested inside students (Level 2). Notice that in this model we have one extra error term for the slope of the time variable. Interpreting this model means that we are allowing each student to have his or her own unique starting value, or random intercept designated by u_{0i}, and his or her own rate of change over all of the time points, or random slope designated by u_{1i}. This may be alternatively stated as modeling each child having a different starting point and different rates of change over time.

In addition to the model in Equation 5, we will be testing two other models. The first model is

$$y_{ti} = \beta_{00} + \beta_{10}T_{ti} + \beta_{01}Gifted_i + u_{0i} + u_{1i} + e_{ti} \qquad (6)$$

where the term β_{01} represents the effect of being identified as a gifted student on the dependent variable and the subscript of i for $Gifted$ means that this is a variable that is measured at the student level, or Level 2. In other words, this effect shows the average amount of difference between the gifted students and all other students.

The final model tested in this chapter adds an interaction effect between time and gifted and is modeled as

$$y_{ti} = \beta_{00} + \beta_{10}T_{ti} + \beta_{01}Gifted + \beta_{11}T_{ti}Gifted_i + u_{0i} + u_{1i} + e_{ti} \qquad (7)$$

where the term β_{11} represents the cross-level interaction effect between time and gifted. In the presence of an interaction effect, the main effects of β_{10} and β_{01} take on slightly different meanings as they now represent the expected value for the effect when the other variable is zero. For example, the slope for time now represents the expected slope of Time for the students not identified as gifted (i.e., $Gifted = 0$), and the slope for gifted represents the effect of being in the gifted group ($Gifted = 1$) at the outset of the study (i.e., $T_{ti} = 0$; Hox, 2002, pp. 56–58).

A NOTE ON STATISTICAL SIGNIFICANCE

Statistical significance testing has come under a considerable amount of fire recently (Cohen, 1994; Schmidt, 1996; Thompson, 1996, 2002). The problems associated with significance testing are even further compounded in HLM. First, a p value in HLM means something slightly different than a p value in OLS. In OLS, the p value for a regression coefficient represents the probability that a given coefficient is statistically significantly different from zero. It would seem then that the p value for a coefficient in HLM would be similarly interpreted. This is not true. In HLM, the test statistic is obtained by dividing the estimate (β_{10} in the case of the slope of time for the repeated measures model) by its standard error. This produces a t-calculated, which can be then be tested against a corresponding t-critical obtained from the appropriate degrees of freedom (this is very similar to testing for the statistical significance of a mean difference when conducting a t test).

There are two problems here. First, just because a grand estimate like β_{10} might not have a p value below .05 does not mean that the corresponding effect is not a good predictor of the dependent variable. For example, suppose that we were observing three gifted students' mathematical abilities over time. As can be seen in Figure 8.2, each of these students is increasing at a different rate, but all of them are increasing at a constant rate. In this case, β_{10} (the slope for time) would represent a maximum likelihood average of each of their individual unstandardized slope coefficients for the relationship between time and mathematics achievement. Because each of the students has a dramatically different rate of growth, the standard error for β_{10} would likely be very large, thus decreasing the probability of obtaining statistical significance. Figure 8.2 clearly shows, however, that there is a strong relationship between time and mathematics achievement for each individual student, but that the relationship has a lot of variability across students. In this case, we would expect the p value for β_{10} to be > .05 and the variance of u_{1j} to be quite large. This does not mean that time is not a good predictor of mathematics achievement, just that the grand estimate for time (β_{10}) is not a good representation of the variability of the random slopes for all three students.

The second problem with statistical significance testing in HLM is that not everyone agrees on which degrees of freedom to use to determine the critical value of t. This is a very complicated problem that is beyond the scope of this chapter. It is noteworthy, however, that the HLM routine "lme4" in the software package R does not report p values, and multiple authors doing research with HLM do not present p values in their findings (e.g., Boston, Hale, Kliegl, Patil, & Vasishth, in press).

Researchers may then wonder how we determine if the addition of a parameter makes a marked improvement in model fit. To do this, we use the Akaike information criterion (AIC; Akaike, 1987) or the Bayesian information criterion (BIC; Schwarz, 1978). These statistics are like the fit criteria that are sometimes used in structural equation modeling (e.g., comparative fit index, normed fit index, root mean square error of approximation) but are on a different scale. They are both computed as a function of chi-square, but

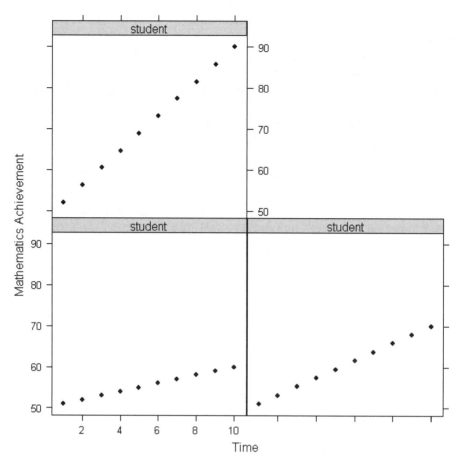

Figure 8.2. Heuristic scores of three students' mathematics achievement across time.

with a "punishment factor" based on the number of parameters estimated. This punishment factor is based on the principle of Occam's razor that states that a more parsimonious answer is preferable because these results produce simpler models that are more likely to replicate in future studies (for a more thorough description, see Gelman & Hill, 2007, pp. 524–526). When comparing competing models, the model with the smallest AIC and BIC is typically the preferred model.

ILLUSTRATION WITH A HEURISTIC DATA SET

Suppose an administrator wants to analyze how a set of gifted students progress through a school year when placed in a class with other nonidentified students. Further suppose that students in this class take an achievement test at 10 regular intervals throughout the school year. One way to analyze such data would be to examine the descriptive statistics of the two groups of students (gifted and nonidentified) across the 10 measurement occasions. Table 8.1 provides the results of such data. Simulation of data can be seen in Appendix A. By analyzing group means, it is clear that the gifted students started the year scoring higher on the achievement test than their counterparts. Furthermore, the administrator can see that the gifted student group continued to outperform the nonidentified group throughout the year. The administrator can also see that, in general, the two groups generally did better on the achievement test each time they took it. Exceptions include Measurement Occasions 3, 5, 6, and 9 for the nonidentified group and Measurement Occasions 4 and 9 for the gifted group. However, the difference between measurement occasions for the nonidentified group appears to be lower than for the gifted group.

Now suppose that the administrator wants to employ inferential statistics to examine group differences in achievement tests scores across time. One way to analyze the data collected would be to conduct a repeated measures ANOVA incorporating a within-subjects and between-subjects factor. The within-subjects factor provides a more sensitive analysis as individuals serve as their own controls, while the between-subjects factor provides the vehicle to examine differences in groups of individuals.

In the scenario presented, the between-subjects factor represents the two groups of interest, and the within-subjects factor represents the 10 measurement occasions. The number of levels for the factors would then be 2 for the between-subjects factor and 10 for the within-subjects factor. Considering all factors, the results of the repeated measures ANOVA will include three analyses—(a) the main effect of group, (b) the main effect of measurement occasion, and (c) the interaction effect between group and measurement occasion. Although the administrator may be most interested in the interaction effect between group and measurement occasion, all three effects are explained.

The *group main effect* tests if there is a significant difference in the mean achievement scores between the two groups. Tables 8.2 and 8.3 illustrate that the difference between 19.82 (mean score on the achievement test for the

TABLE 8.1
Group Means on Achievement Test Results Across Measurement Occasion

Student group	Measurement occasion									
	1	2	3	4	5	6	7	8	9	10
Nonidentified	19.12	19.20	19.19	19.93	19.87	19.77	19.80	20.60	20.27	20.46
Gifted	27.36	28.38	29.92	29.50	30.68	30.90	31.65	32.81	32.77	33.04

TABLE 8.2
Group Means and Averaged Means for Heuristic Data Set

Student group (between subjects)	Measurement occasion (within subjects)										Mean
	1	2	3	4	5	6	7	8	9	10	
Nonidentified	19.12	19.20	19.19	19.93	19.87	19.77	19.80	20.60	20.27	20.46	19.82
Gifted	27.36	28.38	29.92	29.50	30.68	30.90	31.65	32.81	32.77	33.04	30.55
Mean	23.24	23.79	23.53	24.72	25.27	25.33	25.73	26.71	26.52	26.75	

TABLE 8.3
ANOVA Table for Heuristic Data Set

Source	SS	< df	MS	F	p	η^2
Group	3830.78	1	3830.77	372.17	< .001	.94
Error (between subjects)	236.74	23	12.29			
Occasion	207.64	9	23.071	22.28	< .001	.49
Occasion * group	80.87	9	8.98	8.67	< .001	.27
Error (within subjects)	214.31	107	1.03			

Note. SS = sum of squares; MS = mean square.

nonidentified group) and 30.55 (mean score on the achievement test for the gifted group) is statistically, $F(1, 23) = 372.17$, $p < .001$, and practically, $\eta^2 = .94$, different. Overall, what group the students were in explained 94% of the difference in mean scores between the two groups. From a practical perspective, the administrator can see that across measurement occasions, the gifted students scored ~10 points higher than their counterparts.

The *main effect of measurement occasion* tests if there is a significant difference in achievement scores, averaged across group across time. In this case, scores analyzed are the average of the two groups' scores at each measurement occasion (i.e., 23.24, 23.79, 23.53, 24.72, 25.27, 25.33, 25.73, 26.71, 26.52, and 26.75). The main effect of measurement occasion indicates that the averaged scores are statistically significant from each other, $F(9, 207) = 22.28$, $p < .001$, and time explains 49% of their variance. To further understand how the averaged scores changed over time, the administrator could also examine within-subjects contrasts (see Table 8.4) to determine which polynomial trend (linear, quadratic, or cubic) best fits the data. In this example, a linear trend was most representative of the averaged scores over time, $F(1, 23) = 67.44, p < .001$.

The *interaction effect of measurement occasion and group* tests if there is a significant difference between the 20 means identified in Table 8.1. The results of the repeated measures ANOVA indicate that the interaction effect is statistically significant, $F(9, 207) = 8.68, p < .001$, and explains 27% of the variance across the 10 sets of achievement scores. In practical terms, the interaction effect indicates that the effect of time on achievement scores is not identical for the two groups of students. However, further analyses are required to interpret the effect. In addition to graphically representing the interaction effect (see Figure 8.3), the most common technique to interpret the interaction effect involves conducting separate repeated measures ANOVA on each of the two groups. The ANOVA summary tables depicted in Tables 8.5 and 8.6 indicate that although occasion was a statistically significant factor for both groups, $F(9, 180) = 5.69, p < .001; F(9, 27) = 16.82, p < .001$, the effect of time

TABLE 8.4
Tests of Within-Subjects Contrasts

Source	Trend	SS	df	MS	F	p
Occasion	Linear	196.716	1	196.716	676.440	.000
	Quadratic	1.198	1	1.198	1.123	.300
	Cubic	1.719	1	1.719	1.108	.303
	Order 4	.003	1	.003	.002	.964
	Order 5	.115	1	.115	.153	.700
	Order 6	.192	1	.192	.247	.624
	Order 7	7.626	1	7.626	9.060	.006
	Order 8	.004	1	.004	.004	.952
	Order 9	.068	1	.068	.059	.810
Error (occasion)	Linear	6.689	23	.291		
	Quadratic	24.525	23	1.066		
	Cubic	35.696	23	1.552		
	Order 4	38.389	23	1.669		
	Order 5	17.243	23	.750		
	Order 6	17.824	23	.775		
	Order 7	19.360	23	.842		
	Order 8	28.165	23	1.225		
	Order 9	26.418	23	1.149		

on achievement scores was much greater for the gifted students. Whereas time explained 85% of the variance in scores for the gifted group, measurement occasion explained only 22% of the variance in scores for the gifted students' counterparts. Analyzing within-subjects contrasts for each group indicates that a linear trend was most representative of scores across time for both groups, $F(1, 20) = 129.47, p < .001; F(1, 3) = 2,853,963.3, p < .001$.

It is important to note that conducting a repeated measures ANOVA, such as the one outlined in this chapter, dictates a unique set of statistical assumptions. As testing the group main effect is identical to performing a one-way ANOVA on individual achievement scores averaged over mea-

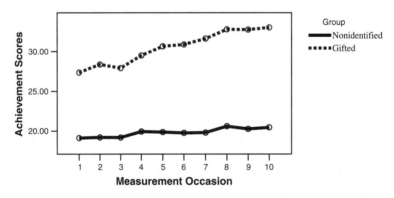

Figure 8.3. Graph of achievement scores by measurement occasion and group.

TABLE 8.5
ANOVA Summary Table for Nonidentified Students

Source	SS	df	MS	F	p	η^2
Subjects	183.12	20	9.16			
Occasion	52.73	9	5.86	5.69	< .001	.22
Error (within subjects)	185.46	180	1.030			

TABLE 8.6
ANOVA Summary Table for Gifted Students

Source	SS	df	MS	F	p	η^2
Subjects	53.62	3	17.87			
Occasion	161.69	9	17.97	16.82	< .001	.85
Error (within subjects)	28.85	27	1.068			

surement occasion, the statistical assumptions are the same as a one-way between-subjects design and include normality, homogeneity of variance, and independence of observations. Because testing the main effect of measurement occasion and the interaction effect of measurement occasion and group parcels out between-subjects error and employs a within-subjects error term, their statistical assumptions extend beyond the usual assumptions of normality and independence of observations. Within each group, the condition of sphericity must exist between measurement occasions (for a more detailed discussion of sphericity, see Hedeker & Gibbons, 2006, pp. 25–26). In addition, each group's variance–covariance matrix must be identical to one another in the population. In general, the F tests resulting from a repeated measures ANOVA with a between-subjects factor are robust to violations of most of the statistical assumptions mentioned herein. The exception is the condition of sphericity. In cases where sphericity does not hold, researchers should consider techniques that do not assume sphericity (i.e., multivariate or adjusted univariate tests).

HIERARCHICAL LINEAR MODELING ANALYSIS OF REPEATED MEASURES DATA

Table 8.7 presents the results from running the multilevel repeated measures with the same heuristic data from above. In this table, Equation 5 is represented in the null model (M_0), Equation 6 is represented in the model M_1, and Equation 7 is represented in the model M_2.

The model M_0 is called both the *null model* and the *baseline model* because it is the model against which we will test all future models. In this

TABLE 8.7
Results of Fitting Data in the Multilevel Model

	M_0: Null model		M_1: + Gifted		M_2: + Interaction	
	Estimate	SE	Estimate	SE	Estimate	SE
	Fixed effects					
Intercept β_{00}	20.441	0.656	19.170	0.213	19.111	0.247
Time β_{10}	0.242	0.045	0.242	0.041	0.158	0.024
Gifted β_{01}			7.950	0.527	8.310	0.618
Time * gifted β_{11}					0.526	0.061
	Random effects					
σ_e^2	1.036		1.121		1.04	
σ_{u0}^2	10.403		0.549		0.93	
σ_{u1}^2	0.038		0.029		< .001	
σ_{u01}					< .001	
	Fit					
χ^2	848.00		822.00		782.00	
AIC	858.00		834.00		796.00	
BIC	876.00		855.00		820.00	

Note. AIC = Akaike information criterion; BIC = Bayesian information criterion.

model, the mean mathematics achievement at time = 0 is predicted to be 20.441 and to increase by 0.242 points for each time point. It is important to note that this is the model that is built for both groups combined, and therefore we cannot yet make speculations as to the growth of the gifted students over the nonidentified students.

Model M_1 includes the Level 2 variable identifying which students are gifted (1 for gifted and 0 for nonidentified). In this case, we can see that the slope for the time variable (coded from 0 to 9 for the 10 time points) did not change very much but that the gifted students had the advantage of starting 7.950 points ahead of the nonidentified students. An easy way to think about this is to write out the regression functions for each of the two groups. For the nonidentified students, their prediction equation would be

$$\hat{y}_{ij} = 19.170 + 0.242 * Time, \tag{8}$$

and the prediction equation for the gifted students would be

$$\hat{y}_{ij} = 19.170 + 0.242 * Time + 7.950 * Gifted$$
$$\hat{y}_{ij} = 27.120 + 0.242 * Time. \tag{9}$$

Notice that because the value of the gifted variable for the gifted students is 1, we can simply add this coefficient back in to the value for the intercept.

In the final model, we allow a cross-level interaction effect between gifted and time (gifted is measured at Level 2, while time is measured at Level 1). It is likewise helpful here to build the prediction equations to aid in the interpretation of the models. For the nonidentified students, their prediction equation reduces to

$$\hat{y}_{ij} = 19.111 + 0.158 * Time \tag{10}$$

because their respective value for the gifted variable is zero. The gifted students, on the other hand, all have a score of 1 for the gifted variable, making their prediction equation as follows:

$$\hat{y}_{ij} = 19.111 + 0.158 * Time + 8.310 * Gifted + 0.526 * Time * Gifted$$
$$\hat{y}_{ij} = 27.421 + 0.158 * Time + 0.526 * Time$$
$$\hat{y}_{ij} = 27.421 + 0.684 * Time. \tag{11}$$

This means that not only are the gifted students starting at a higher level of mathematics achievement than other, nonidentified students in their classroom, they are also making gains in their mathematics achievement at a much faster rate than the other, nonidentified students. This probably makes sense given that gifted students tend to both (a) know more at a given point in time and (b) learn new material at a faster rate than their nonidentified peers. The effect of this model can be seen in Figure 8.4. In this figure, the fitted lines for each student are drawn for their respective data. In this case, the four gifted students appear on the top row at the right four positions. Their respective differences in growth trajectories are readily apparent when plotted against the other students' growth from the same class.

This analysis in model M_2 has several great advantages over the repeated measures ANOVA previously presented. First, we do not encounter the problems of sphericity that often plague repeated measures ANOVA. This is simply not a requirement of the hierarchical linear model. In addition, we can model complex covariance structures in this type of model, where we would not be able to in a repeated measures ANOVA (e.g., autoregressive errors, AR1).

Second, because of the small number of gifted students typical in a general classroom (3%–5%; Davis & Rimm, 2004), ANOVA-type analyses are not plausible because the comparison of cell numbers might be $n = 2$ vs. $n = 24$ for gifted and nonidentified students, respectively. Again, unequal cell sizes are not an issue in HLM because the complete model is based on modeling several individual student models simultaneously and then attempting to find variables that can explain the differences between the students.

Lastly, HLM has a distinct strength over other ANOVA procedures in that it combines the strengths of both OVA and regression techniques. In the repeated measures ANOVA analysis, we are able to ask the question, "Did

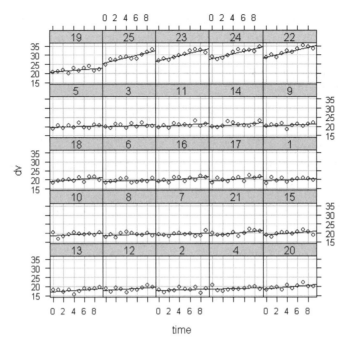

Figure 8.4. Fitted lines from the null model.

the groups differ on the dependent variable across time?" With the multilevel repeated measures model, we can ask not only if the groups differed, but at what rate they differed and what variables contributed to these differences.

FINAL CAUTIONS AND SUGGESTIONS

This introduction to HLM in gifted research is not meant as an exhaustive treatise on the use of multilevel techniques. These models are difficult to construct, and the learning curve is quite steep. However, properly utilized, they could be a powerful tool for investigating gifted students and their change in knowledge over time. There are several books and software packages currently available to both the novice and expert researcher that can help in learning these skills. Many of these resources are made available at HLM-Online (http://www.hlm-online.com/) and at the Centre for Multilevel Modelling (http://www.cmm.bristol.ac.uk/). The first site contains an annotated list of most of the books written on HLM and multilevel modeling, as well as some demonstrations of some of the more simple HLM techniques. The latter has a great resource for investigating all of the software options available for running HLM.

Finally, there seems to be a movement of many researchers to incorporate these types of models into their analyses. Although this is a noteworthy endeavor, many data sets simply do not present themselves as plausible candidates for HLM either because of sample size or because of the nature of the data structure. This isn't to say that HLM is not a powerful tool, but that it should be used with caution. Goldstein (1995) stated this best when he said,

> There is a danger that multilevel modeling will become so fashionable that its use will be a requirement of journal editors, or even worse, that the mere fact of having fitted a multilevel model will become a certificate of statistical probity. That would be a great pity. These models are as good as the data they fit; they are powerful tools, not universal panaceas. (p. 202)

APPENDIX 8.1

R CODE FOR RUNNING GIFTED REPEATED MEASURES MODEL

```
#### Simulating the Roberts, Nimon, and Martin data
#### First, the function "corgen" must be run
#### This new code for corgen is at the bottom of this file

#### Here is where the data is created

#### New data creation
set.seed(12346)
dv<-corgen(x=1:10, r=.3, epsilon=.01, population=T)$y + 20

r.s<-seq(0.2, 0.6, length=20)
int.s<-rnorm(20, 20, 1)

for(i in 1:20){
  test.i<-corgen(x=1:10, r=r.s[i], epsilon=.1,
    population=T)$y + int.s[i]
  dv<-rbind(dv, test.i)
}

int.g<-rnorm(4, 30, 1)

for(i in 1:4){
  test.i<-corgen(x=1:10, r=.9, epsilon=.001, population=T)$y
    + int.g[i]
  dv<-rbind(dv, test.i)
}

id<-rep(1:25, each=10)
time<-rep(0:9, 25)
gifted<-c(rep(0, 210), rep(1, 40))

depend<-data.frame(cbind(id, dv, time, gifted))

#### Run the models in lmer
library(lme4)
dep.null<-lmer(dv ~ time + (time | id), depend)
summary(dep.null)
dep.lmer1<-lmer(dv ~ time + gifted + (time | id), depend)
summary(dep.lmer1)
dep.lmer2<-lmer(dv ~ time * gifted + (time | id), depend)
summary(dep.lmer2)
```

```
anova(dep.null, dep.lmer1, dep.lmer2)

#### Produce Graphs
with(dep.null, {
 cc <- coef(.)$id
 xyplot(dv ~ time | id,
   index.cond = function(x, y) coef(lm(y ~ x))[1],
   panel = function(x, y, groups, subscripts, . . .) {
    panel.grid(h = -1, v = -1)
    panel.points(x, y, . . .)
    panel.lmline(x, y, . . .)
   })
})

###########################################################
#### corgen function
corgen <- function (len, x, r, population = TRUE, epsilon = 0)
{
# remember the sign of the correlation for later
 rsign <- sign(r)
 if (rsign == 0)
   rsign <- 1
 r <- abs(r)

# need to either specify x-data or the desired vector length
 if (missing(x)) {
   if (missing(len)) {
    stop("Must specify x or len.\n")
   }
   else {
    # if x wasn't given, sample it from a normal distribution
    x <- scale(rnorm(len))
    x.orig <- x
   }
}
else {
# can either draw from a population or simulate an exact
# correlation (within epsilon), but not both
 if (population == FALSE) {
   # if x is given, population is set to TRUE
   # but an exact correlation is still generated
   warning("If x is specified population is ignored.\n")
   population <- TRUE
 }
```

```
 len <- length(x)
 x.orig <- x
 x <- scale(x)
}
if (epsilon != 0) {
 if (population == FALSE) {
   warning("If epsilon is specified population is ignored.\n")
   population <- TRUE
 }
}


## Here's where the real work starts
 # First, draw y from a normal distribution
 y <- scale(rnorm(len))
 if (!population) {
   # if exact correlations are desired, use princomp to
   # create uncorrelated data
   # UNLESS x is given-princomp would trash the
   # specified x values
   xy <- princomp(cbind(x, y))$scores
   x <- xy[, 1]
   x.orig <- x
   y <- xy[, 2]
 }


# create a new y based on x and the desired correlation
a <- r/sqrt(1 - r^2)
y <- x * a + y

if (epsilon > 0) {
 # check to see if cor(x, y) meets the given tolerances
 # this is kludgy, but works
 while (abs(cor(x, y) - r) > epsilon) {
   # if not, generate a new y
   y <- scale(rnorm(len))
   if (!population) {
    xy <- princomp(cbind(x, y))$scores
    x <- xy[, 1]
    x.orig <- x
    y <- xy[, 2]
  }
   a <- r/sqrt(1 - r^2)
```

```
    y <- x * a + y
  }
}

# return x and y with the correct sign of r restored
list(x = x.orig, y = y * rsign)
}
```

REFERENCES

Akaike, H. (1987). Factor analysis and the AIC. *Psychometrica, 52*, 317–332.

Beretvas, S. N., & Kamata, A. (2005). The multilevel measurement model: Introduction to the special issue. *Journal of Applied Measurement, 6*, 247–254.

Boston, M. F., Hale, J., Kliegl, R., Patil, U., & Vasishth, S. (in press). Parsing costs as predictors of reading difficulty: An evaluation using the Potsdam Sentence Corpus. *Journal of Eye Movement Research*.

Cohen, J. (1994). The Earth is round (*p* < .05). *American Psychologist, 49*, 997–1003.

Davis, G. A., & Rimm, S. B. (2004). *Education of the gifted and talented* (5th ed.). Boston: Allyn & Bacon.

Gelman, A., & Hill, J. (2007). *Data analysis using regression and multilevel/hierarchical models*. New York: Cambridge University Press.

Goldstein, H. (1995). *Multilevel statistical models*. London: Edward Arnold.

Goldstein, H., Rasbash, J., Plewis, I., Draper, D., Browne, W., Yang, M., et al. (1998). *A user's guide to MlwiN*. London: Multilevel Models Project, Institute of Education, University of London.

Hedeker, D., & Gibbons, R. D. (2006). *Longitudinal data analysis*. Hoboken, NJ: Wiley.

Hox, J. J. (2002). *Multilevel analysis: Techniques and applications*. Mahwah, NJ: Erlbaum.

Raudenbush, S. W., & Bryk, A. S. (2002). *Hierarchical linear models: Applications and data analysis methods* (2nd ed.). Thousand Oaks, CA: Sage.

Robinson, W. S. (1950). Ecological correlations and the behavior of individuals. *Sociological Review, 15*, 351–357.

Schmidt, F. (1996). Statistical significance testing and cumulative knowledge in psychology: Implications for the training of researchers. *Psychological Methods, 1*, 115–129.

Schwarz, G. (1978). Estimating the dimension of a model. *Annals of Statistics, 6*, 461–464.

Skrondal, A., & Rabe-Hesketh, S. (2004). *Generalized latent variable modeling: Multilevel, longitudinal, and structural models*. Boca Raton, FL: Chapman and Hall/CRC.

Thompson, B. (1996). AERA editorial policies regarding statistical significance testing: Three suggested reforms. *Educational Researcher, 25*, 26–30.

Thompson, B. (2002). What future quantitative social science research could look like: Confidence intervals for effect sizes. *Educational Researcher, 31*(3), 24–31.

9

CONTEMPORARY METHODS FOR HANDLING MISSING DATA IN OBSERVATIONAL STUDIES OF GIFTEDNESS

JASON E. KING AND BRIAN G. DATES

Bias attributable to missing data conditions is often ignored by applied researchers. In response, journal editors (e.g., von Elm et al., 2007) and governing bodies (e.g., Wilkinson & APA Task Force, 1999) are increasingly calling for missing data analysis as routine assessment. The term *missing data* is traditionally used in reference to the condition of a study participant missing one or more, but not all, survey responses, test items, or other data points. In addition, methods to control the bias resulting from nonequivalent comparison groups could be viewed as a "missing data" scenario (Dates & King, 2009), though in this chapter we emphasize the former.

Consideration of the effects of missing data is critically needed in studies of giftedness. Frequent causes of missing data include study dropouts in longitudinal studies of children through adolescence and adulthood and incomplete data records due to oversight on the part of respondents, refusal to answer certain questions, or a host of other reasons. Missing values can sometimes be safely ignored if observed for only a very small percentage of items. Yet even a few omitted responses can significantly bias results if the data are missing systematically. For example, consider a hypothetical study of 10,000 children in which 5% are categorized as gifted. Observing a modest missing data rate of 2% may nonetheless be of concern should the absent values all fall within the gifted population (i.e., 40% of gifted children would have missing data). In such an instance, ignoring missing values or applying ineffective adjustments may drastically alter study outcomes and lead to invalid conclusions. It is therefore imperative that giftedness researchers carefully examine the consequences of even modest amounts of missing data and familiarize themselves with best practices for handling these conditions.

This chapter proceeds by briefly describing a typology for categorizing missing data. We then provide a review of the strengths and weaknesses of a number of traditional and contemporary methodologies for handling missing data, followed by discussion and detailed application of a new, "hybrid" approach that is capable of adjusting for both item-level missing data and missing cases in a nonequivalent groups design, a scenario frequently faced by the applied researcher.

ILLUSTRATIVE DATA

All illustrations in this chapter are from an unpublished study investigating the effects of infusing humanities-based metaphors (art, music, poetry) into a gifted enrichment education program in a suburban school district. In reviewing the literature, White, Fletcher-Campbell, and Ridley (2003) found a relative dearth of empirical studies of gifted and talented educational programming. Further, the few educational programs in existence tended to reflect the subjective experiences and curricular preferences of giftedness experts instead of incorporating educational components that have been empirically demonstrated to be effective. White et al. cautioned that modeling gifted programs solely on the ideas of those persons deemed influential in gifted education may result in self-perpetuation and stagnation in the field.

In view of this identified gap, a study was designed that had as its goals to (a) identify evidence-based effective curriculum, (b) investigate the rationale for curricular effectiveness, (c) explore the conditions under which effective curriculum is implemented, and (d) explore the transferability of the conditions for effectiveness. An intermediate (county) school district in Detroit, Michigan, serving as a resource for the school systems developed a gifted curriculum that provided learning experiences in the study and production of art, music, and poetry. To examine the effects of the curriculum on the critical thinking skills of fifth graders, the district randomly chose three gifted classrooms to receive the new curriculum, with the remaining gifted classrooms serving as a comparison group. There were a total of 162 children in the study; 41 received the humanities-based enrichment, and 121 did not.

Critical thinking skills were assessed using the California Critical Thinking Disposition Inventory (CCTDI; Facione, Facione, & Giancarlo, 1996).

The CCTDI consists of 75 items measured on a 6-point Likert-type scale tapping seven critical thinking constructs—Analyticity, Self-confidence, Inquisitiveness, Maturity, Open-mindedness, Systematicity, and Truth-seeking. The sample data yielded a Cronbach's alpha of 0.88 and scale reliabilities ranging from 0.76 to 0.83. Only the composite scores representing the combined constructs were used in the present analyses. Also collected were demographic measures such as age, gender, highest grade level completed by either parent, annual household income, and results of an inventory assessing the availability of art, music, and reading materials in the home (i.e., home stimulation). Although the data were initially complete, with no item-level missing data, missing data conditions were simulated as described below. In addition, the nonrandom assignment of the study arms raised the potential for nonequivalent comparison groups, which is useful in illustrating the hybrid approach that simultaneously corrects for multiple sources of bias.

CAUSES OF MISSING DATA

Data may be missing for a number of reasons, such as requirements related to the study design (e.g., substantial time investment required of participants in longitudinal designs), nature of the data requested (e.g., personal information, private opinions), or procedural mistakes (e.g., unintentional skipping of items). Little and Rubin (1987) offered a typology for categorizing missing data that consists of three classes: data missing completely at random (MCAR), data missing at random (MAR), and data missing not at random (MNAR). These categories are somewhat difficult to grasp and, as such, will not be presented in detail.

In short, a MCAR condition is one in which data are missing due entirely to random processes, such as loss of a questionnaire, sloppy data entry, or an illness preventing a respondent from completing an assessment. One approach to assessing whether the data are MCAR is to divide the participants into two groups—those with and without missing data—and conduct separate variance t tests on all variables in the data set. If there are no statistically significant differences, the data are presumed to be MCAR. A limitation to this approach is the increased Type I error rate arising from the application of multiple t tests. A preferred alternative is to apply Little's MCAR test (Little, 1988), which is an omnibus test that simultaneously compares missing data patterns across all variables. As of this writing, the test is available in SPSS 16.0 in the Missing Value Analysis add-on module. A MAR condition is one in which the reason for scores missing on a given variable can be completely explained by the relationship(s) between the missing scores and other variable(s) in the model. Finally, when data are missing due to the values of the absent scores, the condition is said to be MNAR. The reader is urged to consult Little and Rubin (1987) on these concepts due to the frequency with which they are referenced in the literature. This chapter presents procedures applicable only to MCAR and MAR conditions.

ADJUSTING FOR MISSING DATA CONDITIONS

A large number of approaches have been advanced to adjust for values absent from a variable or item. Several of the more popular traditional approaches are described next, followed by a discussion of better alternatives.

The sample data set was modified for purposes of illustrating each of these procedures. First, we conducted a multiple linear regression on the complete data set using critical thinking as the dependent variable and treatment group, gender, age, highest grade level achievement of either parent, annual household income, and inventory of home stimulation as predictors. Next, critical thinking scores were deleted based on values of grade level to simulate a missing at random condition. This data set was used to calculate treatment effects for the missing data procedures described below (see Table 9.1). Results from the complete case analysis serve as an illustrative baseline against which to compare regression results for each missing data procedure.

Listwise Deletion

A common way to handle missing data is to apply *listwise deletion*, also known as *complete case analysis*. This approach, which is often the default setting in statistical software packages, consists of eliminating from the analysis

TABLE 9.1
Multiple Linear Regression Results for Item-Level Missing
Data Procedures Applied to the Sample Data Set

Procedure	B	SE	β	r_s
Listwise deletion	11.144	2.500	.362	.928
Pairwise deletion	11.419	2.502	.374	.905
Mean substitution	9.936	2.212	.348	.905
Multiple imputation	10.477	2.373	.342	.941
Complete data set	10.371	2.359	.341	.954

Note. r_s structure coefficient. The model was generated by regressing critical thinking on treatment group, gender, age, highest grade level of a parent, annual household income, and home stimulation. The missing data procedures were applied to the sample data set after deleting critical thinking scores based on grade level to simulate a missing at random condition. Results for the complete data set are included for comparison. For illustrative purposes, only regression estimates for the treatment variable are presented here.

any case having missing data on any variable. If five participants are each missing one value on one predictor in a regression analysis, all five participants would be deleted from the entire analysis. This excessive corrective has a tendency to decimate a data set that is sprinkled with missing values. If a mere 3% of responses are absent from each of 10 variables, the resulting loss of cases could total 30% depending on how the missing values are distributed across the variables. A commonly used rule of thumb is that listwise deletion should be avoided if more than 5% of the total cases are removed. Although an appealing approach due to its simplicity, complete case deletion can strongly impact available sample size and reduce statistical power, particularly when the number of deleted cases is large relative to total sample size. In addition, this approach leads to unbiased parameter estimates only if the missing completely at random assumption holds (Little & Rubin, 1987). The first line of Table 9.1 presents regression results from analyzing the data using listwise deletion. The regression coefficient for the treatment group has increased over that obtained for the complete data condition.

Pairwise Deletion

Another popular approach that also assumes MCAR data is *pairwise deletion*, also known as *available case analysis*. In contrast to listwise deletion, under this approach all existing scores for a case are included in the analysis, even if the case is missing data on a subset of variables. Although fewer data points are ignored under pairwise deletion, this procedure results in use of varying subsets of cases when calculating statistics within a single analysis. For example, if a participant reports her age, gender, and income but is missing highest grade level of parents, a regression analysis involving the four predictors would include her age, gender, and income data in estimating beta weights. However, the sample size used to estimate the beta weight for the grade level predictor would contain one fewer observations. This inequality in sample sizes can be particularly problematic in analyses that generate an intercorrelation matrix because the unequal *ns* often lead to a nonpositive definite matrix (i.e., a covariance correlation matrix on which a mathematical operation called *inversion* cannot be performed, which may mean that statistical analysis cannot be conducted). When total sample size is small or the number of cases with missing data is large, pairwise deletion is preferred over listwise deletion, but both deletion approaches are generally inferior to contemporary alternatives. The second line of Table 9.1 displays regression results when applying pairwise deletion. The estimated beta weight is even more biased than that observed under listwise deletion.

Mean and Regression Substitution

A second class of procedures substitutes values for the missing data points rather than deleting cases. *Mean substitution* (or median substitution, if the data are nonnormal) has traditionally been a popular method for imputing (substituting) missing values. Yet significant difficulties with the approach, perhaps best outlined by Cohen, Cohen, West, and Aiken (2003), have led to appreciably decreased use in recent years. The method consists of substituting the mean of the variable for any case having missing data on that variable. Increasing the representation of the mean in the data set may cause a regression to the mean effect, reduction in standard error, and reduced or elevated correlations (depending on the pattern of missing data). A modification of this approach consists of imputing the mean of a subgroup, rather than the grand mean. If an 8-year-old Caucasian student is missing data on the family income variable, the mean of all 8-year-old Caucasian students would be imputed in place of the missing value. Although this modification of mean substitution is more sensible, we do not recommend the procedure because no new data are introduced during the calculation. The third line of results in Table 9.1 was obtained by substituting the mean of critical thinking scores for all missing values. In contrast to the listwise and casewise deletion results, the regression coefficient now underestimates the coefficient obtained when analyzing the complete data set.

In *regression substitution*, a linear regression equation based on cases with complete data is used to predict missing data. Although this improves upon mean substitution to the extent that the imputed data are conditional on other variables measured for the individual, the problem of a reduced standard error persists. Additionally, all cases having identical values on the predictor variable(s) will be assigned the same imputed values.

Hot and Cold Deck Imputation

Hot deck imputation, introduced more than 50 years ago by the U.S. Census Bureau (Scheuren, 2005), involves substituting the value of a case drawn randomly from the current data set. The name references the "hot," or current, batch of computer punch cards, which were being used at the time to store data. Typically, selection is made from among participants sharing similar covariate scores. As with the other substitution methods, hot deck imputation tends to reduce variance and cause regression to the mean effects because it adds values into the data set that have already contributed to the original mean and standard error. This approach is not feasible if sample size is limited or if a sizable percentage of values are missing in the data set.

Unpredictable biases may be introduced by the substitution methods described above if the data are not MCAR. The next approach avoids this pitfall: *Cold deck imputation* consists of randomly drawing a substitute value from an external data set. Cross-validation studies offer the opportunity to easily incorporate this simple imputation approach while also assessing result replicability. Cross-validation consists of withholding from the initial analyses a portion of the sample data, which are then later analyzed using the derived model for purposes of assessing the replicability of study results (Thompson, 1994). Missing data points can be replaced by randomly selecting values from the cross-validation sample (i.e., the cold deck). Combining cold deck imputation with cross-validation provides a reasonable imputation approach while also strengthening the ability to generalize study conclusions. In our opinion, this tactic compares favorably to the more complex approaches described next.

Expectation Maximization

Newer approaches for handling missing data often incorporate *maximum likelihood* or *multiple imputation* (MI) algorithms. A number of variations have been suggested (for a readable introduction, see Peng, Harwell, Liou, & Ehman, 2006), each of which typically requires that the missing data be MAR or MCAR. Dempster, Laird, and Rubin (1977) developed the *expectation maximization* (EM) approach. First, model parameters are estimated based on a combination of the sample data with a theoretical model. After imputing missing values, the parameters are reestimated. This process continues in an iterative fashion until the parameter estimates change negligibly from one iteration to the next. Limitations attendant to EM include the requirement of a large sample size and the dependence of the imputed data estimates on the theoretical model selected. Although the EM parameter estimates are interpretable, statistical significance tests and confidence intervals are invalid due to imprecise estimation of standard errors. An effective alternative is to use the estimates derived from EM as starting values in a multiple imputation strategy, which is described next.

Multiple Imputation

Little and Rubin (1987; see also Allison, 2001, and Schafer, 1999a) defined *multiple imputation* as consisting of three steps. First, a model is specified for the hypothesized variable relationships, and multiple sets of missing data replacements are imputed via Monte Carlo techniques. Rubin (1987) advised setting the number of imputations, m, to between 2 and 10. Next, the m imputed data sets are analyzed individually to obtain a set of m parameter estimates (e.g., setting m to 5 in a linear regression model would yield five estimates of each predictor's beta weight). The estimated parameters are then combined to form confidence intervals. A unique advantage of MI over other options is that the variance of the replicated parameter estimates provides information on the statistical uncertainty of the estimates, making it highly efficient even for small samples. The fourth line in Table 9.1 presents output from the sample data after applying a multiple imputation approach with m set to 5. Results point to more accurate reproduction of the unstandardized and standardized regression weights, standard error, and structure coefficients obtained for the full data set.

Approximate Bayesian Bootstrap

The *approximate Bayesian bootstrap* combines multiple imputation with propensity scoring, which will be briefly described before returning to the approximate Bayesian bootstrap. Although often poorly implemented (Stürmer et al., 2006), propensity scoring methodologies are typically employed to address group inequality (e.g., in a comparative study in which neither group was randomly assigned). The general process consists of replacing all covariates on which the two groups differ by a single variable that is a function of those covariates, and then using the derived scores in a separate analysis to estimate treatment effects (Rosenbaum & Rubin, 1983). Two models are thereby estimated: a propensity score model and an outcomes model. Achieving equivalence on the propensity scores often eliminates group differences. The assumption is that individuals in the treatment and comparison groups having identical propensity scores also have the same probability of falling into the treatment group and so can be compared as if randomly assigned to each group. As Luellen, Shadish, and Clark (2005) explained, "To oversimplify, the idea is that people who have the same propensity score but who choose to be in differential experimental conditions are nonetheless comparable because the distribution of their covariates are in balance" (p. 532). Of course, this holds only to the extent that the modeled covariates equalize the groups.

Step 1: Generate Propensity Scores

A first step is to generate, using logistic regression, an effective propensity score model that predicts membership in treatment group by a set of covariates. The resultant propensity score, $\hat{\pi}$, is the probability that an individual falls into the treatment group given his or her scores on the measured covariates. The goal in selecting covariates is to include in the model indicators for all measures on which the groups may be expected to differ. Neglecting to include all such covariates will cause the study groups to remain nonequivalent, thus limiting the effectiveness of the propensity scoring adjustment.

There is some disagreement as to the type of covariates that should be targeted for inclusion. Many researchers advocate including only those variables for which statistically significant differences are observed in predicting group membership. Rosenbaum (2002) cautioned that such a rigid approach does not consider the effects of nonsignificant covariates, which may also be necessary to obtain group equivalence, and treats covariates in isolation even though the statistical adjustments consider them collectively. Recent simulations by Brookhart et al. (2006) suggest including any covariate thought to be related to the outcome, even if unrelated to the treatment variable. However, Austin (2006) noted that increasing the number of covariates may reduce the degree of propensity score matching while not improving balance. He recommended a studied approach informed by knowledge of previous research and theorized variable relationships. Automated variable selection algorithms such as stepwise logistic regression may not be effective for this purpose because they ignore the cumulative effect of variable combinations (Huberty, 1989; Thompson, 2001). Perhaps of greater value is to obtain input from content experts who are familiar with the variables that would be expected to affect treatment allocation.

It is important to determine whether a preliminary set of covariates achieves balance between the treatment and comparison groups on the propensity scores. This necessitates comparing the groups on each covariate both at baseline and again in relation to the propensity scores. To assess baseline differences, chi-square and *t* tests can be used to model differences between study groups on each covariate. An approach offered by Rosenbaum and Rubin (1984) consists of first rank ordering persons by log of the odds (logit) propensity score and evenly splitting the distribution into quintiles (i.e., five groups). Logits should be used for this purpose rather than the raw propensity scores because logits are normally distributed.

A series of analyses of variance (ANOVAs) are then applied in which each covariate is modeled as a dependent variable explained by the treatment variable, a variable corresponding to the propensity scores split into quintiles, and the treatment by quintile interaction. (Multinomial logistic regression can be used if categorical covariates are present.) Statistically significant effects for the treatment or interaction terms indicate imbalance and require modification of the logistic regression equation by (a) including transformed variables or interaction terms, (b) including additional covariates, or (c) dividing each stratum into finer strata and reassessing. It is imperative to perform this rebalancing before proceeding with estimation of treatment effects. While this may seem self-evident, Austin (2007) reviewed numerous studies and found that only two reported baseline balance and used correct statistical methods to assess for degree of imbalance.

Step 2: Apply Propensity Scores to Estimate the Treatment Effect

Once a satisfactory propensity score model has been achieved, the unbiased treatment effect can be estimated in the outcomes model. There are several classes of propensity scoring methods from which to choose in modeling the outcome: (a) covariance adjustment, (b) stratification, (c) matching, and (d) weighting by the propensity scores. See Dates and King (2009) for an explanation and illustration of each option.

Returning to the approximate Bayesian bootstrap missing data algorithm, propensity scoring is applied in this application not for the purpose of removing group nonequivalence but to obtain replacements for missing data points. Rubin (1987) and Rubin and Schenker (1986; see also Little & Hyonggin, 2003) first outlined this algorithm for use with item-level missing data that are MAR. In the initial step, each case having missing data on Y is dummy coded as 1 (data missing) or 0 (data present). Next, logistic regression is applied using the covariates to predict the dummy variable. Here, the $\hat{\pi}$s represent the probability or propensity of data being missing on Y. Participants are then sorted by logit propensity score and grouped into quintiles. Up to this point, the approach is identical to the propensity scoring approach outlined earlier except that the two groups being compared are not treatment and control groups but missing and present data groups. The methods now diverge.

In each of the quintiles, there are cases with missing data and x number of cases with available data. As in ordinary (percentile) bootstrapping, a random sample of x cases is drawn with replacement from the x available cases. For each case with missing data, one case from the bootstrap sample is randomly selected as a replacement. This is repeated until all missing values are replaced. In addition, the last step is repeated m times to produce m sets of complete data. Parameters are then estimated for each of the m complete data sets and combined to arrive at a final solution.

While this propensity scoring approach might be applied to any variable with missing data, Rosenbaum and Rubin (1983) recommended that it be used to impute values only on the criterion variable. This limitation was strongly supported by research conducted by Allison (2000) indicating that the approximate Bayesian bootstrap may yield biased results when replacing missing data on covariates because it does not take into account the relationships among the covariates.

Software applications for the newer methods are scarce (for a recent review, see Horton & Kleinman, 2007). SOLAS 3.0 (Statistical Solutions, Inc., 2001) is a popular statistical software option for accessing an approximate Bayesian bootstrap algorithm. SAS's PROC MI procedure can be used to perform multiple imputation, while the SPSS Missing Value Analysis module (SPSS, 1997) allows for EM estimation. Schafer (1999b) developed free software (NORM 2.03) that produces EM estimates of means, variances, and standard errors and computes data sets using MI for continuous data fitting a normal distribution. In addition, for multiple imputation, a Microsoft Excel spreadsheet and SPSS syntax are available from the second author upon request (bdates@swsol.org).

Adjusting for Missing Data and Nonequivalent Groups Simultaneously

A given data set may consist of nonequivalent groups yet may also have incomplete responses on items or variables. Propensity scoring has traditionally assumed complete item data. In this section, we describe a recent extension of propensity scoring that incorporates adjustments for both sources of bias in estimating treatment effects. In addition, this approach can be used when data are missing on the covariates, unlike the approximate Bayesian bootstrap.

D'Agostino, Lang, Walkup, Morgan, and Karter (2002) demonstrated that in the presence of missing data with strongly ignorable treatment assignment, a hybrid propensity scoring model can be applied that adjusts for covariance imbalance and missing item-level data. This relatively simple approach consists of adding missing data indicators to the usual propensity score model. For continuous covariates, one dummy-coded variable is defined for each covariate with missing data. For categorical covariates, an extra category representing missing data is added to the coded values. The dummy variables are then combined with the continuous covariates and the recoded categorical covariates in a model that estimates the propensity scores. The remaining steps in propensity scoring continue as usual (e.g., a matching approach could be applied to match treatment and control participants on the obtained propensity scores, followed by estimation of the treatment effect within the outcome model).

Strengths of this procedure include both its simplicity and the inclusion of all study participants in the analysis, even those with missing data on covariates. Interactions between covariates in producing missing data may also be controlled for under this approach. Although generally effective in estimating parameters, D'Agostino et al. (2002) warned that biased results may emerge under some conditions (see Hill, 2004, for an investigation into the relative efficacies of combining propensity score matching with other missing data approaches).

AN ILLUSTRATION

The solution offered by D'Agostino and colleagues (2002) is straightforward and lends itself to the resources most frequently available to the giftedness researcher working in an applied setting. Its ability to adjust for both sources of bias simultaneously makes it broadly applicable. This section illustrates the methodology as applied to our sample data set. The goal is to determine if students in the enriched giftedness classrooms achieved higher critical thinking scores. Recall that because students were not randomly assigned to classrooms, the study groups may be nonequivalent. Variables that may covary with group membership include age, gender, highest grade level completed by a parent, annual household income, and results of an inventory of home stimulation. To simulate item-level missing data that are MCAR, values were deleted at random from the grade level and income covariates.

Step 1: Investigate the Reason for Missingness

Prior to applying any of the missing data algorithms, one must first attempt to determine the mechanism of missingness. Assuming that we do not know the reason for missing values, Little's test can be applied to test the MCAR hypothesis using the SPSS Missing Value Analysis add-on module. If the researcher does not have access to the module, separate variance t tests can be applied as follows. First, a dummy variable is created for each covariate with missing data. We dummy coded grade level and income, arbitrarily assigning values of 0 or 1 to a case if data were missing or not, respectively. An example of coding for the income variable is presented in Table 9.2. Each covariate is then paired one by one with each dummy variable in a separate variance t test. This can be accomplished in the SPSS Base System by requesting an independent t test and interpreting the values in the "equal variances not assumed" column (chi-square analyses can be applied to categorical covariates). Results for the sample data are summarized in Tables 9.3 and 9.4. If the missingness represented by the dummy variable is related to any variable in the analysis, MCAR should be rejected. With the exception of age, no covariates were significantly related to the missing data in grade level or

TABLE 9.2
Dummy Coding to Indicate Presence or Absence of Income Data
(Original and Recoded Data)

Case number	Study group	Age	Gender	Income	IncNoMis[a]
		Original data			
1	1	10	1	105,000	1
2	1	11	2		0
3	0	12	2	60,000	1
4	1	11	1	80,000	1
5	0	11	1		0
		Recoded data			
1	1	10	1	105,000	1
2	1	11	2	0	0
3	0	12	2	60,000	1
4	1	11	1	80,000	1
5	0	11	1	0	0

[a]IncNoMis is a dummy-coded variable indicating presence (1) or absence (0) of income data.

TABLE 9.3
Separate Variance *t* Tests to Assess MCAR Assumption
for Continuously Scaled Variables

Model	*t*	*df*	*p*	Mean difference	*SE* difference
Grade with:					
Age	−2.11	160	.042	−0.22	0.10
Home stimulation	0.92	160	.360	0.35	0.38
CCTDI	1.27	160	.205	4.75	3.73
Income	0.99	132	.326	3,108.67	3,150.68
Income with:					
Age	0.34	160	.733	0.04	0.10
Home stimulation	0.07	160	.948	0.03	0.37
CCTDI	−1.20	160	.232	4.75	4.37
Grade	−1.68	135	.095	−1.03	0.62

Note. CCTDI = California Critical Thinking Disposition Inventory (Facione, Facione, & Giancarlo, 1996); MCAR = missing completely at random. Grade and income, respectively, served as the dependent variable in each set of analyses.

income. Keep in mind that these statistical tests are subject to the usual limitations (e.g., adequate power is required, effect sizes should be consulted, the probability of making a Type I error increases with the number of tests run). Because we know that the mechanism of missingness underlying the data is MCAR, we will not further examine the relationship between age and grade level, assuming that the modest *p* value of .042 arose from random error. However, typically one would have concluded that the missingness mechanism is either MAR, which allows for continuing with the current propensity score analysis, or MNAR, which requires more advanced solutions.

Step 2: Generate Propensity Scores

If the evidence supports the MCAR or MAR assumptions, the process of fitting a propensity score model can begin. First, however, missing values should be recoded so that no cases are deleted from the analysis. As illustrated in Table 9.2, a value of 0 was imputed to the income variable for each case having missing data.

TABLE 9.4
Chi-Square Tests of Gender With Grade and
Income to Assess MCAR Assumption

Model	χ^2	*df*	*p*
Gender with grade	2.15	1	0.142
Gender with income	2.10	1	0.148

Note. MCAR = missing completely at random.

Propensity scores were generated by saving predicted scores from a logistic regression in which treatment group membership was regressed on the five covariates and the two dummy variables (temporarily ignoring the outcome variable). A Compute statement in SPSS was applied to calculate the logit of the propensity scores. For purposes of comparing initial and subsequent results, we gathered a baseline assessment of group imbalance on the covariates by calculating a series of independent t tests for each covariate in relation to the treatment group variable and a t test of the logit propensity scores. The latter test assesses whether baseline differences exist on the latent (propensity score) variable, which incorporates variance contributions from all of the covariates. Results are presented in Table 9.5 under the heading Baseline. Although the groups did not differ significantly on the individual covariates, the combination of the covariates, as represented by the logit propensity score, showed statistically significant differences and a moderate effect size. This illustrates how covariates may combine in unexpected ways to cause group disparities.

It is possible that the selected propensity score model could be improved upon through the inclusion of transformed covariates or interaction effects. One way to check the balance of study groups on the propensity scores is to (a) sort cases within each study group by logit propensity score and divide the scores into quintiles, then (b) regress each covariate on the treatment indicator, the quintile variable, and the interaction of treatment and quintile using ANOVA. Illustrative output for one of the covariates is displayed in Figure 9.1. Statistically significant treatment or interaction effects suggest nonequivalence. None were observed, so we conclude that the current form of the propensity score model effectively removes group differences with no need to include transformations.

The propensity scores can now be matched to derive two data sets having equivalency on the covariates. Using a nearest-neighbor matching algorithm, each of the 41 treatment group members was matched to a comparison group member. This was facilitated by a SPSS macro developed by Painter (n.d.). To determine whether the matching approach was effective at removing group differences, an additional set of independent t tests were calculated for the matched data set (although dependent t tests would typically be preferred when analyzing matched data, here the resultant increase in statistical power would make pre-to-post comparisons incommensurate.) Because no effects, including that associated with the propensity score, were statistically significant or large (see Table 9.5 under Matched Propensity Scores), we determined that the covariates are no longer related to treatment condition. Graphic comparisons confirm that group equivalence has been achieved (see Figures 9.2 and 9.3).

TABLE 9.5
Study Group Comparisons on Covariates and Logits With and Without Propensity Score Matching

Variable	Baseline				Matched propensity scores			
	t	df	p	SDIFF%	t	df	p	SDIFF%
Age	−1.214	160	.226	−21.978	−0.721	80	.472	−15.920
Grade	−1.192	160	.235	−23.136	−0.336	80	.737	−7.423
Income	1.103	160	.272	18.827	−0.036	80	.971	−0.800
Home stimulation	0.430	160	.668	7.776	0.124	80	.901	2.740
Logit propensity score	−2.303	160	.023	−41.618	0.005	80	.996	0.118
	χ^2	df	p		χ^2	df	p	
Gender	2.098	1	.148		.467	1	.494	

Note. The standardized mean difference in percent (SDIFF%) is the mean difference expressed as a percentage of the average standard deviation: $100(\bar{X}_1 - \bar{X}_2)/[(s_1^2 + s_1^2)/2]^{1/2}$.

Source	Type III Sum of Squares	df	Mean Square	F	Sig.	Partial Eta Squared
Corrected Model	54.397(a)	9	6.044	2.228	.030	.218
Intercept	2286.800	1	2286.800	842.962	.000	.921
Treatment	.002	1	.002	.001	.976	.000
Quintile	50.792	4	12.698	4.681	.002	.206
Treatment * Quintile	3.495	4	.874	.322	.862	.018
Error	195.323	72	2.713			
Total	3819.000	82				
Corrected Total	249.720	81				

R Squared = .218 (Adjusted R Squared = .120)

Figure 9.1. SPSS output of analysis of variance assessing balance on home stimulation after propensity score matching.

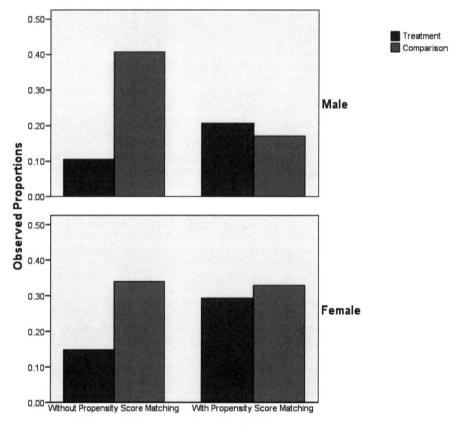

Figure 9.2. Frequency distributions of gender by study group with and without propensity score matching.

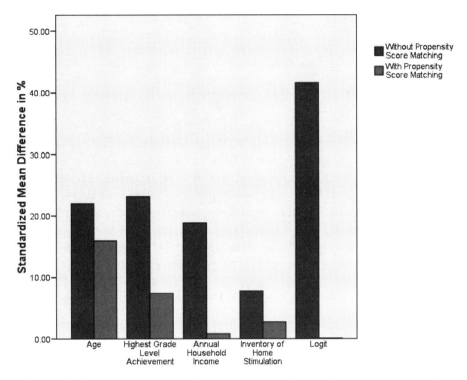

Figure 9.3. Standardized mean difference in percent for continuous covariates with and without propensity score matching.

Step 3: Apply Propensity Scores to Estimate the Treatment Effect

Our ultimate interest lies in comparing critical thinking scores, rather than propensity scores, between study groups. A dependent *t* test can be applied to quantify mean differences in CCTDI scores between the matched samples from the treatment and comparison groups. Results depicted in Figure 9.4 allow us to conclude that the group having received the enriched

		Paired Differences							
		Mean	Std. Deviation	Std. Error Mean	95% Confidence Interval of the Difference		t	df	Sig. (2-tailed)
					Lower	Upper			
Pair 1	Treatment and Control	29.659	20.3478	3.178	23.236	36.081	9.333	40	.000

Figure 9.4. SPSS output of dependent *t* test comparing matched samples on critical thinking outcome.

curriculum achieved higher critical thinking scores than the comparison group after correcting for initial differences on measured covariates.

CONCLUSION

The intent of this chapter has been to present a set of tools for handling the missing data conditions faced by researchers studying gifted populations. These conditions have traditionally been handled using listwise deletion, pairwise deletion, or mean imputation. We encourage the use of newer, more effective techniques such as multiple imputation. The chapter also described and illustrated the use of a more general propensity scoring approach capable of adjusting for both missing data and nonequivalent group conditions simultaneously. Although some of the strategies described here are sophisticated and technically involved, their use is often necessary to avoid reaching faulty conclusions arising from inappropriate treatment of missing data. Happily, more user-friendly software is constantly being developed to facilitate the use of powerful methods for this purpose.

REFERENCES

Allison, P. D. (2000). Multiple imputation for missing data: A cautionary tale. *Sociological Methods and Research, 28,* 301–309.

Allison, P. D. (2001). *Missing data.* Thousand Oaks, CA: Sage.

Austin, P. D. (2006). A comparison of propensity score methods: A case study estimating the effectiveness of post-AMI statin use. *Statistics in Medicine, 25,* 2084–2106.

Austin, P. D. (2007). A critical appraisal of propensity-score matching in the medical literature between 1996 and 2003. *Statistics in Medicine, 26,* 258–277.

Brookhart, M. A., Schneeweiss, S., Rothman, K. J., Glynn, R. J., Avorn, J., & Stürmer, T. (2006). Variable selection for propensity score models. *American Journal of Epidemiology, 163,* 1149–1156.

Cohen, J., Cohen, P., West, S. G., & Aiken, L. S. (2003). *Applied multiple regression/correlation analysis for the behavioral sciences* (3rd ed.). Mahwah, NJ: Erlbaum.

D'Agostino, R., Lang, W., Walkup, M., Morgan, T., & Karter, A. (2002). Examining the impact of missing data on the propensity score estimation in determining the effectiveness of self-monitoring of blood glucose (SMBG). *Health Services and Outcomes Research Methodology, 2,* 291–315.

Dates, B. G., & King, J. E. (2009). *Contemporary methods for handling missing cases in observational studies of giftedness.* Unpublished manuscript.

Dempster, A. P., Laird, N. M., & Rubin, D. B. (1977). Maximum likelihood from incomplete data via the EM algorithm. *Journal of the Royal Statistical Society B, 39*, 1–38.

Facione, P. A., Facione, C. F., & Giancarlo, C. A. (1996). *The California Critical Thinking Disposition Inventory Test Manual*. Millbrae, CA: California Academic Press.

Hill, J. (2004). *Reducing bias in treatment effect estimation in observational studies suffering from missing data* (Columbia University Institute for Social and Economic Research and Policy Working Paper 04-01). New York: Columbia University.

Horton, N. J., & Kleinman, K. P. (2007). Much ado about nothing: A comparison of missing data methods and software to fit incomplete data regression models. *American Statistician, 61*, 79–90.

Huberty, C. J. (1989). Problems with stepwise methods—better alternatives. In B. Thompson (Ed.), *Advances in social science methodology* (Vol. 1, pp. 43–70). Greenwich, CT: JAI Press.

Little, R. (1988). A test of missing completely at random for multivariate data with missing values. *Journal of the American Statistical Association, 83*, 1198–1202.

Little, R., & Hyonggin, A. (2003). *Robust likelihood-based analysis of multivariate data with missing values* (University of Michigan Department of Biostatistics Working Paper Series No. 5). Ann Arbor, MI: University of Michigan.

Little, R., & Rubin, D. (1987). *Statistical analysis with missing data*. New York: Wiley.

Luellen, J., Shadish, W., & Clark, M. H. (2005). Propensity scores: An introduction and experimental test. *Evaluation Review, 29*, 530–558.

Painter, J. (n.d.) *SPSS propensity matching program description*. Chapel Hill, NC: Jordan Institute for Families, School of Social Work, University of North Carolina at Chapel Hill. Retrieved April 15, 2008, from http://sswnt5.sowo.unc.edu/VRC/Lectures/index.htm

Peng, C. Y., Harwell, M., Liou, S. M., & Ehman, L. H. (2006). Advances in missing data methods and implications for educational research. In S. S. Sawilowsky (Ed.), *Real data analysis* (pp. 31–78). New York: Information Age Publishing.

Rosenbaum, P. R. (2002). *Observational studies* (2nd ed.). New York: Springer-Verlag.

Rosenbaum, P. R., & Rubin, D. B. (1983). The central role of the propensity score in observational studies for causal effects. *Biometrika, 70*, 41–55.

Rosenbaum, P. R., & Rubin, D. B. (1984). Reducing bias in observational studies using subclassification on the propensity score. *Journal of the American Statistical Society, 79*, 516–524.

Rubin, D. B. (1987). *Multiple imputation for nonresponse in surveys*. New York: Wiley.

Rubin, D. B., & Schenker, N. (1986). Multiple imputation for interval estimation from simple random samples with ignorable nonresponse. *Journal of the American Statistical Association, 81*, 366–374.

Schafer, J. L. (1999a). Multiple imputation: A primer. *Statistical Methods in Medical Research, 8*, 3–15.

Schafer, J. L. (1999b). *NORM: Multiple imputation of incomplete multivariate data under a normal model* [Computer software]. Retrieved August 11, 2009, from www.stat.psu.edu/~jls/misoftwa.html

Scheuren, F. (2005). Multiple imputation: How it began and how it continues. *American Statistician, 59,* 315–319.

SPSS. (1997). *SPSS missing value analysis 7.5* [Computer software]. Chicago: Author.

Statistical Solutions. (2001). *SOLAS for missing value analysis 3.0* [Computer software]. Saugus, MA: Author.

Stürmer, T., Joshi, M., Glynn, R. J., Avorn, J., Rothman, K. J., & Schneeweiss, S. (2006). A review of the application of propensity score methods yielded increasing use, advantages in specific settings, but not substantially different estimates compared with conventional multivariable methods. *Journal of Clinical Epidemiology, 59,* 443–447.

Thompson, B. (1994). The pivotal role of replication in psychological research: Empirically evaluating the replicability of sample results. *Journal of Personality, 62,* 157–176.

Thompson, B. (2001). Significance, effect sizes, stepwise methods, and other issues: Strong arguments move the field. *Journal of Experimental Education, 70,* 80–93.

von Elm, E., Altman, D. G., Egger, M., Pocock, S. J., Gotzsche, P. C., Vandenbroucke, J. P., & STROBE Initiative. (2007). Strengthening the reporting of observational studies in epidemiology (STROBE) statement: Guidelines for reporting observational studies. *British Medical Journal, 335,* 806–808.

White, K., Fletcher-Campbell, F., & Ridley, K. (2003). *What works for gifted and talented pupils: A review of recent research* (LGA Research Rep. 51). Slough, Berkshire, England: National Foundation for Education Research.

Wilkinson, L., & APA Task Force on Statistical Inference. (1999). Statistical methods in psychology journals: Guidelines and explanations. *American Psychologist, 54,* 594–604.

III

REFLECTIONS FROM
LEADERS IN THE FIELD

10

TWO PERSPECTIVES ON STATISTICS IN GIFTED EDUCATION

PAULA OLSZEWSKI-KUBILIUS

Given my interest in statistics and design, I was pleased to be able to read the chapters in Parts 1 and 2 of this book and think about applying the concepts within them to my own work. I am going to respond to the earlier chapters from two different perspectives—as a former editor of two of the major journals in the field of gifted education and as a current reviewer for several others, and as a researcher in the field of gifted education.

FROM AN EDITOR'S PERSPECTIVE

I learned a great deal from these chapters and am grateful for the challenging opportunity to digest and reflect on them. Though I am no longer a journal editor, when I review articles, I will certainly do so with a more critical eye. Specifically, I will be looking to see that authors using rating scales and instruments to assess psychological and social variables specify instrument reliabilities for their study samples, or at least explicate how their sample compares to those used to generate reliability indices published in test construction manuals. I myself have been guilty of relying on reliability estimates published by instrument authors and believing that if these were good, it meant the "instrument was reliable" and a good one to use. I succumbed to the erroneous thinking that once good psychometric data were available on an instrument, I had no obligation or reason to assess it in my own research, except for my own interest—so I thought. However, I now see that this assessment is not only good methodology and best practice, so to speak, but can contribute to conceptual understandings of issues as well. If an instrument had very different reliabilities from those reported in a technical manual and if other issues such as reduced variability due to restriction in range are not at play, one is left questioning whether the construct being assessed is meaningful within the gifted population, or at least within the sample of gifted students under study.

Similarly, in response to my exposure to the chapters in this book, I will also look for researchers to check the factor structure of instruments they employ to determine whether the factors reported by the instrument developers are robust for gifted samples. That factor structures can vary within the gifted population is demonstrated by the following two research examples on social coping and self-perceptions.

First Example—Social Coping

The first example revolves around a series of studies that used the Social Coping Questionnaire (SCQ), originally developed by Swiatek (1995, 2001; Swiatek & Dorr, 1998). The SCQ was created to assess how gifted students deal with the social stigma attached to being identified as gifted. Through factor analysis, Swiatek and others have identified several coping strategies used by gifted children such as denying their giftedness to peers so as to fit in, engaging in lots of activities to develop and maintain a positive social persona beyond one of being smart, denying that there are negative social implications of being gifted, and using humor to gain peer acceptance. Swiatek has revised and reassessed the factor structure of the SCQ with various populations of gifted students and has published studies detailing these investigations of its psychometric qualities (see Swiatek, 1995, 2001; Swiatek & Dorr, 1998).

Other researchers have also used the instrument in their studies, and a few have assessed the factor structure specifically with their study samples (Chan, 2005; Rudasill, Foust, & Callahan, 2007). Rudasill et al. (2007), for example, examined the factor structure of the SCQ with several different samples of gifted students, and Chan examined it using a translated version of the SCQ with a sample of gifted Chinese students. The results across these various investigations suggested that there were six social coping strategies that were consistently found across the various samples and studies, but there were also differences in factor structure depending upon the age of the subjects, gender, and how giftedness was operationalized. The various samples used across the studies included students whose scores placed them in the top 1% of middle school students taking the ACT (American College Testing Program); high school students in honor or advanced placement (AP) classes; Chinese students nominated by their teachers as being intellectually gifted or having special talents; students selected to participate in a summer residential camp based on IQ scores, achievement tests scores, teacher recommendations, and essays; and students attending a special state-supported, residential high school for academically gifted students.

Rudasill et al. (2007) acknowledged that differences in factor structures are also likely due to differences in factor analytic techniques, such as the use of oblique versus orthogonal rotations of factors, decision rules for keeping or eliminating items from factors, and interpretation and labeling of factors. But the results across studies suggest that some coping strategies may function differently or may not be as salient for some groups of gifted students as for others. For example, Chan (2005) found that the strategy of discounting the importance of popularity with peers loaded under both of two general categories/types of coping strategies, one of which included strategies centered on diminishing how obvious the student's giftedness was to peers and the other of which included strategies centered on increasing different types of social interactions with peers. He theorized that this is because the younger Chinese students he used in his studies might view discounting popularity as a way of being more like their peers, whereas the older children used in other studies might view this same coping strategy as a way of distancing themselves from their peers. In other words, the same strategy has different meanings for different-age students. Developmental factors (e.g., how younger versus older adolescents view the importance of popularity among their friends and peers) and cultural factors (e.g., how Chinese students value popularity) may be interacting here to produce different factor structures.

Second Example—Self-Perceptions

Another great example of the utility of examining the factor structure of well-known and highly used instruments to determine their robustness with gifted students is found in a study by Worrell (1997). He tested the reliability of the factor structure of the Self-Perception Profile for Adolescents, developed by Harter (1985), with a group of 7th- through 11th-grade students who participated in a summer program for academically talented students on a university campus. This scale has often been used in studies with gifted students (I have used it myself) because it is multidimensional, it purports to measure several important areas of self-concept including social self-concept and scholastic self-concept, and its question format is especially appealing for children. Worrell examined the factor structure via exploratory factor analysis. As recommended by Henson (chap. 1, this volume), Worrell conducted a parallel analysis and found that among his sample of students, seven factors emerged, compared to eight identified by Harter, but none of his seven exactly replicated any of Harter's factors. Worrell concluded that four of Harter's original factors—scholastic competence, athletic competence, job competence, and behavioral conduct—were relatively robust, while the "items representing social acceptance, close friendship, physical appearance, and romantic appeal may simply be tapping the two broader domains of general attractiveness and peer support" (p. 1023). Worrell speculated that romantic appeal may not be a salient aspect of self-perceptions for the early adolescents that comprised his sample but could be for older adolescents.

Interestingly, Worrell initially involved 414 students in the study, the entire body of participants in the summer program, but due to missing data, which were deleted listwise, the sample whose data were analyzed consisted of only 248 students. As you might expect, given the broad age range in the sample (12 to 17 years), younger students were more likely to skip questions on the Self-Perception Profile for Adolescents (46%) compared with older students (34%). Missing data were more prevalent for items on certain subscales, including Job Competence and Romantic Appeal, compared to the other six subscales. As King and Dates (chap. 9, this volume) suggest, listwise deletion of missing data, often the only option open to researchers, can "decimate" a sample and reduced Worrell's by nearly half. Also, it appears that the missing data are not missing at random, given that job competence and romantic appeal are probably less salient as dimensions of one's self-concept for younger adolescents, the same group that more often skipped these items. One wonders if the factor structure that Worrell obtained, particularly his results for the Romantic Appeal subtest, was affected by the listwise deletion that resulted in the loss of more of the younger subjects for whom this construct is not particularly salient.

Other Examples and Applications

Checks on the factor structure with study samples are rare, and the findings of Rudasill et al. (2007) and Worrell (1997) suggest that such checks are necessary. There are other instruments that are used frequently in gifted research. The ACT and Stanford Achievement Test (SAT) are used to assess the abilities of middle school students who score at the ceiling on in-grade achievement tests with several hundred thousand students annually. Minor and Benbow (1996) compared the factor structure of the SAT-Math test for Talent Search students, seventh graders who qualified to participate in Talent Search programs but did not end up enrolling, and high-school-age students who typically take the test for college entrance. Minor and Benbow found similar factor structures but also indications that the younger students relied more on arithmetic reasoning to solve SAT-Math questions, as opposed to the older students, who relied on content knowledge of algebra. This finding lent credence to the contention that the SAT-Math serves more as an assessment of mathematics reasoning than mathematical achievement for the younger students.

The Harter (1985) Self-Perception Profile for Adolescents is also used frequently as a measure of self-concept in studies of gifted children. Very few studies in gifted education check factor structures, largely because of the difficulty of getting large enough samples to be able to do the analyses, although this would be possible in some cases.

I must admit that my views on null hypothesis significance testing (NHST) are forever changed. I recall learning about the relationships between sample size and power and about confidence intervals, but now I will cast a much more critical eye toward studies that rely solely on NHST. Especially important is the concept that much more helpful to researchers and educators than a mean or point estimate is an understanding of how much that point estimate can vary across different samples and the degree of precision with which the true difference can be estimated. It is likely that within giftedness research, typically small sample sizes will often result in large confidence intervals; nevertheless, it would be instructive to report CIs so that the reader understands the impreciseness of means and that they are only estimates of population parameters.

The authors of the chapters in this volume collectively urge researchers of giftedness to use more meta-analytic techniques. Practitioners and researchers in the gifted field often point to the meta-analyses done by Kulik and Kulik (1992) on grouping and acceleration as the most rigorous and probably widely used pieces of research to support gifted education practices. Rogers (2002) similarly conducted meta-analyses on a range of types of gifted programs, but overall, these are efforts are relatively rare in our field.

Chapter 5 of this volume, on reliability generalization methods, brought home the point that reliability estimates are dependent upon the variance within the scores on instruments one is using. This is a particularly prevalent problem for researchers of giftedness since we necessarily restrict our sample and thus, often, the range of scores on an instrument. Kieffer and his coauthors urge us to find instruments with sufficient ceiling to eliminate this problem. There is controversy over whether gifted children tend to have psychological profiles that go along with giftedness and distinguish them from nongifted children. Gifted children, operationalized typically as children with higher IQs and achievement, tend to score more positively on broad-scale measures of psychological functioning (Neihart, 1999) than groups of children with a wide range of intelligence and achievement scores. So high-achieving, high-ability children tend to have very positive psychological profiles. On the other hand, other groups of gifted children, particularly children with very high IQs, may not evidence such positive profiles. Clearly, then, restriction of range may be a problem depending on the sample under study, but this is rarely checked in research on giftedness, particularly with psychosocial measures. I suspect that restriction of range might be more of problem with psychosocial measures that involve a cognitive component—say, measures of social problem solving—than with instruments that measure constructs less dependent upon IQ. Nevertheless, this needs to be routinely checked.

Restriction of range is rarely taken seriously in attempts to measure achievement of gifted children, yet there is a huge body of research emanating from Talent Search programs (Lee, Matthews, & Olszewski-Kubilius, 2008) that off-level or above-grade-level testing is needed to adequately assess the intellectual or achievement growth of gifted children. Standardized achievement tests used on level will yield inherently unreliable scores for gifted children due to severe ceiling effects. It is relatively easy for researchers to use measures of achievement off level since most standardized achievement tests have different tests for different grade groups, and the tests designed for students several grades above the study sample can easily be obtained and employed.

I was happy to see the emphasis in chapters 3 and 4 of this volume on examining the results of tests of inference with an eye toward understanding the nature of effects rather than strictly in terms of their statistical significance. The idea of thinking meta-analytically and looking for the direction of effects across different samples or studies, taking into consideration the power of the study to detect small differences and valuing nonsignificant results, resonated with me. As an editor, I was lenient regarding the reporting of nonsignificant findings and small effect sizes and encouraged authors to include these in their thinking in order to obtain a broader picture of what was actually happening in their study sample. However, reviewers would often comment that nonsignificant effects need not be reported and even should not be interpreted. In a field that is relatively unsophisticated in terms of empirical research, latitude around reporting and interpreting NHST results is important to refining and developing models and new hypotheses and should be encouraged within reason, and as long as researchers look for patterns in a data set pointing to a particular hypothesis rather than reporting lots of isolated findings.

The field of gifted education, like many other fields, I suspect, is divided into camps of quantitative researchers and qualitative methodologists. Individual researchers tend to conduct one form of research rather exclusively. This is unfortunate. While I was editor of *Gifted Child Quarterly* from 2002 to

2007, I noticed an increase in the number of papers I received that used some form of qualitative methodology, and these approaches to research questions seem to be growing in popularity in gifted education. Given the typically small samples in gifted education research, combining both methodologies is sensible. As Onwuegbuzie, Collins, Leech, and Jiao point out in chapter 6 of this volume, one research approach can inform and enhance the other. A central issue within the field is whether special programs for gifted students are effective, particularly in terms of altering participants' educational and career outcomes and paths. The most important questions to ask and answer are, Do gifted children need gifted programs? Do these programs make any difference in their lives? Will gifted children succeed without them? Will some succeed, and if so, who? Which students need gifted programming the most?

Demonstrating that gifted children benefit from programs in significant ways is critical to obtaining funding for programs and services as well as for developing policies that support gifted education. Program effects are difficult to demonstrate given the combination of small sample sizes and the fact that most gifted programs are "weak treatments" because they typically do not involve a great deal of students' time. Yet those of us who work in this field can share many instances where individual students were profoundly affected by participation in a gifted program, mainly, I believe, because involvement in just one good program makes students aware of the fact that there are educational contexts that are a good fit to them and that there are other students like them who thrive on challenge and intellectual rigor. Expert use of qualitative methodologies can look in depth at individual students and capture the complexity of forces at play in talent development. Such efforts are needed to provide support for gifted programming and to inform the development of generalizable models of talent development that could be tested empirically and quantitatively.

FROM A RESEARCHER'S PERSPECTIVE

I have spent the last 25 years crafting and running programs for academically talented learners. I have been a scholar and a practitioner, developing program models and assessing them. These programs have taken many different forms, including weekend programs, summer programs, distance learning programs, and programs that had both in-school and outside-of-school components. The common thread is that they have all been supplementary educational experiences for gifted students. Through my organization, the Center for Talent Development (CTD), I have been involved heavily in the provision of supplementary gifted education to gifted students of all types and varieties. In fact, one of the most interesting aspects of the field of gifted education is the extent to which significant talent development takes place outside of the main arena for education, meaning schools. The Talent Search organizations, of which CTD is one, are the main providers of supplemental gifted education in academic areas of learning within the United States, serving 240,000 students annually in off-level testing programs and 33,900 students in educational programs (Lee et al., 2008).

Supplementary educational programs supply important ingredients to the talent development process, such as academic rigor, access to intellectual peers, and teachers with high levels of content expertise. Additionally, supplementary programs may be the only source of support and stimulation for many gifted children (Olszewski-Kubilius & Lee, 2008). Consequently, it is important to understand more about the role of supplementary programs in the process of talent development. That is, how important are they from students' perspectives? What are their effects on students? What are their short and long-term impacts, and what are the processes that underlie these impacts? What are the direct effects on students, and what are the indirect ones? For example, how do parents' views of their child's educational needs change as a result of program participation? How do effects and the mechanisms underlying these effects vary by subgroups of students—for example, low-income or minority students? These are largely unanswered questions for supplementary gifted education programs, yet the answers are important if we are to design the most effective supplementary educational programs for talented students.

There is a considerable body of research on middle school students who take the SAT and ACT as off-level identification instruments and then subsequently participate in summer programs offered by Talent Search organizations and other institutions of higher education. Students who participate in residential, 3-week summer programs experience greater academic challenge and subsequently have higher educational aspirations and take a more rigorous course of study throughout high school. They also experience increased use of accelerative educational options, apply to and attend more academically selective institutions of higher education, and are more likely to participate in math-related extracurricular activities while in high school (see Olszewski-Kubilius, 2007, or Olszewski-Kubilius & Lee, 2008, for a review). These effects suggest that summer programs for gifted youngsters impact them beyond the duration of the program, such that they affect future academic choices, goals, and aspirations. While this is good, we do not understand how programs achieve such long-term effects.

I have suggested elsewhere that participation in rigorous academic programs with other talented students may alter students' self-perceptions. Success in a class with students who are equally able may increase a student's confidence and beliefs that he or she is gifted and can be successful in other difficult and rigorous courses. Students may become less fearful of challenging and stretching themselves and more accepting of learning and growth as primary goals rather than simply attaining good grades. For minority students, successfully competing against nonminority peers in a summer program may be vital to choosing advanced classes in school, especially in situations where there will be few other minority students making that choice. Thus, self-concept and self-perceptions may be intervening variables mediating the effects of the challenging coursework and peer environments characteristic of special supplementary gifted programs on students. Additionally, a child's success in a challenging summer program may directly affect parents' perceptions of their child's abilities, reaffirming them or changing them, as well as their expectations regarding their child's achievement. This may then indirectly affect children's academic and achievement-related choices via parental push for more rigorous classes or support for further involvement in special supplementary programs or extracurricular talent-developing activities.

PROJECT EXCITE

Figure 10.1 is an attempt to model the effects of a particular supplemental educational program designed for a special group of gifted students who are typically underrepresented in school-based gifted programs. Specifically, Figure 10.1 (Lee, Olszewski-Kubilius & Peternel, in press) was generated for Project Excite, whose purpose is to prepare talented minority children to enter advanced academic tracks in high school, and it is meant to be exemplary rather than exact or comprehensive. For each year of Project Excite, we identify 25 third-grade students with above-average achievement in math, science, and reading via standardized testing from several schools in a district in Evanston, Illinois. Students receive a variety of programmatic interventions during the next 6 years, until they enter high school. These interventions include after-school sessions in science during the third grade, participation in math or science classes in CTD's Saturday Enrichment Program during Grades 4 through 8, special supplementary Saturday classes for Project Excite students in mathematics, one-on-one tutoring, group drop-in tutoring in mathematics available on a weekly basis, mentoring by college students from Northwestern University, participation in summer programs through CTD's Spectrum program or ones designed specifically for Excite students, field trips, family meetings to discuss future educational options and goals, and one-on-one support to families in the form of counseling or resources for individual student's needs.

Once Excite students reach ninth grade, they are placed into existing support programs run by their high school for minority students, and Project

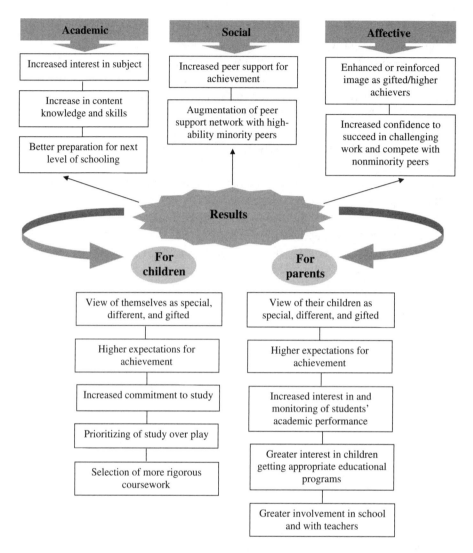

Figure 10.1. Influences and results of participation in special programs on minority gifted students.

Excite continues to supply tutoring in math and counseling via group or individual sessions. We currently have eight cohorts of students in the program. Attrition per cohort ranges from 30% to 50%, mostly due to families moving out of the district. To accommodate this, for the last few years, we adopted a policy of replacing students who left with other similarly qualified students. Although Figure 10.1 is still in development as Project Excite is ongoing, it is an attempt to capture effects based on previous research and my experiences with students and their families. In the next few paragraphs, I will discuss it in light of the issues raised within the chapters in this book.

Assessing the model shown in Figure 10.1 has many challenges. Unlike some of the other supplemental programs I run that have large enrollments, this model attempts to depict the influence of a program that serves a small number of students. Project Excite typically recruits only 25 students annually from the third grade and follows them longitudinally. We have about 130 total students based on eight cohorts and subsequent attrition. Additionally, there would be good reasons to not group the cohorts together for any kind of quantitative study and analysis. Although basic program components have been identified as key supports for the academic achievement of the students involved, these program components are tweaked, modified, and changed as we learn about what works best with students. For example, tutoring via weekly drop-in sessions was added after the program had been operating for a few years and after trying to arrange for one-on-one tutoring for individual students. The nature of the educational programs has also changed because of a greater understanding of participants' needs.

Even the identification battery has changed. Initially, we used a non-verbal ability test along with teacher recommendations to find students we thought needed and would benefit from the program. We have since added a standardized achievement battery to the identification and selection protocol that gives us measures of math and reading achievement. For the first few cohorts of Excite students, we did not include reading achievement in the selection criteria, but based on concerns about students who had ability in math but were deficient in reading, and thus not able to read advanced science content, we now look for at least grade-level achievement in reading along with above-grade-level achievement in math. Given these changes over the years, the annual cohorts of Excite students differ in terms of cognitive characteristics and also perhaps in other ways (e.g., higher achievement is likely correlated with motivation to achieve and excel). Analyzing within individual cohorts and across cohorts would likely result in a fuller understanding of how Project Excite affects students. Therefore, computing point estimates for various variables (or changes in scores on various variables) and confidence intervals for these would be preferred, given the small sample sizes and the low power of NHST analyses performed on individual cohorts to detect differences.

Understanding the way in which Project Excite affects students would require a complicated design—one that involves repeated measures of students over time (perhaps yearly) and by cohort. We have already used a mixed methods approach in our evaluation of Project Excite. We have collected data primarily on student achievement, such as how many Excite students have completed algebra before Grade 9, how many students were placed in honors-level math and science classes in Grade 9, how many students eventually matriculate into the high school's most advanced math science program (the Chem/Phys Program), and students' performance on standardized tests that their school district uses (the Illinois Scholastic Achievement Test and the Explore test). We do not have a constructed control or comparison group, but we have compared data on Excite students to data on minority students districtwide or schoolwide. We have measured variables such as students' interest in and enthusiasm for math and science. We have also interviewed Excite students and their parents as well as school administrators involved in the program to get a better idea about how the program is impacting families, whether it is changing parents' behavior, and whether the program is affecting children's school achievement since Excite is mainly an outside-of-school program. Through interviews, we learned a couple of interesting things that would help us to create a more accurate model of program effects.

For example, we had been concerned that one of the factors potentially affecting minority students' school achievement would be negative feedback from minority peers that achieving well in high school is "acting White." Project Excite was designed to give students access to other high-ability minority students who would augment their peer networks and thereby increase social support from minority peers for high achievement. But interviews with students and parents indicated that few students perceived negative messages from minority peers for school achievement or for their participation in Project Excite. Students commented on the fact that they had to forgo activities with friends on Saturday mornings to participate in Excite activities and that, though this was difficult, they did so, prioritizing their Project Excite activities over other attractive options. Excite students did make new friends among other Excite students, many of whom did not go to their neighborhood school, but these friendships existed mainly within the program and did not extend to outside-of-school time. So, while the students indicated they felt increased support to be high achievers, the effect was probably less than what we had expected. However, it is likely that outside-of-school gifted programs like Project Excite are less stigmatizing for minority students than in-school programs, and this may be an advantage of these programs.

Interview data also revealed that the Project Excite students liked the fact that through the Saturday and summer classes, they got ahead of their peers in school. That is, they learned content in advance of when they would study it in school, and this gave them a "leg up," which they perceived as a benefit of participation in the program. Finally, interviews with parents revealed that they took great pride and joy in their child being identified as talented and subsequently participating in special programs at a major private university. Parents expressed how Project Excite caused them to view their child differently and to expect more from him or her. In summary, the use of qualitative data gleaned from interviews helped to refine many aspects of the model for how Project Excite impacts students.

Another challenge in evaluating the model is the measurement of many of the constructs involved. Some of these constructs may be captured by existing questionnaires or surveys, and some will need to be developed. Factor analytic techniques would be useful here, but their use will be limited by the small sample size. Ideally, I would want to create a model that could be evaluated using structural equation modeling (SEM). Questionnaire items to assess various outcomes could be combined into a single questionnaire and factor analysis used to determine whether the items for different constructs correlate and can be combined into factor scores for SEM.

While qualitative data gleaned from interviews is vital in the construction and refinement of the model, they are also needed for a deeper understanding of the processes involved. For example, if students report that they do have more minority peers in their social networks as a result of meeting students from other schools in Project Excite activities, but this does not result in perceptions of increased support for high achievement, is it because these new peers are not available in the student's school environment to buttress commitment, provide encouragement, and help students resist negative influences? Or if students report that they are more confident about their ability to succeed in challenging courses after being in Project Excite, yet do not enroll in honors-level courses in high school, what other factors are influencing this decision? Does anticipation of the new high school environment trigger stereotype threat (Steele & Aronson, 1995) for minority students, resulting in a fear of competing with nonminority students?

Combining qualitative and quantitative data to understand and assess programs like Project Excite will also likely result in changes in the design of the program. For example, if students make friends among other Excite students, but this does not increase their feelings of support for high achievement within their schools, then perhaps the school environment needs to be constructed differently by, for example, gathering all Project Excite students together on a weekly basis for a group meeting aimed at providing encouragement and an opportunity to mutually support one another. There is much to be learned here from the use of mixed methods research, in terms of both how interventional, supplementary programs like Project Excite impact students and how to craft programs to maximize positive benefits.

I am enlightened as to better statistical procedures that will improve my research thanks to the authors of the chapters in this book. I was able to apply their suggestions and methods only at the broadest level in my own chapter at this point, but I will, no doubt, go back to and use their specific and detailed recommendations and procedures in the future.

REFERENCES

Chan, D. W. (2005). The structure of social coping among Chinese gifted children and youths in Hong Kong. *Journal for the Education of the Gifted, 29*, 8–29.

Harter, S. (1985). *Manual for the social support scale for children and adolescents*. Denver, CO: University of Denver.

Kulik, J. A., & Kulik, C. C. (1992). Meta-analytic findings on grouping programs. *Gifted Child Quarterly, 36*, 73–77.

Lee, S. Y., Matthews, M., & Olszewski-Kubilius, P. (2008). A national picture of Talent Search and Talent Search educational programs. *Gifted Child Quarterly, 52*, 55–69.

Lee, S.-Y., Olszewski-Kubilius, P., & Peternel, G. (2009). Follow-up with students after six years of their participation in Project EXCITE. *Gifted Child Quarterly, 53*, 137–156.

Minor, L., & Benbow, C. P. (1996). Construct validity of the SAT-M: A comparative study of high school students and gifted seventh graders. In C. P. Benbow & D. Lubinski (Eds.), *Intellectual talent* (pp. 347–361). Baltimore, MD: Johns Hopkins University Press.

Neihart, M. (1999). The impact of giftedness on psychological well-being: What does the empirical literature say? *Roeper Review, 22*, 57–64.

Olszewski-Kubilius, P. (2007). The role of summer programs in developing the talents of gifted students. In J. VanTassel-Baska (Ed.), *Serving gifted learners beyond the traditional classroom* (pp. 13–32). Waco, TX: Prufrock Press.

Olszewski-Kubilius, P., & Lee, S.-Y. (2008). Specialized programs serving the gifted. In F. A. Karnes & K. P. Stephens (Eds.), *Achieving excellence. Educating the gifted and talented* (pp. 192–208). Columbus, OH: Pearson Education.

Rogers, K. B. (2002). *Re-forming gifted education: Matching the program to the child*. Scottsdale, AZ: Great Potential Press.

Rudasill, K. M., Foust, R. C., & Callahan, C. M. (2007). The Social Coping Questionnaire: An examination of its structure with an American sample of adolescents. *Journal for the Education of the Gifted, 30*, 353–371.

Steele, C. M., & Aronson, J. (1995). Stereotype threat and the intellectual performance of African Americans. *Journal of Personality and Social Psychology, 69*, 797–811.

Swiatek, M. A. (1995). An empirical investigation of the social coping strategies used by gifted adolescents. *Gifted Child Quarterly, 39*, 154–161.

Swiatek, M. A. (2001). Social coping among gifted high school students and its relationship to self-concept. *Journal of Youth and Adolescence, 30*, 19–39.

Swiatek, M. A., & Dorr, R. M. (1998). Revision of the Social Coping Questionnaire: Replication and extension of previous finding. *Journal of Secondary Gifted Education, 10*, 252–259.

Worrell, F. C. (1997). An exploratory factor analysis of Harter's Self-Perception Profile for Adolescents with academically talented students. *Educational and Psychological Measurement, 57*, 1016–1024.

11

MOVING THE FIELD OF GIFTED STUDIES TOWARD INCREASINGLY SOPHISTICATED APPROACHES TO RESEARCH: AN HOMAGE TO MICHAEL PYRYT

TRACY L. CROSS AND JENNIFER R. CROSS

The chapters in Parts 1 and 2 of this book provide considerable detail about myriad approaches to quantitative and mixed method research designs and important issues to consider when using those designs. The authors build a compelling case for the importance of using those designs in moving the research base in gifted studies toward greater sophistication. The first author's awareness of the need to enhance the literature base by incorporating increasingly sophisticated research approaches crystallized in November 1997 at the National Association of Gifted Children conference just after a symposium on research methodology had ended, when Laurence J. Coleman, Michael Pyryt,[1] and I stood talking about the session. I asked Michael if he thought the field of gifted studies was ready to move in a postpositivistic direction. As he was known to do, he thought about what I had asked him and carefully responded with his own question: "How can the field of gifted studies become postpositivistic when our research base is still prepositivistic?"

That was Michael's way of critiquing our field as being reliant on too many studies that were theoretically unsound and poorly conducted. The

---

[1]Michael C. Pyryt was a revered researcher and professor of gifted education at the University of Calgary whose untimely death at the age of 54 (January 15, 2008) shocked and saddened the entire community.

symposium had emphasized the epistemological and ontological assumptions of qualitative and quantitative approaches to research. Arguments were made during the session for the utility of both approaches, but with an emphasis being placed on the limitations of each in terms of the nature of the research questions that can and cannot be addressed by either. While few academics these days still question the usefulness of either quantitative or qualitative research (see Capraro & Thompson, 2008; Larabee, 2003), what Michael did in few words was summarize the research in the field of gifted studies circa 1997. This book is intended to be both a catalyst and a primer for future research in gifted studies to help us move from prepositivistic to positivistic and postpositivistic approaches. Michael would be pleased.

In this chapter, we describe the various research approaches we have utilized over the years, including both qualitative and quantitative techniques. Other chapters in this volume have provided fodder for additional discussions about our research. As a result of the ideas generated by our fellow authors in this volume, we propose an enhancement to our existing research through the use of structural equation modeling (SEM) as described by Kline in chapter 7 of this volume.

SOME EXAMPLES OF ADVANCED STATISTICAL APPROACHES: FROM RESEARCH TO APPLICATION

For several years, Laurence Coleman and the first author explored the lived experiences (Husserl, 1962) of students with gifts and talents. From that research, we pursued some foundational questions about these students in school settings, developing a questionnaire, the Student Attitude Questionnaire (SAQ). In 1988, we published a study in the *Journal of Education for the Gifted* called "Is Being Gifted a Social Handicap?" Because we were attempting to uncover lived experience, we began with phenomenology and descriptive research, as recommended by Gall, Gall, and Borg (2004). That piece led to a longstanding collaboration between the first author and Mary Ann Swiatek (e.g., T. L. Cross & Swiatek, 2009; Swiatek & Cross, 2006). Swiatek built on Coleman and Cross (1988); T. L. Cross, Coleman, and Terhaar-Yonkers (1991); and others by extending research into social coping in differing settings with various subgroups of gifted students. By incorporating factor analysis in several studies, Swiatek has been able to hone her Social Coping Questionnaire (SCQ; Swiatek, 2000; Swiatek & Dorr, 1998).

Beginning a study with phenomenology and then continuing to scale development using factor analytic procedures was touted by the first author's professors Howard Pollio and Michael Patton at the University of Tennessee. This process is exemplified in our research over the past several decades. We began with uncovering and describing lived experience of students with gifts and talents, then creating an initial questionnaire about being gifted in school, followed by generating and vetting a more sophisticated questionnaire, the SCQ, employing factor analytic techniques. The culmination of this process has been the use of the SCQ at a residential academy for gifted high school juniors and seniors as a way to help identify students who might benefit from proactive counseling. The staff at the academy has been trained to use the SCQ as a tool to lead discussions with new students about issues of transitions relative to the students' previous experiences as gifted students. These discussions encourage and begin the process of the students' efforts to reevaluate the prior social coping behavior that they engaged in given their assessment of the social milieu of their schools. In essence, the SCQ accelerates children's efforts to break free from self-imposed constraints and reinvent themselves in a more accepting environment. Given that the academy experience is only 2 years long, it is important to make a positive transition very quickly. As evidenced by the effective implementation of these measures, this research has led to tangible benefits for students with gifts and talents.

The need for such studies investigating the coping skills of gifted students became apparent following a cluster suicide of three gifted students in 1994. From several studies exploring suicide among gifted students (Cassady & Cross, 2006; T. L. Cross, Cook, & Dixon, 1996; T. L. Cross, Gust-Brey, & Ball, 2002), it was hypothesized that intellectually gifted students are not more likely to engage in suicide ideation than the general population on which the Suicidal Ideation Questionnaire (Reynolds, 1987) was normed and that the intellectual processing of suicide ideation may be more complex among the gifted population than the general population. These hypotheses were tested using factor analysis (Cassady & Cross, 2006). The results supported our hypotheses, pushing the knowledge base forward toward fuller understanding of suicide ideation in this special population.

AN EVOLUTION OF RESEARCH METHODS: LOOKING FOR STRUCTURE IN THE DATA

These examples of the progression of research to enhance the lives of students with gifts and talents indicate how we have come to employ increasingly sophisticated methods of research. As the data we have collected have become more complex, new methods for discovering their deeper meaning were needed. Statistical methods exist for identifying the underlying structure of the data. These methods differ in a number of ways from other statistical techniques. They are not required to meet the same assumptions necessary to the accuracy of most other techniques such as normality, linearity, and homoscedasticity (Hair, Black, Babin, Anderson, & Tatham, 2006). Cluster analysis and latent class analysis (LCA) are two techniques for grouping together observations that are similar, finding the greatest homogeneity within clusters and greatest heterogeneity between clusters. Similar to the Q-technique factor analysis described in chapter 2 in this volume by Thompson, cluster analysis identifies patterns between *cases* as opposed to *variables*. We have used both the traditional methods of analyzing the relationships among variables through factor analysis and the less common technique of cluster analysis to gain a "big picture" perspective of our data. When carried out thoughtfully, cluster analysis can point to relationships otherwise not obvious in the data and can lead to hypotheses for further testing.

Cluster Analysis in Gifted Studies

Cluster analysis was used to positive effect in a recent study exploring a unique population of gifted and nongifted students and their teachers (T. L. Cross, al Lawati, Frazier, & Cross, 2007). In this study, factor analytic and cluster analytic techniques were combined to address complicated questions about the contexts in which gifted students attend school. The study was conducted in a unique setting in which two schools (a K–12 university laboratory school [lab school] established to carry out the preservice teacher education mission of the college and a public statewide residential academy for intellectually gifted students in Grades 11 and 12) had coexisted for 18 years in the same building. The lab school enrolled approximately 550 students, of whom about 35% were identified as gifted. The academy hosted 300 students, all of whom were identified as gifted. Students from both schools attend some classes in the other school, and both take classes at the university campus on which they exist.

The study originated because a new initiative was being put in place in which gifted education practices were expected to be implemented across all grades in the lab school. Previous efforts to that end had met with limited success. While executive director of the academy, the first author of this chapter had observed that two relatively distinct cultures existed in the two schools and, along with these cultures, evidence of some negative feelings on the part of the lab school faculty and students toward the academy students. Moreover, some of the faculty of the lab school had been critical of gifted education and proffered opinions that the lab school was an effective learning environment already because they met the needs of all students without labeling them or participating in gifted education practices. Other faculty members had received training in gifted education and were in various stages of trying to implement aspects of it in their classrooms.

In order to identify these hypothesized cultures in the two schools, 189 faculty members and students participated in a survey based on Gagné and Nadeau's

(1985, 1991) Opinions About the Gifted and Their Education, which consisted of statements concerning beliefs about the need for special services for students with gifts and talents, the value of specialized gifted services, the appropriateness of acceleration, and so forth. Through factor analysis, the following four factors were found: (a) effectiveness of traditional schooling in meeting the needs of gifted youths (Needs), (b) value of gifted education (Elitism), (c) attitudes toward gifted education and gifted people (Support), and (d) attitudes toward grade skipping (Acceleration). These factors were used to group questions from the survey to determine whether there were differences between the schools by each factor. Using multiple analysis of variance (MANOVA), significant differences were found between respondents from the two schools in all but the fourth factor concerning grade skipping. The factor scores were then used in a cluster analysis to determine how students and teachers clustered together in their different attitudes. Factor scores may, in fact, reduce the ability to discriminate that is the heart of cluster analysis (Hair et al., 2006), but in this case, a reduction in the large number of items to be analyzed was needed.

Hierarchical cluster analysis in SPSS was used, with the four factor scores—Elitism, Support, Needs, and Acceleration—as the cluster variables. Three to five clusters were suggested by jumps in the coefficients (squared Euclidean distance). Analysis of the cluster memberships among these options indicated the best solution was three clusters. Three clusters produced homogeneous, interpretable groups, with a different profile of membership in each cluster.

A second MANOVA was conducted with the cluster group as the independent variable and the four factor scores as the dependent variables. The results of this multistep analysis identified a group of gifted students with attitudes that may have been inhibiting their intellectual development. In our sample, a large proportion of the academy students (79%) fell into the cluster we named the Conflicted Gifted. These students recognized the needs of gifted students but had difficulty expressing their support for it. Another cluster consisted primarily of teachers who supported gifted education, but without acknowledging that students with gifts and talents have unique educational needs. We called this cluster the Supporters. They were blind to the needs of this special population but enthusiastically supportive nonetheless. The third cluster we called the Nonsupporters. Made up largely of lab school students and teachers, this group indicated that students with gifts and talents have few unique educational needs and expressed very little support for gifted education. Elitism was a major concern only for the Conflicted Gifted. These students appeared to worry about their status as gifted persons, agreeing with such statements as "Special educational services for gifted children are a mark of privilege" or "When the gifted are put in special classes, the other children feel devalued."

This research design using cluster analysis allowed us to make policy suggestions and garner support for strategic faculty development opportunities. Study data were used as evidence to influence hiring decisions. A counselor with training in the special needs of students with gifts and talents was hired to assist in establishing individual learning plans for gifted students in the lab school environment, addressing the unacknowledged needs of these students among the teachers who were both Supporters and Nonsupporters. A simple analysis of academy or lab school students or teachers would not necessarily have identified attitudinal differences among the students and teachers who clustered together.

Latent Class Analysis in Gifted Studies

Whereas numerous procedures exist as part of the technique called *cluster analysis,* LCA is a single statistical procedure for grouping cases together. LCA functions differently from cluster analysis. Rather than assigning cases to a cluster based on similarity, LCA can be used with binary, categorical, or Likert-type data to determine the probability that a case will fall into a latent class, a categorization that is not directly observed but inferred from the observed data (Uebersax, 2008).

LCA produces models based on the prevalence of specific response patterns to the variables being tested. The probability that each case has the response pattern of each class is determined through the maximum likelihood criterion. Similar to cluster analysis, the researcher must choose the most appropriate number of classes. This decision is based on measures of model fit such as the Bayesian information criterion (Sclove, 1987) or the likelihood ratio χ^2 statistic (G^2; Uebersax, 2008). Once the number of classes has been determined, membership can be assigned either based on the highest probability or by degree of membership in a specific class. There is less dependence on the researcher's judgment in LCA than in cluster analysis.

This method of grouping data was used in an analysis of supporters of gifted education (J. R. Cross, Cross, & Finch, in press). After many years in the field, we had developed the hypothesis that supporters of gifted education actually represent two different groups. Through our work with lobbying on behalf of gifted children, running a school for gifted students, and engaging in research, we had seen evidence of different belief systems about and goals for students with gifts and talents (J. R. Cross & Cross, 2005). We hypothesized that one group supported gifted education for purposes of maintaining the dominance of their group over others. For example, minority students are found less frequently in gifted programs than we would expect from their numbers in the general population (Ford, Harris, Tyson, & Trotman, 2002; Office of Educational Research and Improvement, 1993). Such discrepancy may be due to an unconscious bias among those more highly represented in gifted education: White, middle- to upper-class Americans. To test this hypothesis, we designed a study to evaluate the preference for inequality (social dominance orientation [SDO]; Sidanius & Pratto, 1999) and deference to authority (right-wing authoritarianism [RWA]; Altemeyer, 1981) among supporters of gifted education with different preferences for educational practice.

In this study, the preferences of 218 self-identified supporters of gifted education for various educational practices were reported: best method of identification of gifted students, use of cooperative learning with nongifted peers, benefits of cooperative learning in mixed-ability groups, and preferred placement for gifted students (e.g., heterogeneous classrooms with differentiated instruction, pull-out programs, cluster groups). These preferences were used as the variables for classification in the LCA. The number of latent classes with the best model fit was two. Coincidentally, each class had 109 members. Members of the two classes, which we named Individualists and Communitarians, differed in their preference for cooperative learning and preferred placement. Individualists opposed cooperative learning with nongifted classmates and preferred placements that removed gifted students from learning with their nongifted peers. In this group, self-contained classes were by far considered "best" for gifted students, with 69% of Individualists choosing this option. Communitarians, on the other hand, felt that cooperative learning should be used frequently, and 40% chose heterogeneous classrooms with differentiated instruction as their preferred placement for students with gifts and talents.

The next step was to use logistic regression, with the latent class as the dependent variable and SDO, RWA, and a measure of socially desirable responding, the Marlowe–Crowne Social Desirability Scale (MCS; Reynolds, 1982), as the independent variables. Class membership was associated with SDO and RWA, with higher scores on SDO increasing the likelihood of being in the Individualist group and higher scores on RWA associated with a lower likelihood of being in the Individualist group. SDO and MCS did not differ between the two classes, but RWA was higher among Communitarians than among Individualists. We interpreted this relationship to indicate that, for some supporters of gifted education, there is a powerful societal norm to maintain community over developing individual potential. As the Communitarians defer to this societal norm—a behavior that may be predicted by their higher deference to authority—they prefer educational practice that may inhibit individual success. Individualists would be dissatisfied with a classroom in which such inhibition of individual potential exists. We propose that both groups of supporters can be satisfied by providing high-quality community-oriented practice in the classroom, such as cooperative learning or curriculum differentiation that will appeal to both Communitarians and Individualists.

Although all participants in this study considered themselves supporters of gifted education, they did not all agree on what is "best" for students with gifts and talents. By grouping participants according to the likelihood of each response preference through LCA, we were able to consider other psychological constructs that may be underpinning their support for different practices. Compromise between supporters of gifted education who are Individualists and Communitarians may be facilitated by the findings of this study. Prior to this exploration of attitudes using sophisticated research methods, supporters could only speculate about the reasons for support of different educational practice.

EXTENDING THE RESEARCH WITH NEW METHODS

Our study of supporters of gifted education has led us to much questioning about the idea that some individuals support gifted education for maximizing potential in their own children but have no concern that this be accomplished for other children. Dictionary definitions of *elitism* include an exclusiveness or selectivity that may be represented by this lack of concern for others. In the language of research on prejudice, from which SDO and RWA derive, an ingroup favoritism and outgroup bias result in this type of exclusiveness and selectivity (Whitley & Kite, 2006). If we adopt this lack of concern for the development and enhancement of others as a working definition of elitism, based on our interpretation of the results of our study, we can accurately say that some supporters of gifted education are elitist. We achieved this understanding through the constructs of social dominance orientation and right-wing authoritarianism, along with a measure of social desirability.

The chapters in this volume have generated ideas about how we might extend our study to clarify the relationships among these factors that appear to be contributing to elitism in gifted education. Structural equation modeling (SEM; see chap. 7, this volume) can provide a useful means of understanding the relationships between specified variables in our study and the latent variable we call *elitism*. Using SEM, our measure of elitism would be indicated by responses to the questions regarding preference for practice in gifted education. As suggested by Kline in chapter 7, the sample size must be large enough to conduct the SEM. An acceptable model would identify the strength and direction of the relationships among the preference for inclusive or exclusive classroom practice, SDO, RWA, and socially desirable responding. The position of variables in the suggested model (Figure 11.1) could be altered to find the model with the best fit indexes. In contrast to our LCA analysis, this approach would allow us to see the relationships between the various pieces of information in the model. Whereas LCA indicated groups, with SEM we would have a continuous measure (elitism) and thus could distinguish gradations of support. Research indicates that SDO and RWA are affected by ethnicity, gender, occupation or major, and education level (Jost

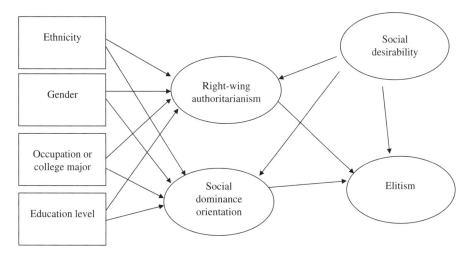

Figure 11.1. Proposed model of the psychological foundations of elitism in gifted education.

& Thompson, 2000; Sidanius & Pratto, 1999; Sidanius, Sinclair, & Pratto, 2006; Sidanius, van Laar, Levin, & Sinclair, 2003). The variability of elitism among these groups, as well as their direct relationship to the latent variable, could be explored as a result of the model.

CONCLUSION

Ambrose, Van Tassel-Baska, Coleman, and Cross (2006) described the research base in gifted studies as fractured feudal states built on a lack of theory and with a relative lack of sophistication in research design. While the evidence for this assessment is persuasive, there are increasing examples of studies using sophisticated designs and data analysis techniques emerging in the literature. Although Michael Pyryt's critique of the field of gifted studies as prepositivistic is still relatively accurate, we believe that there has been a changing tide that emphasizes theoretically sound and sophisticated research methodologies, either quantitative or qualitative, being employed by the current generation of scholars. In time, this changing tide has the potential to affect all boats. Through encouragement of high-quality, philosophically sound research, the field can achieve the substantive research base that Pyryt envisioned.

REFERENCES

Altemeyer, R. A. (1981). *Right-wing authoritarianism*. Winnipeg, Manitoba, Canada: University of Manitoba Press.

Ambrose, D., Van Tassel-Baska, J., Coleman, L. J., & Cross, T. L. (2006, November). *Unified–insular–firmly policed or fractured–contested–porous gifted education?* Presentation at the annual meeting of the National Association for Gifted Children, Charlotte, NC.

Capraro, R. M., & Thompson, B. (2008). The educational researcher defined: What will future researchers be trained to do? *Journal of Educational Research, 101,* 247–253.

Cassady, J. C., & Cross, T. L. (2006). A factoral representation of gifted adolescent suicide. *Journal for the Education of the Gifted, 29,* 290–304.

Coleman, L. J., & Cross, T. L. (1988). Is being gifted a social handicap? *Journal for the Education of the Gifted, 11,* 41–56.

Cross, J. R., & Cross, T. L. (2005). Social dominance, moral politics, and gifted education. *Roeper Review, 28,* 21–29.

Cross, J. R., Cross, T. L., & Finch, W. H. (in press). Maximizing student potential versus building community: An exploration of right-wing authoritarianism, social dominance orientation, and preferred practice among supporters of gifted education. *Roeper Review.*

Cross, T. L., al Lawati, F., Frazier, A. D., & Cross, J. R. (2007, November). *Two schools for gifted students in one building: A quantitative exploration of different cultures.* Paper presented at the annual meeting of the National Association of Gifted Children, Minneapolis, MN.

Cross, T. L., Coleman, L. J., & Terhaar-Yonkers, M. (1991). The social cognition of gifted adolescents in schools: Managing the stigma of giftedness. *Journal for the Education of the Gifted, 15,* 44–55.

Cross, T. L., Cook, R. S., & Dixon, D. N. (1996). Psychological autopsies of three academically talented adolescents who committed suicide. *Journal of Secondary Gifted Education, 7,* 403–409.

Cross, T. L., Gust-Brey, K., & Ball, B. (2002). A psychological autopsy of the suicide of an academically gifted student: Researchers' and parents' perspectives. *Gifted Child Quarterly, 46,* 247–264.

Cross, T. L., & Swiatek, M. A. (2009). Social coping among academically gifted adolescents in a residential setting: A longitudinal study. *Gifted Child Quarterly, 53,* 25–33.

Ford, D. Y., Harris, J. J., Tyson, C. A., & Trotman, M. F. (2002). Beyond deficit thinking: Providing access for gifted African American students. *Roeper Review, 24,* 52–58.

Gagné, F., & Nadeau, L. (1985). Dimensions of attitudes towards giftedness. In A. H. Roldan (Ed.), *Gifted and talented children, youth and adults: Their social perspective and culture* (pp. 148–170). Monroe, NJ: Trillium Press.

Gagné, F., & Nadeau, L. (1991). *Opinions about the gifted and their education.* Unpublished instrument.

Gall, J. P., Gall, M. D., & Borg, W. R. (2004). *Applying educational research: A practical guide* (5th ed.). Upper Saddle River, NJ: Merrill.

Hair, J. F., Jr., Black, W. C., Babin, B. J., Anderson, R. E., & Tatham, R. L. (2006). *Multivariate data analysis*. Upper Saddle River, NJ: Pearson Prentice Hall.

Husserl, E. (1962). *Cartesian meditations* (D. Cairns, Trans.). The Hague, the Netherlands: Martinus Nijhoff.

Jost, J. T., & Thompson, E. P. (2000). Group-based dominance and opposition to equality as independent predictors of self-esteem, ethnocentrism, and social policy attitudes among African Americans and European Americans. *Journal of Experimental Social Psychology, 36*, 209–232.

Larabee, D. F. (2003). The peculiar problems of preparing educational researchers. *Educational Researcher, 32*(4), 13–22.

Office of Educational Research and Improvement, U.S. Department of Education. (1993). *National excellence: A case for developing America's talent*. Washington, DC: U.S. Government Printing Office.

Reynolds, W. M. (1982). Development of reliable and valid short forms of the Marlowe–Crowne Social Desirability Scale. *Journal of Clinical Psychology, 38*, 119–125.

Reynolds, W. M. (1987). *Suicidal Ideation Questionnaire*. Odessa, FL: Psychological Assessment Resources.

Sclove, S. L. (1987). Application of model-selection criteria to some problems in multivariate analysis. *Psychometrika, 52*, 333–343.

Sidanius, J., & Pratto, F. (1999). *Social dominance: An intergroup theory of social hierarchy and oppression*. Cambridge, England: Cambridge University Press.

Sidanius, J., Sinclair, S., & Pratto, F. (2006). Social dominance orientation, gender, and increasing educational exposure. *Journal of Applied Social Psychology, 36*, 1640–1653.

Sidanius, J., van Laar, C., Levin, S., & Sinclair, S. (2003). Social hierarchy maintenance and assortment into social roles: A social dominance perspective. *Group Processes and Intergroup Relations, 6*, 332–352.

Swiatek, M. A. (2000). Social coping among gifted high school students and its relationship to self-concept. *Journal of Youth and Adolescence, 30*, 19–39.

Swiatek, M. A., & Cross, T. L. (2006, May). *Social coping among gifted adolescents: Validity of the social coping questionnaire and longitudinal changes after enrollment at a residential high school*. Paper presented at the Wallace National Research Symposium on Talent Development, Iowa City, IA.

Swiatek, M. A., & Dorr, R. (1998). Revision of the social coping questionnaire: Replication and extension of previous findings. *Journal of Secondary Gifted Education, 10*, 252–259.

Uebersax, J. S. (2008). *LCA frequently asked questions (FAQ)*. Retrieved July 28, 2008, from http://ourworld.compuserve.com/homepages/jsuebersax/faq.htm

Whitley, B. E., & Kite, M. E. (Eds.). (2006). *The psychology of prejudice and discrimination*. Belmont, CA: Thomson Wadsworth.

12

RESEARCH METHODS FOR GIFTED STUDIES: COMMENTS AND FUTURE DIRECTIONS

D. BETSY MCCOACH

To understand and better serve the needs of the gifted, the field must produce quality research to inform practice. Far too often, recommendations in the field of gifted education are based on conventional wisdom or anecdotes instead of data-driven research. This book provides accessible introductory treatments of several modern analytic methods that can be used to advance our knowledge within the field of gifted education. It also alerts researchers about potential pitfalls of inferential statistics in general as well as analytical areas of particular concern within the field of giftedness. As someone who is passionate about both gifted education and research methodology, I am honored to be able to provide some comments about the techniques contained in this volume and to provide thoughts about future methodological directions for our field.

This chapter contains three sections. First, I describe some of my own research within the field of gifted education. Then, I briefly describe studies that I am planning or contemplating that utilize some of the methodologies described in this book. Finally, I offer some thoughts on methodological issues that researchers in the field of gifted education should consider as they are planning their studies.

BACKGROUND AND RESEARCH INTERESTS

For the last decade, I have been involved in research within the field of gifted education, and much of my work has been focused on the under-achievement of gifted students. In particular, I am interested in understanding why some gifted students underachieve and how educators, psychologists, and parents can help students to perform at academic levels that are commensurate with their abilities. I became interested in the area of underachievement when I was a gifted specialist in Pennsylvania. At the time, gifted education in Pennsylvania fell under the umbrella of special education and had to abide by all special education regulations. Therefore, we held annual individual educational programming (IEP) planning meetings for all identified gifted students every year. Many parents of middle school and high school children (who were predominantly male) came to their gifted children's annual IEP conferences both frustrated and confused. "He used to be a good student in elementary school," they lamented. "He used to enjoy school." "Now he doesn't want to take honors courses, and he's content to get Cs and Ds." Some of these students were the most colorful characters in the school: bright, artistic, outspoken, and unconventional. Others were lethargic and uncommunicative. Some seemed as perplexed by their own underachievement as their parents were. These underachievers came in a variety of packages. As I began to read about underachievers, I realized that many of the studies describing the characteristics of underachievers were based on single case studies or anecdotes. Thus, the descriptions that were painted in the literature seemed to fit some but not all of my charges. When I began my own research, I decided to try to better understand the phenomenon of under-achievement within the gifted population in the hopes of being able to help parents and teachers to reverse underachievement behaviors.

Whereas much of the research on underachievement was qualitative in nature, I tend to be a more quantitatively oriented researcher. In addition, I was most interested in understanding whether there were similarities or patterns across the range of gifted underachievers. Therefore, my first research endeavor involved developing an instrument to measure some of the affective constructs that my review of literature had suggested were characteristics of underachievers. The School Attitude Assessment Survey—Revised (SAAS–R) represented the culmination of the first phase of that research. The validation of the SAAS–R involved conducting both exploratory and confirmatory factor analyses, as well as a study of criterion-related validity that examined whether the SAAS–R was effective at distinguishing known groups of gifted underachievers from gifted achievers (McCoach & Siegle, 2003b). The SAAS–R measures five factors that the literature suggests are related to underachievement: academic self-perceptions, motivation/self-regulation, attitudes toward teachers, attitudes toward school, and goal valuation. We found that generally the self-regulation and the goal-valuation factors tend to be the most predictive of underachievement behavior and the most related to measures of academic achievement for gifted students (Baslanti & McCoach, 2006; McCoach & Siegle, 2003a, 2003b), although the academic self-perceptions factor is highly related to academic achievement in general education populations (Suldo, Shaffer, & Shaunessy, 2008).

More recently, Ugur Baslanti and I developed a second instrument: the Challenges to Scholastic Achievement Scale (CSAS; McCoach & Baslanti, 2008). Whereas all of the questions on the SAAS–R are positively worded and measure traits that should be related to achievement, all of the questions on the CSAS are negative. Thus, the CSAS measures negative characteristics and behavior. The CSAS is designed to measure lack of self-regulation, low academic self-perceptions, negative attitudes toward school, low goal valuation, and alienation. We are in the process of completing exploratory and confirmatory factor analyses of the CSAS. It is my hope that one day, both the SAAS–R and the CSAS could be given to students who are at risk of underachievement to understand their attitudes and motivations. This should enable educators to better provide interventions to combat students' underachievement behaviors.

Having described some of my own substantive research, I now consider the ways in which the research methods described in this volume could be used within my own research agenda for future scholarship. I already utilize exploratory and confirmatory factor analysis, structural equation modeling, and multilevel modeling. Thus, I focus my attention here on two less utilized methods: Q-technique factor analysis and propensity score analysis.

USING Q-TECHNIQUE FACTOR ANALYSIS
TO STUDY UNDERACHIEVERS

Chapter 2 of this volume, on Q-technique factor analysis, captured my attention. Although I use factor analysis on a regular basis, I have never utilized Q-technique factor analysis. The Q-technique represents an effective way to probe similarities and differences among a small number of people quantitatively. This technique appears to be particularly well suited to studying gifted underachievers. After having read this chapter, I can envision a study that would utilize Q-technique factor analysis to explore possible typologies of underachievers. In such a study, I would solicit approximately 15 highly gifted, chronically underachieving high school students to participate. Each of the participating students would be asked to complete several instruments, including the SAAS–R, the CSAS, the Achievement Motivation

Profile (Friedland, Mandel, & Marcus, n.d.), and the Revised NEO Personality Inventory (NEO–PI–R; Costa & McCrae, 1992).

The Achievement Motivation Profile is a commercially available instrument that was designed to be used to evaluate underachieving students on personality traits and motivation. It measures 15 constructs across four domains: motivation for achievement, interpersonal strengths, work habits, and inner resources. The NEO–PI–R measures 30 constructs across five broad domains: neuroticism, extraversion, openness, agreeableness, and conscientiousness. Thus, the combination of these four instruments would measure 65 traits. Given a sample size of 15 gifted underachievers, the trait:person ratio would be slightly more than 4:1, which is higher than the minimum of 2:1 recommended by Thompson in chapter 2 of this volume. Using Q-technique factor analysis would allow me to examine different "types" of underachievers empirically and to determine which characteristics are most representative of the different types of underachievers.

GROUP NONEQUIVALENCE AND PROPENSITY SCORE ANALYSIS

Within chapter 9 of this volume, on missing data, is a treasure: a lucid discussion of the dangers of group nonequivalence. King and Dates describe the issues surrounding the analysis of quasi-experimental and observational data, and they present four approaches for minimizing group differences due to nonrandom assignment. The importance of these techniques for our field cannot be overemphasized. King and Dates are correct when they assert that it is often impossible to randomly assign gifted students to treatment and control conditions. Further, it is never possible to assign the construct of "giftedness." Therefore, very few experimental studies have been conducted within the field of gifted education.

For example, one of the most important questions that our field has yet to answer involves the effectiveness of gifted programs. Do gifted programs benefit students who participate in them? At the surface, this seems like such a simple question. Yet it is an incredibly difficult question to answer in practice. Why? Students cannot be randomly assigned to be placed into gifted programs. As a field, we assume that the programs that we offer are differentiated to meet the needs of an exceptional clientele. Thus, in theory, gifted programs should provide no positive benefit (and could theoretically even result in negative outcomes) for nongifted students. This phenomenon is sometimes referred to as an *aptitude treatment interaction*. Following this logic, randomly assigning students to gifted programs would likely result in no appreciable main effect, as only a small proportion of the students who were assigned to the treatment (the gifted) would be likely to show any positive benefit from it.

A second possible design would involve randomly assigning some gifted students within a school to receive gifted programming while others are denied access to gifted programming. Some researchers within the field of gifted education may consider such a study to be unethical because they assume that the effects of the gifted programming are beneficial. Of course, that is precisely the question that such a study would be designed to answer empirically. Although some researchers may be willing to conduct such a study, convincing schools, teachers, and parents to randomly assign gifted students to a condition in which gifted programming is withheld from some students would be virtually impossible. What parent would want his or her gifted child assigned to the no-treatment control group? Even if a school agreed to such a design, the random assignment mechanism would be in peril, as some parents of gifted students who were not selected for the gifted program would attempt to have their children reassigned to the gifted program treatment group. Note the irony here: The question that we seek to answer (are gifted programs effective?) becomes difficult to answer because the answer is assumed (yes, they are).

A third possibility involves randomly assigning schools either to offer gifted programs or to offer no specialized programming for the gifted. Again, convincing schools to succumb to such a randomization scheme would be virtually impossible. For schools that do not offer gifted programming, requiring such services would have large fiscal repercussions, including adding and/or training additional staff members. Thus, answering such a seemingly simple and straightforward question using experimental methods is far more complex than it seems at first glance.

Using propensity score analysis provides the gifted education researcher with a powerful tool to examine program effectiveness using nonexperimental data. Currently, Jill Adelson and I are working on just such an analysis (Adelson, 2008) using the Early Childhood Longitudinal Study—Kindergarten Cohort database to examine the effects of gifted programming. The research examines three separate research questions. First, what is the average effect of having a gifted program on academic achievement at the school level? Specifically, we are interested in determining the effect of having a gifted program on a school's average academic achievement in both math and reading. The net effect of a gifted program could be positive. For example, there could be carryover effects from the gifted program that positively impact the achievement of other students. Perhaps the implementation of a gifted program improves the climate of the school, the teaching practices of the faculty, or the educational enrichment opportunities for all students. In such a scenario, "a rising tide lifts all ships" (Renzulli, 1998, p. 104).

On the other hand, opponents of gifted education might speculate that having a gifted program could negatively impact the overall achievement of the school. Some of the most common arguments against gifted programs are that they funnel valuable resources away from the rest of the school population and that they deprive the nongifted classes of the gifted students, who can serve as powerful role models, tutors, and intellectual resources for the rest of the class. Proponents of this viewpoint would hypothesize that the impact of gifted programs on school achievement could actually be negative. Finally, the net impact of gifted programming at the school level could be zero or negligible. In other words, after matching schools based on their propensity to have gifted programs, there may be no difference in the average achievement of schools with and without programs. To determine the impact of gifted programs on school achievement in the absence of random assignment, we are utilizing propensity score analysis. Specifically, we are creating propensity scores at the school level, and we will stratify schools based on their propensity scores. Then we will compare the average achievement levels of schools within those strata. By comparing schools that exhibit similar propensities to have gifted programs, we are essentially balancing or matching schools on a large number of covariates simultaneously. This allows us to estimate the effect of gifted programming for schools that are similar on a wide variety of variables that are related to the likelihood of having a gifted program and school achievement.

A lack of overall effect at the school level could occur because gifted programming positively impacts the achievement of gifted students but negatively impacts the achievement of other students, or it could occur because gifted programming has no impact on the achievement of the gifted or nongifted students. Thus, it is also necessary to look separately at the effects of gifted programs on gifted students and nongifted students, and two additional analyses examine the impact of gifted programs on gifted students and the impact of gifted programs on nongifted students.

Therefore, the second research question examines the effect of gifted programming on those students who receive gifted services. Does gifted programming seem to have a positive impact on those who receive it? To answer this question, we will estimate how much higher or lower gifted students' achievement would be if they attended schools that did not offer gifted programming. These analyses become a bit more complex as there are essentially two levels of analysis that must be considered. The school or school district determines the availability of gifted programming; however, individual students are selected to receive the treatment. For this reason, answering this research question requires explicitly modeling both the school level and the student level within the analysis. For these analyses, we plan to combine multilevel modeling techniques and propensity score stratification to estimate the effect of gifted programming on gifted students. The use of propensity score stratification allows us to "match" students who receive gifted programming with similar students who do not receive gifted programming. These students will be balanced both on school-level characteristics and student-level characteristics.

Finally, our third research question involves estimating the average effect of gifted programming on students who are not involved in a gifted program. In other words, (1) does gifted programming lift the average achievement of the non-participating students? (2) Does catering to the needs of the gifted negatively impact the average achievement of non-participating students? Or (3) is there essentially no effect of offering gifted programming on those who are not identified as gifted? Again, using a combination of multilevel modeling and propensity score analysis, we will estimate the effect of being in a school with a gifted program for students who have a near null probability of being chosen for such a program. The nongifted students will also be balanced both on school-level characteristics and student-level characteristics. The analytic strategy that we are using for this research project is patterned after Hong and Raudenbush (2005), and readers who are interested in pursuing similar analyses are strongly encouraged to consult their excellent article.

THOUGHTS FROM INSIDE THE FIELD

Although my substantive research is in the field of gifted education, I am employed as a professor of measurement, evaluation, and assessment at the University of Connecticut, where I teach courses in research design, educational measurement, and educational statistics. Thus, I straddle the worlds of methodology and gifted education. I believe that this gives me a unique vantage point for seeing the methodological needs within the field of gifted education. I would like to take advantage of my expertise in the areas of both gifted education and research methodology to offer a few comments about using quantitative research methodology to address substantive issues within the field of gifted education.

Restriction of Range Versus Nonnormality?

Although all of the chapters in this volume address the issue of restriction of range, none of them mention the possibility that studying such an extreme group could result in outcome variables that are not normally distributed. It might be reasonable to expect certain outcome variables to be negatively skewed in a gifted population, such that most people score at the top of the scale, with a long tail representing infrequent scores throughout the lower portion of the scale. For example, academic self-concept might be negatively skewed within a gifted population. In such a scenario, the majority of gifted students would exhibit high self-concept, but a small minority of gifted students would have lower academic self-concept.

In fact, our work on underachievers follows a similar logic. Del Siegle and I have proposed a model of underachievement in which deficits in academic self-efficacy, goal valuation, environmental perceptions, and self-regulation lead to underachievement (Siegle & McCoach, 2004, 2005). According to the model, being low on any one of the four factors can lead to academic underachievement. Thus, underachievement is not an additive phenomenon; instead, it is interactive. It is our hypothesis that underachievers do not necessarily score low on all four of the factors but, rather, that they are students who exhibit low scores in one of the four areas. An unpublished analysis of the data from McCoach and Siegle (2003a) revealed that 55.4% of gifted underachievers in their sample scored at least one standard deviation below the mean on at least one of the following three SAAS–R subscales: self-regulation, goal valuation, and/or academic self-perceptions. In contrast, only 7.5% of high achievers scored at least one standard deviation below the mean on one of those three subscales. Further, using a student's lowest score on one of those three subscales predicted his or her achievement status nearly as well as using all of the subscales. These findings lend some credence to the notion that underachievement is related to a deficit in at least one of the factors identified by the achievement motivation model. Under such circumstances, it is easy to imagine a case where a variable of interest is negatively skewed within a gifted population, such that most gifted students exhibit high scores on the variable of interest and very few gifted students (in our example, a subset of gifted underachievers) exhibit low scores on the variable.

Researchers tend to assume that all constructs of interest are normally distributed. However, that is most certainly not true. Nonnormally distributed variables include count variables, especially those that represent the frequency of rare events. In the area of gifted education, a classic example is creative productivity. The distribution of creative productivity, when measured by rare events, such as publications, patents, and awards, may not follow a normal distribution at all. Instead, these events may reflect a Poisson distribution. The shape of a Poisson distribution is determined by μ, the rate, or the expected number of times that an event has occurred per unit of time (Long, 1997). As μ increases, the shape of the Poisson distribution approximates the normal distribution. However, when μ is low, the Poisson distribution is severely positively skewed, such that low rates or counts occur with high frequency and high rates or counts are exceptionally rare. If the events or counts in question are so rare that they do not even occur for most of the sample, these extraordinarily rare events or counts follow a Poisson distribution with a preponderance of zeros (zip). Garcia-Cepero (2007) conducted a study of creative productivity among faculty. She used publications, patents, and products as indicators of creative productivity, and she found that these indicators followed a zip distribution. For example, many of the faculty in the sample had no publications during the time period in question. Thus, she used a confirmatory factor analytic model in which creative productivity, her latent variable, was modeled using zip distributed indicators.

Finally, when restriction of range is a problem, researchers may want to consider models for censored data (Long, 1997). When a test exhibits a ceiling or floor effect, we do not know how much higher or lower a student might have scored if the test had a more adequate range. Imagine the case of ceiling effects on an achievement test. Many of the gifted students who take an on-grade-level achievement test may answer all of the questions correctly. This causes the scores for the gifted students to be bunched together at the ceiling of the test. Not only is the range restricted, but the distribution of the variable no longer appears to be normally distributed. Instead, the distribution is likely to look negatively skewed. In this scenario, however, the actual distribution of achievement may be normally distributed. However, we are unable to observe the true distribution of scores because values above the ceiling of the test are censored. The most common model for censored data is the Tobit model (details about this model are available in Long, 1997). Recently, M. McBee (personal communication, July 15, 2008) has begun to champion the use of censored data models in gifted education.

Is Giftedness Qualitative or Quantitative?

Is giftedness a qualitative or a quantitative phenomenon? Are gifted individuals qualitatively different from nongifted individuals, or do they simply exhibit certain traits in greater magnitude than nongifted individuals? Clearly, the field lacks any sort of consensus on this issue. However, researchers with differing notions about the nature of giftedness will use different methods to explore and explain the phenomenon. Simplistically, one could purport that those who view gifted individuals as being qualitatively different from nongifted individuals would tend to invoke more qualitatively oriented research methods to study the phenomenon of giftedness, while those who perceive gifted individuals as manifesting greater degrees of certain traits would tend to utilize quantitative methods for studying giftedness. However, even quantitatively oriented researchers can use quantitative methods to study gifted individuals as qualitatively distinct from nongifted individuals. Latent structure analysis lends itself to just such research questions.

Factor analysis assumes that the latent variable being measured is normally distributed and measured at the interval level. Thus, when conducting factor analyses to define constructs such as academic self-concept, intelligence, or creativity, one assumes that people are normally distributed on such constructs; some people have more of the trait and some have less of the trait, but all people fall somewhere on a continuum of the trait. However, if one views giftedness as being qualitatively different from nongiftedness, then factor analysis would be inappropriate, as the construct of giftedness is categorical rather than continuous. Latent structure analysis is analogous to factor analysis for a categorical latent variable. Two basic types of latent structure analyses are latent class analysis and latent profile analysis. Using latent class analysis, researchers can "empirically identify discrete latent variables from two or more discrete observed variables" (McCutcheon, 1987, p. 7). In contrast, latent profile analysis enables researchers to identify discrete latent variables from two or more continuous observed variables (McCutcheon, 1987).

The underlying assumption of latent class–latent profile analysis is that the data set contains a mixture of two or more different subpopulations. For latent profile analysis, the scores within each subpopulation are normally distributed; however, the overall distribution of scores within the total data set is not assumed to be normally distributed. In latent class analysis, both the observed indicators and the latent variable are categorical. Thus, there are no distributional assumptions placed on the indicators or the latent variable. Using latent structure analysis, researchers can identify different typologies, taxonomies, or subpopulations within a given data set. For example, latent structure analysis could be used to try to model giftedness as a discrete latent variable. In such a scenario, giftedness is unobserved, and we infer membership within the gifted population based on a person's pattern of scores on the manifest variables within our model.

Using similar logic, growth mixture modeling (GMM) resembles a combination of latent structure analysis and growth modeling (described in chap. 8, this volume). Again, instead of assuming that all subjects come from the same population, growth mixture modeling allows the researcher to empirically identify different growth classes, or subgroups that have qualitatively different growth patterns. For example, one might hypothesize that gifted students start higher and grow more quickly in their reading or math skills than nongifted students. Thus, using growth mixture modeling, a researcher could try to identify qualitatively different growth patterns and identify the different subpopulations that exhibit these different patterns. Again, the categorical variable of interest is latent, not observed. Thus, we infer group membership based on people's growth patterns. Given the ease with which modern computer packages such as MPLUS (Muthén & Muthén, 1998–2007) and AMOS (Arbuckle, 2007) allow researchers to estimate mixture models, these models have increased in popularity over the last several years. For more information about mixture models, see Hancock and Samuelson (2007) and Lubke and Muthén (2005). Latent class analysis and GMM are both fairly exploratory techniques, and as such they may lend themselves to mixed methods research designs. For example, prototypical cases from each of the classes could be selected for interviews or other qualitative follow-up to more fully understand the nature of the different classes.

As mentioned earlier, it is unclear whether the construct of giftedness is qualitative or quantitative in nature. Taxometric analysis (Meehl, 1965) is a technique that enables researchers to empirically examine the latent structure of constructs to determine whether they are qualitative or quantitative in nature (Ruscio & Ruscio, 2004). While taxometric analysis has not been utilized in gifted education, it is increasingly used in psychopathology research to determine whether psychological disorders represent qualitatively different states or extreme levels on a quantitative continuum (Haslam, 2007). This research has led to the conclusions that certain disorders, such as attention-deficit/hyperactivity disorder, hypomania, and social anxiety, represent extreme states on one or more quantitative dimensions, whereas other disorders, such as dissociation and specific language impairments, probably represent qualitatively distinct categories (Haslam, 2007). Applying taxometric techniques to the study of giftedness could yield important insights into the nature of the very construct that we seek to study. Such insight could have a profound impact on the discourse and research within the field.

CONCLUSION

Methodological advances allow us to ask and answer more interesting, sophisticated, and nuanced research questions than ever before. However, these abilities come with a price: the time necessary to master these newer techniques. It is my hope that a new generation of gifted education researchers will emerge and that these young scholars will combine passion and interest in gifted education with expertise in quantitative and qualitative research methods. It is this marriage that will enable us to answer some of the most important and pressing research questions in the field of gifted education.

REFERENCES

Adelson, J. L. (2008). *A gift for all? Examining the effects of gifted programming on all students.* Unpublished doctoral dissertation proposal, University of Connecticut, Storrs.

Arbuckle, J. L. (2007). AMOS *user's guide.* Chicago: SPSS.

Baslanti, U., & McCoach, D. B. (2006). Factors affecting the underachievement of gifted students. *Roeper Review, 28,* 210–215.

Costa, P. T., Jr., & McCrae, R. R. (1992). *NEO PI–R professional manual* Odessa, FL: Psychological Assessment Resources.

Friedland, J. G., Mandel, H. P., & Marcus, S. I. (n.d.). *Achievement Motivation Profile.* Los Angeles: Western Psychological Services.

Garcia-Cepero, M. C. (2007). *Institutional and individual factors associated with faculty scholarly productivity*. Unpublished doctoral dissertation, University of Connecticut, Storrs.

Hancock, G. R., & Samuelson, K. M. (Eds.). (2007). *Advances in latent variable mixture models*. Charlotte, NC: Information Age Publishing.

Haslam, N. (2007). The latent structure of mental disorders: A taxometric update on the categorical versus dimensional debate. *Current Psychiatry Reviews, 3,* 172–177.

Hong, G., & Raudenbush, S. W. (2005). Effects of kindergarten retention policy on children's cognitive growth in reading and mathematics. *Educational Evaluation and Policy Analysis, 27,* 205–224.

Long, J. S. (1997). *Regression models for categorical and limited dependent variables*. Thousand Oaks, CA: Sage.

Lubke, G., & Muthén, B. (2005). Investigating population heterogeneity with factor mixture models. *Psychological Methods, 10,* 21–39.

McCoach, D. B., & Baslanti, U. (2008, March). *Development and validation of the Challenges to Scholastic Achievement (CSAS) Scale*. Paper presented at the annual conference of the American Educational Research Association, New York.

McCoach, D. B., & Siegle, D. (2003a). Factors that differentiate underachieving gifted students from high achieving gifted students. *Gifted Child Quarterly, 47,* 144–154.

McCoach, D. B., & Siegle, D. (2003b). The SAAS–R: A new instrument to identify academically able students who underachieve. *Educational and Psychological Measurement, 63,* 414–429.

McCutcheon, A. L. (1987). *Latent class analysis*. Thousand Oaks, CA: Sage.

Meehl, P. E. (1965). *Detecting latent clinical taxa by fallible quantitative indicators lacking an accepted criterion* (Rep. No. PR-65-2). Minneapolis: University of Minnesota, Research Laboratories of the Department of Psychiatry.

Muthén, L. K., & Muthén, B. O. (1998–2007). *Mplus user's guide* (5th ed.). Los Angeles: Muthén & Muthén.

Renzulli, J. S. (1998). A rising tide lifts all ships: Developing the gifts and talents of all students. *Phi Delta Kappan, 80,* 104–111.

Ruscio, J., & Ruscio, A. M. (2004). A non-technical introduction to the taxometric method. *Understanding Statistics, 3,* 151–194.

Siegle, D., & McCoach, D. B. (2004). *Motivating gifted students*. Waco, TX: Prufrock Press.

Siegle, D., & McCoach, D. B. (2005). Making a difference: Motivating gifted students who are not achieving. *Teaching Exceptional Children, 38,* 22–27.

Suldo, S. M., Shaffer, E. J., & Shaunessy, E. (2008). An independent investigation of the validity of the School Attitude Assessment Survey—Revised. *Journal of Psychoeducational Assessment, 26,* 69–82.

INDEX

Circulation Research, 77

CIs. *See* Confidence intervals

Clark, M. H., 200

Classes, 148

Classical test theory, 91–93, 96

Cleaning data, 105, 151

Clinical significance, 73

Cluster analysis, 232–234

Coding form, for reliability generalization
studies, 102–103

Coefficient alpha, 93

Cognitive Abilities Test, Form 6
(CogAT), 102–104

Cohen, J., 59, 80, 84, 198

Cohen, P., 198

Cold deck imputation, 199

Coleman, Laurence, 230

Collins, K. M. T., 115, 117, 119, 124,
126, 130

Common factor analysis, 17

Communality coefficient, in factor
analysis, 26

Comparative fit index (CFI), 153

Comparison groups, 5, 125

Complete case analysis, 196

Complete data set, 196

Conceptions of Giftedness
(Sternberg & Davidson), x

Confidence intervals (CIs), 53–54,
67–68

calculating and interpreting, 85

in ESCIMAT, 55–56

in giftedness research, 57, 58, 61–62

p values vs., 62–65

and replication, 56–58

as standard of evidence, 77–78

Confirmatory factor analysis (CFA),
12, 158–161

Constrained estimation (optimization),
152

Construct measurement, 13–14

Construct validity, 14, 33

Cook, R. S., 231

Correlation matrix, in structural equation
modeling, 152

Covariance matrix, in structural equation
modeling, 152

Covariances, in structural equation
modeling, 163

Covariance structure, 148

Covariance structure analysis, 148

Covariance structure modeling, 148

Cramond, B., 156, 158

Creativity, 4

Creswell, J. W., 118–119

Crocker, L., 91

Cross, J. R., 232–236

Cross, T. L., 230–236

Cross-validation studies, 199

Crowley, S., 92–93

CSAS (Challenges to Scholastic
Achievement Scale), 243

CTD (Center for Talent Development),
221–223

Cumming, G., 56–58, 67, 72, 78, 79, 85

D'Agostino, R., 203

Daniel, L. G., 13, 20

Data analysis

cleaning, dummy coding, and
recording data, 105

entering data, 104–105

for mixed research, 121–123,
126–130

in studies of reliability generalization,
104–106

Data collection

for mixed research, 120–121, 124

for Q-technique factor analysis,
36–37

for reliability generalization studies,
103–104

Data matrix (factor analysis), 34–36

Data missing at random (MAR), 195

Data missing completely at random
(MCAR), 195

Data missing not at random (MNAR),
195–196

Data reduction, factor analysis for, 13

Data screening, in structural equation
modeling, 150–151

Davidson, J. E., x

Decision making

dichotomous, 74

in exploratory factor analysis, 15

unjustified by data, 55

Definitions of giftedness, 4, 125

Deković, M., 161, 162

Dellinger, A. B., 117

DeMarco, G. M. P., 115

Individual educational programming (IEP), 242
Instrument development, factor analysis in, 11–12
Instrument fidelity, 124–125
Instrument reliability, 215–216
Integrated methods, 114. *See also* Mixed research
Interaction effect of measurement occasion and group, 181–182
Internal replication, 150
International Committee of Medical Journal Editors (ICMJE), 76, 77
International Handbook of Giftedness and Talent (Heller, Mönks, Sternberg, & Subotnik), x
Intravenous streptokinase study, 82–83
Inverse probability fallacy, 55
Ipsative ratings, 43–44
   as criterion for giftedness, 4
   gifted children's scores for, 219–220
Item deletion, in factor analysis, 23–24

Jiao, Q. G., 117
Johnson, R. B., 114–115, 120–122, 139
Journal of Abnormal and Social Psychology, 80
Journal of Abnormal Psychology, 81
Journal of the American Medical Association, 77
Journal of Wildlife Management, 78

KABC-I (Kaufman Assessment Battery for Children), 159–161
KABC-II (Kaufman Assessment Battery for Children), 162
Karter, A., 203
Kaufman, A. S., 159–160
Kaufman, N. L., 159–160
Kaufman Assessment Battery for Children (KABC-I), 159–161
Kaufman Assessment Battery for Children (KABC-II), 162
Keith, T. Z., 161
Kennedy, R. S., 100
Kerlinger, F. N., 36
Kirk, R. E., 74
Kline, R. B., 55, 58
Kogan, L. R., 96–99

Kulik, C. C., 218
Kulik, J. A., 218

Laird, N. M., 199
Lancet, 77
Lang, W., 203
Latent class analysis (LCA), 234–236, 250
Latent growth models (LGMs), 161–162
Latent structure analysis, 250
Latent variables, in structural equation modeling, 148–149, 165
LCA. *See* Latent class analysis
Leech, N. L., 117, 118, 120, 126
Levin, J. R., 154, 155
LGMs (latent growth models), 161–162
Listwise deletion, 196–197
Literature review, for reliability generalization studies, 103
Little, R., 195–196
Little's MCAR test, 195
Lived experiences, 230
Loading, in factor analysis, 22, 23
Lohman, D. F., 164–165
Luellen, J., 200

MacCallum, R. C., 26, 152
Main effect of measurement occasion, 181
MAR (data missing at random), 195
MAT. *See* Meta-analytic thinking
Mathematics assessments, factor analysis of, 13
Matthews-Morgan, J., 156
Maximum likelihood (ML)
   in handling missing data, 199
   in structural equation modeling, 151, 152
Maxwell, S. E., 81
MCAR (data missing completely at random), 195
McCoach, D. B., 151, 242–243, 247–248
McCutcheon, A. L., 250
McGaw, B., 85
Meaningfulness, 73–74
Meaningfulness fallacy, 80
Mean structure, in structural equation modeling, 148–149

Naming fallacy, 160–161
NEO-PI-R (Revised NEO Personality Inventory), 244
New England Journal of Medicine, 77
Newman, C., 115
Newman, I., 115
Neyman–Pearson approach, 55, 79
NHST. *See* Null hypothesis significance testing
Nil null hypotheses, 75, 100
Nonequivalent groups
    adjusting for missing data with, 203
    and propensity score analysis, 244–247
Nonnormality, restriction of range vs., 247–249
Normative ratings, in Q-technique factor analysis, 43–47
Null hypothesis, 75
Null hypothesis significance testing (NHST), 67, 68, 219. *See also* Statistical significance
    and confidence intervals, 56, 63
    in ecology research, 78
    and falsification, 74–76
    in giftedness research, 57, 58
    limitations of, 54, 55
    in medical research, 76, 77
    misconceptions about, 55
    potential damage from using, 79–83
    in psychology research, 78–79
    and replication, 54–58
    as standard of evidence, 76
Null model, 183–184
Nunnally, J. C., 28, 33–34, 48

Oblique rotations of factors, 21–22
Observed score, 91
Occam's razor, 178
O'Connor, B. P., 20
Odds against chance fantasy, 73
Off-level testing, 5
OLS analysis. *See* Ordinary least squares analysis
Onwuegbuzie, A. J., 115, 117–122, 126–127, 130, 132, 137, 139
Ordinary least squares (OLS) analysis, 171–173, 175, 177
Orthogonal rotations of factors, 21–22
O-technique factor analysis, 35

PAF (principal axis factoring), 17
Pairwise deletion, 196, 197
Parallel analysis, for number of factors, 19–21
Participants
    attrition of, 5–6, 125
    pool of, 67
Pashler, H., 153
Path models, 156–157
PCA (principal components analysis), 17
Pearson correlation matrix, in exploratory factor analysis, 16–17, 23, 24
Pearson's r
    in giftedness research, 58
    intuitions about, 59, 65–66
    in Q-technique factor analysis, 44, 47
Pedhazur, E. J., 90, 152
Pituch, K. A., 154, 155
Planning stage, in mixed research, 119–120
Poisson distribution, 248
Popper, K., 75
Popperian falsification, 74–76
Practical intelligence, 4
Practical significance, 73
Principal axis factoring (PAF), 17. *See also* Factor analysis
Principal components analysis (PCA), 17. *See also* Factor analysis
Process/experience-oriented analyses, 132, 133–135, 138–139
Program effects, 221, 244–247
Project Excite, 223–227
Promax, 22, 46
Propensity scores, 200–203
    in estimation of treatment effect, 209–210
    generating, 205–209
    and group nonequivalence, 203, 244–247
Psychology, standards of evidence in, 78–79
PsycINFO, 103
P-technique factor analysis, 35
Public schools, 7
p values
    confidence intervals vs., 62–65, 67
    erroneous beliefs about, 58

ABOUT THE EDITORS

Bruce Thompson is a distinguished professor and distinguished research fellow of educational psychology and a distinguished professor of library sciences, Texas A&M University. He is also an adjunct professor of family and community medicine, Baylor College of Medicine (Houston). He has been coeditor of the teaching, learning, and human development section of the *American Educational Research Journal* (*AERJ:TLHD*), and past editor of *Educational and Psychological Measurement*, the series, *Advances in Social Science Methodology*, and two other journals. He is the author/editor of 202 articles, and several books, including the recently published *Foundations of Behavioral Statistics*. His contributions have been especially influential in moving the field as regards greater emphasis on effect size reporting and interpretation, and promoting improved understanding of score reliability.

Rena F. Subotnik, PhD, began her position as director of the Center for Psychology in the Schools and Education at the American Psychological Association (APA) in January 2002. From 1986 through 2001, Dr. Subotnik was a professor at Hunter College, where she coordinated the secondary education program and served as research and curriculum liaison to the Hunter College

265

laboratory schools for gifted children (grades PK–12). From 1977–1984 she was a gifted education specialist in the Seattle Public Schools.

Dr. Subotnik is also director of the Center for Gifted Education Policy at the APA. The center's mission is to generate public awareness, advocacy, clinical applications, and cutting-edge research ideas that will enhance the achievement and performance of children and adolescents with special gifts and talents in all domains (including the academic disciplines, the performing arts, sports, and the professions).

Dr. Subotnik has been awarded grants from the McDonnell Foundation, the Institute for Education Sciences, Jack Kent Cooke Foundation, Camille and Henry Dreyfus Foundation, the American Psychological Foundation, National Science Foundation, U.S. Department of Education Javits program, and the Spencer Foundation.

She is co-editor of *Developing Giftedness and Talent Across the Life Span* (with F. D. Horowitz and D. Matthews), *Optimizing Student Success with the Other Three R's: Reasoning, Resilience and Responsibility* (with R. J. Sternberg), *The Scientific Basis of Educational Productivity* (with H. Walberg), *The International Handbook of Research on Giftedness and Talent* (2nd Edition; with F. Monks K. Heller, R. J. Sternberg), *Remarkable Women: Perspectives on Female Talent Development* (with K. Arnold and K. Noble), and *Beyond Terman: Contemporary Longitudinal Studies of Giftedness and Talent* (with K. Arnold). She is the first author of *Genius Revisited: High IQ Children Grown Up* (with L. Kassan, A. Wasser, and E. Summers).

Dr. Subotnik was the 2002 recipient of the National Association for Gifted Children NAGC Distinguished Scholar award. She was also selected as a 2009 American Educational Research Association Fellow.